D0139713

Second Edition

STAFF DEVELOPMENT
for Education in the '90s
New Demands, New Realities, New Perspectives

ANN LIEBERMAN & LYNNE MILLER
Editors

TEACHERS COLLEGE PRESS

Teachers College, Columbia University
New York and London

Published by Teachers College Press, 1234 Amsterdam Avenue
New York, NY 10027

Library of Congress Cataloguing-in-Publication Data

Staff development for education in the '90s : new demands, new
    realities, new perspectives / Ann Lieberman & Lynne Miller, editors.
    —2nd ed.
            p.   cm — (Professional development and practice series)
        Rev. ed. of: Staff development.
        Includes bibliographical references and index.
        ISBN 0-8077-3100-5.—ISBN 0-8077-3099-8 (pbk.)
        1. School personnel management—United States.   2. Teachers—In
-service training—United States.   I. Lieberman, Ann. II. Miller,
Lynne, 1945-   III. Staff development. IV. Series.
LB2831.58.S73   1991
371.1'46—dc20   91-9913
                                                                              CIP

ISBN 0-8077-3100-5
ISBN 0-8077-3099-8

Printed on acid-free paper
Manufactured in the United States of America
98 97 96 95 94 93 92   8 7 6 5 4 3 2

Contents

Preface

This volume is part of the *Professional Development and Practice Series*, in which we are trying to highlight the contemporary work on professionalizing teaching, restructuring schools, and rethinking teacher education. In so doing we seek to give recognition to several important perspectives that must inform the practices of those who teach in our schools and who work with teachers. This volume, the second edition of *Staff Development: New Demands, New Realities, New Perspectives*, presents a fresh look at one of the most vexing problems of educational change: the continuous growth and development of teachers.

In 1979, when the first edition of this book was published, it was one of the few books that spoke of the need to look at staff development not as an isolated set of workshops but as a means of working with teachers over time. Our understanding, although teacher oriented, lacked the perspectives that have since developed that see staff development as part of the school culture, taking many different forms. For example, while district and local levels of support must be present, coupling staff development with the growing move to professionalize teaching puts teachers at the center of helping to create and participate as central figures in their own development. This new volume, then, deepens our understandings of the nature of staff development, building on the foundation of our knowledge of the social realities of teachers and their connection to students.

Several themes that illuminate this new perspective can be found in the work of many authors of this volume:

- Understanding the importance of the teacher as a learner, leader, and colleague in helping shape a professional community
- Confronting the fact that serious staff development involves personal learning about self in relation to one's students
- Seeing staff development as a continuous means for "growth in practice"
- Recognizing the significance of informal networks as a means for intellectual learning and social support

Part I of the book looks at staff development from different points of view. We believe that no one theory or set of ideas is sufficient to mount a successful staff development program precisely because no one theory encompasses all the important perspectives that must be considered. We begin with Maxine Greene's chapter on the quest to find a personal reality as a teacher. Greene confronts the individual with the necessity of challenging oneself as teacher and the world as given. This chapter, the only one that is the same as in the first edition, still retains both its timelessness and its relevance.

In Chapter 2 Susan Loucks-Horsley revisits her chapter in the first edition and puts "teacher concerns," a long-term line of research that documents the stages teachers go through as they adopt new ideas, into historical context. She takes another look at the ideas and adds some new understandings gained from looking at the teacher as an individual as well as a member of a school faculty. The historical context illuminates teacher concerns as they existed two decades ago while considering them in relation to the impact of new constructs that deal with people, processes, practices and policies, power and philosophy.

Sharon Oja in Chapter 3 presents a comprehensive view of theories of adult development and their importance for a fuller understanding of teacher learning. This area of research has often been overlooked by staff developers and, as we learn, is critical to the success of how we think about the way adults grow and change.

In Chapter 4 Milbrey McLaughlin revisits her earlier contribution in which she and David Marsh wrote of the implications for staff development of the landmark Rand Change Agent Study. McLaughlin deepens this chapter in the light of new research that highlights the importance of differing school contexts and the variety of institutional factors that work to "enable" or "constrain" staff development opportunities for teachers. She enriches her earlier work, focusing on the significance of context and organizational conditions, such as "developing and nurturing structures for communication, collegiality, and feedback." We see that both district *and* school level strategies affect the teacher's sense of professionalism and continued growth and development.

Myrna Cooper in her earlier chapter described the organized profession's views and concerns about how staff development was practiced in the 1970s. In this version, Chapter 5, she argues persuasively that we have learned that we need to work collectively in order to enable us to create the new skills and abilities needed to restructure schools. With her characteristic clarity of voice and penetrating understanding of teachers, she urges a transformation of not only what we do, but how we think about schools, teachers, and teaching.

In Chapter 6 we go back to our chapter on the social realities of teaching and link some of the conditions that appear to be unchanged for teachers with some of the burgeoning possibilities for change embedded within the move to restructure schools and professionalize teaching. Attempting to link theory with practice, we integrate the personal, pragmatic, organizational, and constructivist perspectives of the preceding authors. Staff development work, we emphasize, should not be eclectic, but rather the product of a systematic way of looking at the connections between the school culture and the teacher as an individual craftsperson.

The second part, "Staff Development at Work," digs deeply into a variety of strategies that people are using to involve teachers in staff development—not simply as recipients of someone else's ideas, but as leaders in their own research and development. This part of the book begins with Anna Richert's description of the use of the case method as a means of staff development (Chapter 7). Teachers write case studies of particular students and, meeting in a group, try to help each other to better understand these students. Using a method borrowed from the case conference procedures in other professions, teachers get help from colleagues who are also helping themselves. Teachers expand their knowledge of child development and pedagogy as they learn together how to better serve their students.

In Chapter 8 Peter Holly gives us a comprehensive look at the historical, theoretical, and practical understanding of collaborative or "action research." As an ardent teacher of the method himself, he argues convincingly for this type of research as a necessity for not only improving teaching but improving schools as well. His examples compel us to look favorably on his avowed advocacy of the method.

Patricia Wasley, in Chapter 9, takes us into the lives of three teachers who have become leaders. We not only get an inside view of the differences in the way people lead, but she makes us aware of the many conflicting issues surrounding colleagueship: the power of the bureaucratic structure, the paucity of genuine organizational forms that promote colleagueship, and the lack of legitimacy for teachers teaching teachers. We also gain insights into teachers' views of what teachers should know and how they should be taught, and recognize the hard work yet to be done to change school structures so that they welcome perhaps their richest untapped resource—their own colleagues.

In Chapter 10 Judith Schwartz takes over where Wasley leaves off. She describes the growth and development of a districtwide teacher center that not only accommodates teacher leadership roles but in a real sense creates those roles and responsibilities as the teachers themselves develop and define them. Teacher research and development, the creation of new roles, joint teacher-administrator programs, peer review and continuous teacher initiatives in curriculum and instruction show us what teacher professionalism means in practice.

In Chapter 11 Hilton Smith and Eliot Wigginton, with their colleagues Kathy Hocking and Bob Jones, describe the challenge inherent in the growth and expansion of the Foxfire approach to teaching and learning. Their candid description of the teacher outreach networks is both enlightening and encouraging. As Milbrey McLaughlin suggests in her chapter, these new networks may play a very powerful role in propelling teachers to rethink how they engage students in their own learning. By modeling their own strong beliefs, these networks provide "opportunities for teachers to develop leadership," to become empowered in their own schools and classrooms, and as a result to break their isolation and become part of a larger move toward a focus on student-centered schools.

Robert McClure in Chapter 12 demonstrates another means of networking, as he describes the Mastery In Learning Project, a national network that involved the National Education Association in a site-based, faculty-led school improvement project. This network, as did Foxfire, started with a set of principles that included students as active participants with faculty in making decisions concerning teaching and learning. The processes by which this network grew, and how and what its members learned about the complexities of changing schools, provide us with important tools for and insights into organizing, supporting, and maintaining a network. In their words, "faculty-led school improvement efforts that are context specific, student-outcome oriented, intellectually valid, and professionally enabling embody the essence of effective staff development programs."

In the Afterword Gary Griffin helps us to integrate our current knowledge and understanding of staff development by summarizing what we know about teachers, teaching work, and leadership related to the function of "interactive staff development." Making us aware of the comprehensive set of factors that go into mounting a significant staff development program that becomes an integral part of school life, he challenges us to deal with the complexities described in this book. More than an intellectual exercise, this may help in the building of more productive lives for students and teachers in this expansive and fruitful time of educational change.

Part I

PERSPECTIVES
ON STAFF DEVELOPMENT

1 Teaching
The Question of Personal Reality

Maxine Greene

The realities of teaching are multiple. Three points of view, three tones of voice begin to suggest the range. The first is John Dewey's (1938/1963):

> The principle that development of experience comes about through interaction means that education is essentially a social process. This quality is realized in the degree in which individuals form a community group. It is absurd to exclude the teacher from membership in the group. As the most mature member of the group he has a peculiar responsibility for the conduct of the interactions and intercommunications which are the very life of the group as a community. (p. 58)

The second is B. Othanel Smith's (1963):

> Our most general notion is that teaching is everywhere the same, that it is a natural social phenomenon and is fundamentally the same from one culture to another. . . . In our view, teaching is a system of action involving an agent, a situation, an end-in-view, and two sets of factors in the situation—one set over which the agent has no control (for example, size of classroom and physical characteristics of pupils) and one set which the agent can modify with respect to the end-in-view (for example, assignments and ways of asking questions). (p. 4)

The third is Martin Buber's (1947/1957). He, too, was writing about the teaching situation—always, he thought, a situation "that has never been before and will never come again."

> It demands of you a reaction which cannot be prepared beforehand. It demands nothing of what is past. It demands presence, responsibility; it demands you. (p. 114)

3

To talk about the personal reality of teachers is to consider their lived lives and their pursuits of meaning in contexts that include a concern for the social dimensions of teaching, for the strategic, *and* for the existentially unique. It is, if possible, to avoid the kinds of either/ors or dichotomies that arise when the social is viewed as antithetical to the individual, or when the cognitive and conceptual are treated as if they were at odds with the affective, the authenic, the humane.

What we understand to be "reality" is interpreted or reflected-on experience. We live in continuing transactions with the natural and human world around us. Perceived shapes, colors, lights, sounds, present themselves to our embodied consciousness. Only as we begin moving into the life of language, thematizing, symbolizing, making sense, do we begin to single out certain profiles, certain aspects of the flux of things to attend to and to name (see Merleau-Ponty, 1964). Once we begin doing that, we begin orienting ourselves to what we think of as the "real." The patterns or schemata we use in the process of sense-making are those made available to us by "our predecessors and contemporaries" (Schutz, 1967, p. 15). We are, after all, functions of a culture; most of those teaching in the public schools speak the same language. The realities we construct— schools, for example, time clocks, running tracks, political parties, dining room tables, public squares—mean what they mean because we have internalized common ways of thinking about them and talking about them. But, at the same time, each of us looks upon the common world from a particular standpoint, a particular location in space and time. Each of us has a distinctive biography, a singular life history. Each of us, to use George Herbert Mead's words, is both an "I" and a "me." The "I" gives us our "sense of freedom, of initiative." It is, Mead said, "the response of the organism to the attitudes of others; the 'me' is the organized set of attitudes of others which one . . . assumes. The attitudes of the others constitute the organized 'me', and then one reacts toward that as an 'I'" (p. 175). The "me," therefore, is social; it refers to the shared social reality we respond to as we live. There is always, however, the perspective and the agency of the "I"; and this means that there is always the possibility of self-consciousness, of choosing, and of unpredictability. It is with these that I wish to associate the idea of personal reality.

When we look back, most of us realize that we somehow knew about teachers and classrooms very early in our lives, long before we went to school. The specific teachers and classrooms with which we later came in contact, therefore, appeared within a horizon of "pre-acquaintanceship" (Schutz, 1967, p. 59). We were already familiar with the difference between larger and smaller people, with the spaces and surfaces prohibited to us—and the spaces and surfaces we were expected to explore. We were accustomed to hands that helped and hands that restrained, voices that disapproved and voices that tried to point things out, to help us understand, to help us see. If there were bookshelves in our homes, and sheets of paper, and memo pads, these simply belonged to the world of daily life. They were part of the background or the scenery, taken for granted as what they appeared to be. It was only when we actually became pupils in actual classrooms that we began to identify unique instances of teaching behavior, to select out something called "teaching" against what we had taken for granted. It was then that we began perceiving books and paper in terms of a specified kind of use. It was then that we began noticing chalkboards, charts, attendance sheets, grade books, as indicators, somehow, of a new kind of social world. We did not, of course, see all this in identical ways. We constituted them, as we constituted our classrooms, in the light of the particular problems we faced in becoming pupils (or "third-graders," or "bluebirds") among other children in a regularized, oddly public place away from home. The nature of our "interest" and what Alfred Schutz described as "the system of relevances involved" (p. 60) originated in our own biographical situations and in the circumstances that prevailed in our lives at the time we first went to school.

As we grew older along with others and experienced diverse teachers and teaching situations, we built up a structure of meanings. Many of these meanings derived from the ways in which our choices and purposes were supported or frustrated by other people's choices and purposes in the shifting social worlds of the classrooms we came to know. Some derived from our developing commonsense understanding of the workings of those worlds. Then, at least for some of us, there were the meanings that emerged from our reflections on our commonsense understandings, reflections made possible by an ability to "do" psychology or one of the social sciences, by a developed skill in tracing certain political currents in the schools, or by an achieved capacity to think in terms of teaching strategies.

There came a time, finally, when we began thinking about teaching as a way of spending our working lives. Like all other human beings, we could not but "future," in some sense, think about what might be. As Jean-Paul Sartre (1963) has written, our behavior is not only determined by our relation "to the real and present factors which condition it," but by "a certain object, still to come, which it is trying to bring into being." And Sartre went on to say, "This is what we call *the project*" (p. 91). We may be moved to choose our project because of certain lacks in a social situation in which we are involved: We may want to repair those lacks and make that situation what it might be, rather than what it is. Or our choice of project may be connected with our notion of what we want to make of ourselves, of the kinds of identity we want to create. In either case, we are trying to become what we are not yet by acting on perceived deficiency, or on perceived possibility.

Dewey (1916) wrote that "the self is not ready-made, but something in continuous formation through choice of action" (p. 408). He said that if an individual, say, was interested in keeping at his or her work even if his or her life were endangered, that would be because the individual found his or her self "*in* that work." People who give up in the face of danger or threat or discomfort are people who, in choosing their own security or comfort, are declaring their preference to be people of that sort; they are creating prudent, comfortable selves. Dewey stressed the fact that "self and interest are two names for the same fact; the kind and amount of interest actively taken in a thing reveals and measures the quality of selfhood which exists" (p. 408). To think of the self in this fashion or to define personal reality in this fashion is very different from placing one's credence in "self-actualization" or in any approach focused on an unfolding or realization of an original, authentic self. Dewey believed, as does Sartre, that what we become, what we make of ourselves, depends upon what we do in our lives. And what we do cannot be simply routine and mechanical; it must be conscious, interested, committed. If it is not, if we content ourselves with being behaving organisms rather than reflective persons engaged in ongoing *action*, the quality of our selfhood becomes thin and pallid. We begin to resemble those T. S. Eliot (1952) called "hollow men," or those Thoreau (1854/1963) described as living their lives in "quiet desperation" (p. 69).

We who choose to become teachers obviously have an "interest" when we do so. As has been suggested, that interest arises out of our biographical situation as much as it does out of a sense of what we are trying to bring into being. There are those who select out the nurturant dimension of teaching and focus on creating themselves as caring persons, motherly or fatherly persons, interested very often in open-ended growth. There are those who attend most particularly to the social dimension of the educational process: the transmission or communication of a way of life; the fostering of the democratic ideal; the shaping of community. There are those who find themselves so challenged, so enlightened by engagement with an academic discipline that they turn toward teaching as a way of introducing others to the domain of history or physics or sociology or literary studies, in the hope that their perspectives also will be expanded, even as they become initiates in the community of scholars—or (perhaps) sophisticated technicians, bibliophiles, mediators for another generation of the young. And there are always persons who turn toward teaching because they see themselves as people committed to arousing others to critical thinking or to "conscientization" (Freire, 1970, p. 157) or even to bringing about social change. And there are a few who want especially to stimulate awareness and understanding of the arts, and a few who want to train apprentices for one of the fields of scientific inquiry. I am speaking of the interests that appear to motivate persons when they decide to enter into teaching, interests that may be refined or eroded or totally transformed in the course of teacher training, but that remain present in the individual's historical situation, no matter what happens in his or her everyday.

What happens, of course, when we have our initial experiences with teaching in public schools, is that we become sharply aware of limits, of structures and arrangements that cannot easily be surpassed. No matter how practical, how grounded our educational courses were, they suddenly appear to be totally irrelevant in the concrete situation where we find ourselves. This is because general principles never fully apply to new and special situations, especially if those principles are thought of as prescriptions or rules. Dewey (1922/1957) spoke of principles as methods of inquiry and forecast "which require verification by the event" (p. 221). They provide standpoints, ways of interpreting or making sense of what is happening; they are not practical, as rules are practical; they do not tell us specifically what to do. Yet, when we first enter into the classrooms for which we are responsible, or when we confront groups of students who are resistant or undisciplined or inept, we long for rules or for someone to tell us "what to do at 9 o'clock." We forget that, for a rule to be universally applicable, all situations must be fundamentally alike; and, as most of us know, classroom situations are always new and never twice alike. Even so, we yearn oftentimes for what might be called a "technology of teaching," for standard operating procedures that can be relied upon to "work." Devoid of these, we project our frustration back upon whatever teacher education we experienced; or (in cases of extremity) we project our frustration outward to the young people in our classes, the creatures who seem to be rejecting what we offer them—an alienated and alienating crowd who do not seem to care about learning how to learn.

Obviously, this does not always happen. But there are few teachers who avoid the anxiety of beginning, few who can see beyond the limits or succeed in breaking through. It is difficult to gain the capacity "of going beyond created structures" (to use the words of Maurice Merleau-Ponty, 1967b) "in order to create others" (p. 175). And yet, as Merleau-Ponty saw it, this capacity—like the power to choose and vary points of view—is what defines the human being. There are obstacles that inhere in the organization of the public schools, particularly if they are bureaucratically run and visibly hierarchical. There are obstacles raised by the pressures of parents and school boards, perhaps especially in suburban or middle-class communities. There are obstacles to be found in the emphasis on "competencies," in "accountability" arrangements, in the technological language so often spoken, in the ubiquity of testing and measurement.

The problem is that, confronted with structural and political pressures, many teachers (even effectual ones) cope by becoming merely efficient, by functioning compliantly—like Kafkaesque clerks. There are many who protect themselves by remaining basically uninvolved; there are many who are so bored, so lacking in expectancy, they no longer care. I doubt that many teachers deliberately choose to act as accomplices in a system they themselves understand to be inequitable; but feelings of powerlessness, coupled with indifference, may permit the so-called hidden curriculum to be communicated uncritically to students. Alienated teachers, out of touch with their own existential reality, may contribute to the distancing and even to the manipulating that presumably take place in many schools. This is because, estranged from themselves as they are, they may well treat whatever they imagine to be selfhood as a kind of commodity, a possession they carry within, impervious to organizational demand and impervious to control. Such people are not personally *present* to others or in the situations of their lives. They can, even without intending it, treat others as objects or things. This is because human beings who lack an awareness of their own personal reality (which is futuring, questing) cannot exist in a "we-relation" with other human beings. They cannot know what it means to live through a "vivid present in common" with another, to share another's "flux of experience in inner time" (Schutz, 1964, p. 173). Unable to come in touch with their own inner time, they cannot experience what Schutz called "the mutual tuning-in relationship, the experience of the 'We', which is at the foundation of all possible communication" (p. 173). It appears to me that without the ability to enter a "mutual tuning-in relationship," the teacher is in some manner incapacitated; since teaching is, in so many of its dimensions, a mode of encounter, of communication. This is one of the several reasons why I am arguing the importance of a recovery of personal reality.

Dewey, it will be recalled, said that the self is "something that is in continuous formation through choice of action." This suggests that teachers lacking a sense of self are the kinds of people who sit back and affirm that they are defined, indeed identified by their roles. Dewey (1916) stressed "*continuous* formation" and meant that persons are forever in process, forever growing and reconstructing their experiences

(p. 408; emphasis added). They are forever in pursuit of themselves. To deny that is to deny possibility, to deny the power to risk and to choose. As Sartre (1956) has said, we cannot be obliged to be *what* we are; we must continue making ourselves what we might be. A teacher who has become his or her role resembles the café waiter Sartre has described, the man whose "movement is quick and studied, a little too precise, a little too rapid." He moves like a mechanism, as if "imitating the quickness and pitiless rapidity of things" (p. 60). It is as if he is performing a part, as if he is nothing *but* a café waiter (as an inkwell is an inkwell, as a glass is a glass). He cannot transcend his role; he cannot imagine himself as anything *but* a café waiter; and so he is in bad faith. Sartre has given another example as well: "The attentive pupil who wishes to *be* attentive, his eyes riveted on the teacher, his ears open wide, so exhausts himself in playing the attentive role that he ends up by no longer hearing anything" (p. 60). In all these cases, the individual person (teacher, café waiter, or attentive child) is refusing to confront the fact that it was his or her free choice to get up in the morning and go to the school or the café, and that it is he or she who confers meaning and value on the work being done, the role being played. The crucial point is that the individual, conscious of multiple possibilities, must be aware that he or she is choosing to wait on tables, to study, to teach, choosing each day that he or she lives.

The "choice of action" must be interested as well as reflective; if not, the teacher is likely to be bored, as well as without care. I think of characters in literature who are bored in this sense, who drift without commitment through their lives. There is Frederic Moreau, in Gustave Flaubert's *A Sentimental Education* (1869/1976), the young man who can never choose a coherent line of action, who can never feel involved. At the end of the novel, he is sitting with his friend, who has also failed to realize any of his hopes. Typically, they are looking backward rather than forward. "They had both failed, one to realize his dreams of love, the other to fulfil his dreams of power. What was the reason?" (p. 417). They had dreamed; they had wandered; they had taken no responsibility. "Then they blamed chance, circumstances, the times into which they were born" (p. 418). And that is another mode of bad faith, not unknown among teachers: the habit of blaming ineffectuality on the institution, on circumstances, and the times.

Another example, perhaps more fearful, is to be found in Toni Morrison's novel *Sula* (1975). A vibrant, rebellious girl and woman, Sula is capable of watching from a distance when a child drowns and when her mother burns to death. Also, she drifts around the cities of the country in pointless boredom, finding that all the cities "held the same people, working the same mouths, sweating the same sweat" (p. 104). And then:

> In a way, her strangeness, her naivete, her craving for the other half of her equation was the consequence of an idle imagination. Had she paints, or clay, or knew the discipline of the dance, or strings; had she anything to engage her tremendous curiosity and her gift for metaphor, she might have exchanged the restlessness and preoccupation with whim for an activity that provided her with all she yearned for. And like any artist with no art form, she became dangerous. (p. 105)

This may be another way of talking about the necessity of a life project, of some purposeful work to do. It is also another way of suggesting the need for a medium or a meaningful activity if a self is to come into being, if a personal reality is to be achieved. A contrary example, one that dramatizes such an achievement, is Ralph Ellison's *Invisible Man* (1952). At the end, when the narrator (having lived underground) is about to emerge and move back into the social world, he says:

> In going underground, I whipped it all except the mind, the *mind*. And the mind that has conceived a plan of living must never lose sight of the chaos against which that pattern was conceived. That goes for societies as well as individuals. Thus, having tried to give pattern to the chaos which lives within the pattern of your certainties, I must come out, I must emerge. (p. 502)

He had given "pattern to the chaos" by taking the action of telling about it, writing about it, because he was unable to "file and forget." And, in the course of acting according to a "plan of living," he had attained a version of visibility; he had begun to create a self.

I would lay particular emphasis on choice. I believe that teachers willing to take the risk of coming in touch with themselves, of creating themselves, have to exist in a kind of tension; because it is always easier to fall back into indifference, into mere conformity, if not into bad faith. In Albert Camus's *The Plague* (1948), Tarrous sees the sickness that has befallen the town of Oran to signify, among other things, abstractness and indifference. He tells Dr. Rieux that everyone has the plague within him, that "what's natural is the microbe." He goes on to explain:

> All the rest—health, integrity, purity (if you like)—is a product of the human will, of a vigilance that must never falter. The good man, the man who infects hardly anyone, is the man who has the fewest lapses of attention. And it needs tremendous will-power, a never ending tension of the mind, to avoid such lapses. Yes, Rieux, it's a wearying business, being plague-stricken. But it's still more wearying to refuse to be it. That's why everybody in the world today looks so tired; everyone is more or less sick of plague. (p. 229)

Self-awareness, self-discovery, self-actualization: These are often made to seem affairs of feeling, mainly, or of intuition. Teachers are asked to heighten their sensitivity, to tap the affective dimension of their lives, to trust, to love. Of course it is important to reach out, to feel, to experience love and concern. But I believe that, if teachers are truly to be present to themselves and to others, they need to exert effort in overcoming the weariness Camus described—a weariness all teachers, at some level, recognize. I believe that, for teachers as well as plague-fighters, "health, integrity, purity," and the rest must be consciously chosen. So must interest and good faith.

I have talked about the original interests that move persons to decide to take up teaching as a career. I have touched on the ways in which the demands of institutional situations make certain teachers set those interests aside. A lover of poetry, for instance, once eager to open the world of poetry to the young, may find it impossible to reconcile that desire (and that love) with the requirements of socialization and control. A person with an interest in physics or chemistry, hoping to inspire young apprentices, may find it too difficult to engage students with actual inquiries and at once maintain order in the classroom. The consequence may be a repression of the original enthusiasm and a resigned decision to have things the way they are "spozed to be" (Herndon, 1969). Understandable though this is, the decision is evocative of the one Dewey has in mind when he spoke of people who give up in the face of discomfort or danger: Such teachers are declaring their preference to be teachers who choose to keep order and simply disseminate as many bits of knowledge as they can. This is quite different from the choice to create a situation in which knowledge can be sought and meanings pursued. It is quite different from the choice to institute the kind of dialogue that might move the young to pose their own worthwhile questions, to tell their own stories, to reach out in their being together to learn how to learn. And it may well be that the teachers who make such decisions are alienating themselves still more from what they think of as their personal reality.

For one thing, it is important to move back in inner time and attempt to recapture the ways in which the meanings of teaching (and schooling) were sedimented over the years. It should not be impossible for individual teachers to reflect back upon the ways in which they have constituted what they take to be the realities of their lived worlds. To look back, to remember is to bind the incidents of past experience, to create patterns in the stream of consciousness. We identify ourselves by means of memory; and, at once, we compose the stories of our lives. In Sartre's *Nausea*, Roquentin points out that "everything changes when you tell about life" (1959). There are beginnings and endings; there are significant moments;

banal events are transformed. Hannah Arendt (1974) has written of the importance of "enacted stories" and the ways in which stories disclose a "who," an "agent; she has made the point that every individual life between birth and death can eventually be told as a story with beginning and end" (p. 184).

Looking back, recapturing their stories, teachers can recover their own standpoints on the social world. Reminded of the importance of biographical situation and the ways in which it conditions perspective, they may be able to understand the provisional character of their knowing, of all knowing. They may come to see that, like other living beings, they could only discern profiles, aspects of the world. Making an effort to interpret the texts of their life stories, listening to others' stories in whatever "web of relationships" (p. 184) they find themselves, they may be able to multiply the perspectives through which they look upon the realities of teaching; they may be able to choose themselves anew in the light of an expanded interest, an enriched sense of reality. Those who wished to become nuturant beings may—having entered new "provinces of meaning" (Schutz, 1967, p. 231) looked at from different vantage points—come to see that nurturing too can only be undertaken within social situations, and that the social situation in the school must be seen in relation to other situations lived by the young. Those who chose themselves as keepers of the academic disciplines may come to realize that the perspectives made possible by the disciplines are meaningful when they illuminate the experience of the learner, when they enable him or her to order the materials of his or her own lived world. Those who focused primarily on the social process may come to see that existing individuals, each in his or her own "here" and own "now," act in their intersubjectivity to bring the social reality into being, and that attention must be paid to the person in his or her uniqueness even as it is paid to the community. Seeing more, each one may be more likely to become "a network of relationships" (Merleau-Ponty, 1967a, p. 456) and perhaps be more likely to act in his or her achieved freedom to cut loose from anchorage and choose anew.

The diversification of perspectives has much to do, I think, with the sense of personal reality; but I would add that it is equally important for those engaged in seeking themselves to involve themselves in critique. By that I mean critical reflection upon the social situation, especially the situation they live in common. The dangers of submergence are multiple, as we have seen. Teachers suffer in many ways what they experience as conditioning or manipulation by their superiors or by the "system" itself. To reflect upon the situation, even the bureaucratic situation, is to try to understand some of the forces that frustrate their quests for themselves and their efforts to create themselves as the teachers they want to be. At once, it is to identify the kinds of lacks in that situation that require naming and repair: impersonality, for example; reliance on external criteria of "performance"; inequitable tracking; mindless routines. Coming together to determine what is possible, teachers may discover a determination to transcend.

I am suggesting that a concern for personal reality cannot be divorced from a concern for cooperative action within some sort of community. It is when teachers are together as persons, according to norms and principles they have freely chosen, that interest becomes intensified and commitments are made. And this may open pathways to expanded landscapes, richer ways of being human—unique and in the "we-relation" at one and the same time.

Hannah Arendt (1961) has told a story about some former members of the French Resistance who felt that they had "lost their treasure" when the war was over and they returned to ordinary life; and what she wrote seems to apply to teachers and their search for their personal reality.

> What was this treasure? As they themselves understood it, it seems to have consisted . . . of two interconnected parts: they had discovered that he who "joined the Resistance, found himself," . . . that he no longer suspected himself of "insincerity," of being "a carping, suspicious actor of life," that he could afford to "go naked." In this nakedness, stripped of all masks—of those which society assigns to its members as well as those which the individual fabricates for himself in his psychological reactions against society—they had been visited . . . by an apparition of freedom, not, to be sure, because they acted against tyranny . . . but because they had become "challengers," and had taken the initiative upon themselves and therefore . . . had begun to create that public space between themselves where freedom could appear. (p. 4)

I want to see teachers become challengers and take the initiative upon themselves. As they do so, as *we* do so, there will emerge a "public space" where personal reality can be at last affirmed.

REFERENCES

Arendt, H. (1961). *Between past and future*. New York: Viking.

Arendt, H. (1974). *The human condition* Chicago: University of Chicago Press.

Buber, M. (1957). *Between man and man*. Boston: Beacon. (Original work published 1947)

Camus, A. (1948). *The plague*. New York: Knopf.

Dewey, J. (1916). *Democracy and education.* New York: Macmillan.

Dewey, J. (1957). *Human nature and conduct.* New York: Modern Library. (Original work published 1922 by Henry Holt)

Dewey, J. (1963). *Experience and education.* New York: Collier. (Original work published 1938)

Eliot, T. S. (1952). The hollow men. In *The complete poems and plays.* New York: Harcourt, Brace.

Ellison, R. (1952). *Invisible man.* New York: Signet.

Flaubert, G. (1976). *A sentimental education.* New York: Penguin. (Original work published 1869)

Freire, P. (1970) *Pedagogy of the oppressed.* New York: Herder & Herder.

Herndon, J. (1969). *The way it spozed to be.* New York: Bantam.

Mead, G. H. (1934). *Mind, self and society.* Chicago: University of Chicago Press.

Merleau-Ponty, M. (1964). *The primacy of perception.* Evanston, IL: Northwestern University Press

Merleau-Ponty, M. (1967a). *Phenomenology of perception.* New York: Humanities.

Merleau-Ponty, M. (1967b). *The structure of behavior.* Boston: Beacon

Morrison, T. (1975). *Sula.* New York: Bantam.

Sartre, J. (1956). *Being and nothingness.* New York: Philosophical Library.

Sartre, J. (1959). *Nausea.* New York: New Directions.

Sartre, J. (1963). *Search for a method.* New York: Knopf.

Schutz, A. (1964). *Collected Papers: Vol 2. Studies in social theory.* The Hague: Martinus Nijhoff.

Schutz, A. (1967). *Collected Papers: Vol 1. The problem of social reality.* The Hague: Martinus Nijhoff.

Smith, B. (1963). Toward a theory of teaching. In A. A. Bellack (Ed.), *Theory and research in teaching.* New York: Teachers College, Bureau of Publications.

Thoreau, H. D. (1963). *Walden.* New York: Washington Square. (Original work published 1854)

② Using Knowledge of Change to Guide Staff Development

Susan Loucks-Horsley & Suzanne Stiegelbauer

Throughout the country and, indeed, around the world, educators are engaged in rethinking what learning, teaching, and schooling are all about and making some major changes in their practice as a result. Discussions that take place in meetings, conferences, workshops, and staff lounges provide evidence of the typical frustrations with change. The following comments from a range of individuals associated with schools illustrate the various reactions to the process of change:

Teacher: How can they be so sure that changing everything will be for the better?

Building administrator: It seems that restructuring means that the school will be run by a committee.

Teacher: I need some good ideas for what to do on Monday, not more theory.

Community member: Why are school people so unclear about what the outcomes of schooling ought to be? I wonder if I can be helpful in setting this school to rights.

Teacher: I'm really comfortable with my kids in my classroom, but I'm not sure how good I'll be as a member of the leadership team.

Building administrator: I think I've been a good school leader by my definition, but I'm not sure I'll be able to function well in the new role they're talking about.

Teacher: I can't wait to get started on the new restructuring project.

District administrator: They're talking about getting rid of centralized curriculum and staff development. What will I do then?

Judging from where we have started, there is no doubt that the 1990s will be characterized by efforts to restructure, redesign, and generally transform schools into systems that are built to focus on learning (rather than teaching and administering) and where decisions are made in a much more participative way than they have been in the past. Traditional distinctions such as teaching and learning, teacher and administrator, testing and instruction, school and community, will be blurred in the interest of richer, more meaningful student outcomes.

In all the grand thinking, however, it is often easy to ignore, or even miss altogether, the pros and cons, complaints and praise, moans and musings, such as those above: the real reactions and concerns of the people closest to the changes that are occurring or are likely to occur. While their roles and experiences to date have varied widely, the greatest common denominator seems to be that all are awash in a sea of complexities. The kinds of changes everyone from parents to the President of the United States imagine will only succeed if the needs of those closest to children are attended to. Staff developers can and should play a critical role.

In the first edition of this book (1978), one of us (Susan Loucks-Horsley) and Gene Hall wrote the precursor to this article, "Teacher Concerns as a Basis for Facilitating and Personalizing Staff Development." It remains one of our favorite articles about the Concerns-Based Adoption Model (CBAM), largely because it captured some of the liveliness and the meaning that were beginning to emerge from an exciting area of research on how individuals experience the change process and what that might imply for staff development. For that reason, we have drawn on that article to supply the core descriptive material for this chapter.

Knowing something about the context in which the CBAM was born and developed can serve to illustrate its usefulness over 20 years later. In the late 1960s and early 1970s, when the CBAM was conceived, there were enormous resources being expended on innovation in schools. Most people who were writing about and conducting research on change were focused on the organizational level. Organization development specialists were concerned about the communication, problem-solving, and decision-making structures in schools, and about their climate (Schmuck & Miles, 1971; Schmuck, Runkel, Arends, & Arends, 1977). They were designing strategies to improve these elements in schools. Yet there was little if any attention to teaching and learning, to the individual teachers who were being called upon to change their practice overnight.

The CBAM filled that gap, focusing on, as we describe in detail in this article, the developmental process individuals go through as they experience a change (Hall & Hord, 1987). The CBAM does not prescribe a specific set of strategies for change; rather it provides useful information for those whose role it is to help teachers change their curriculum and instructional approaches. Staff developers can design their programs to anticipate the kinds of questions teachers would have as they grow in their knowledge and skills. Program planners and administrators can set goals for change and monitor their achievement. Evaluators can assess implementation.

Enter the 1980s, when we learned that effective schools could in fact exist in hostile environments and the correlates of such schools were the focus of change efforts nationwide (Cohen, 1982; Edmonds, 1979). Effective schools programs broadened the scope of innovation beyond the classroom to such school-level factors as leadership and school mission and goals, although the best of them also remembered how critical instructional and curriculum change were to learning. By the late 1980s, with attention directed to reform of the entire education system, such organizational variables as leadership, decision making, and culture were the focus of change efforts (Fullan, 1990a, 1990b; Goodlad, 1984; Rosenholtz, 1989; Sizer, 1984).

What we have learned in our work with the CBAM over the past two decades is that there is still and will always be a critical place for consideration of the individual in the change process. The CBAM never pretended to include everything staff developers, school administrators, and others responsible for change needed to know to succeed in change efforts. Yet as we become smarter about how to think about and manage the organizational dimension of change, the CBAM takes its place in the new frameworks to remind us of the critical individual dimension.

The development of the CBAM was based on extensive experience with educational innovations in school and college settings (Hall, Wallace, & Dossett, 1973). The following principles were derived from that experience, and they establish the model's perspective on working with change:

1. Change is a process, not an event. Too often policy makers, administrators, even teachers assume that change results from a policy mandate, an administrative requirement, adoption of new curricula, or a revised procedure. They assume that a teacher will put aside a tried-and-true practice and immediately use a new one with great facility. In the most absurd situations, there is the companion assumption that the new program can soon be evaluated for its impact on students. In reality, change takes time and is accomplished only in stages.

2. Because the *individual* is a key player in the change process, his or her

needs must be the focus of help and support designed to facilitate change. Other approaches to change view the organization as the primary unit of intervention. The CBAM, however, emphasizes working with individuals—both teachers and administrators—as they are involved with innovations. The CBAM holds firmly to the conviction that organizations cannot change until the individuals within them change.

3. Change is a highly *personal* experience. Unfortunately, people responsible for change often attend closely to the innovation itself and ignore the people experiencing the change. The CBAM holds that the personal dimension is often more important to the success or failure of a change effort than the technological dimension. Since change is made by individuals, their personal satisfactions, frustrations, concerns, motivations, and perceptions all contribute to the success or failure of a change initiative.

4. The change process is *developmental*. Individuals involved in change go through stages in their perceptions and feelings about an innovation, as well as in their skill and sophistication in using the innovation.

5. Well-designed staff development results from a measure of *diagnostic/prescriptive* thinking. Too many staff development offerings address the needs of staff developers rather than those of the participants. The most relevant and supportive staff development can be planned only if staff developers diagnose where participants are in the change process and design activities that resolve their expressed needs.

6. Staff developers need to have a *systemic* view of change and constantly *adapt* their behaviors as the change progresses. They need to stay in constant touch with the progress of individuals within the context of the total organization that is supporting the change. They must be able to assess and reassess the state of the change process and be able to tailor help and support to the latest information. They must also be aware of the "ripple effect" that change in one part of the system has on the system's other parts.

To accomplish all this, a conceptual model of the change process must provide practical reference points in a constantly changing array of events. The Concerns-Based Adoption Model provides a structure that takes these ideas into account. Three aspects of change form the basic frame of reference of the model: the concerns that individuals experience about an innovation or change, how the innovation is actually used, and the ways in which the innovation is adapted to the needs and styles of particular individuals. The first dimension, that of Stages of Concern, is the primary focus of this chapter. The other dimensions, Levels of Use and Innovation Configurations (also called Innovation Components), provide helpful information for monitoring progress and tailoring activities and support. They are discussed briefly later in the chapter.

STAGES OF CONCERN ABOUT THE INNOVATION

Those responsible for staff development, whether principals, teachers, consultants, assistant superintendents, or formally designated staff development coordinators, will find all too familiar the comments in the opening of this article. How can you think about these statements? How can you address them within a framework of a comprehensive staff development program? How can that program influence and be favorably influenced by critical organizational dimensions of the change process? These and other questions will be addressed as we describe and discuss applications of the CBAM.

Because Stages of Concern address the "people response" to change, and because change does not occur until "someone" changes, we begin there. As noted earlier, the process of change is a personal experience for each individual involved. Everyone approaching a change, initially implementing an innovation, or developing skill in using an innovation will have certain perceptions, feelings, motivations, frustrations, and satisfactions about the innovation and the change process.

In the CBAM, the concept of concerns has been developed to describe these perceptions, feelings, and motivations. Concerns are also preoccupations; they reflect what is on an individual's mind about a change at a single point in time.

The research on Stages of Concern verified a set of stages that people appear to move through when they are involved in implementing a change. We learned that their response to change is developmental and to a certain degree predictable, although some may move through the stages quickly and others slowly.

The concept of concerns was first described by Frances Fuller (1969). In her research, Fuller identified four general levels of concerns that preservice and inservice teachers expressed as they moved through their teacher education program. These concerns moved from initial concerns *unrelated* to teaching (I'm concerned about getting along with my roommate), to concerns about *self* in relation to teaching (I wonder if I can do it), to concerns about the *task* of teaching (It's taking so long to prepare my lessons every night), to *impact* concerns (Are the students learning what they need?). The progression of concerns shows considerable resemblance to Maslow's hierarchy of needs.

As we shared the concept of teacher concerns with people across the country, it became apparent that the idea applied in a similar way to individual teachers and college professors involved in implementing various educational innovations. Seven Stages of Concern (SoC) about the innovation were identified (see Figure 2.1; Hall et al., 1973). Apparently a person's concerns moved generally through the progression from self, to task, to impact that Fuller had described.

Research on Stages of Concern

Research on the concept of Stages of Concern initially focused on the development of a reliable and valid measurement procedure for assessing concerns (Hall, George, & Rutherford, 1979) and then on a series of cross-sectional and longitudinal studies that verified the existence of such stages (Hall & Loucks, 1978).

FIGURE 2.1 Stages of Concern About the Innovation

6 REFOCUSING. Concerns focus on exploration of more universal benefits from the innovation, including the possibility of major changes or replacement with a more powerful alternative. Individual has definite ideas about alternatives to the proposed or existing form of the innovation.

5 COLLABORATION. Concerns focus on coordination and cooperation with others in use of the innovation in order to better meet the needs of students.

4 CONSEQUENCE. Concerns focus on the impact of the innovation on students in their immediate spheres of influence. The focus is on relevance of the innovation for students, evaluation of student outcomes, and changes needed to increase student outcomes.

3 MANAGEMENT. Concerns focus on the processes and tasks of using the innovation and the best use of information and resources. Issues related to efficiency, organization, management, scheduling, and time are crucial.

2 PERSONAL. The individual is uncertain about the demands of the innovation, his or her inadequacy to meet those demands, and his or her role with the innovation. Concerns focus on his or her role in relation to the reward structure of the organization, decision making, and consideration of potential conflicts with existing structures or personal commitment. Concerns about financial or status implications of the program for self and colleagues may also be reflected.

1 INFORMATIONAL. Concerns focus on developing a general awareness of the innovation and learning more detail about it. The individual is interested in substantive aspects of the innovation such as general characteristics, effects, and requirements for use.

0 AWARENESS. There is little concern about or involvement with the innovation.

Note. Original concept from Hall, Wallace, and Dossett (1973).

The data gathered in these studies elaborated the concept of concerns as it appears in the real world. Individuals grow and mature as they gain experience. The concerns they have often reflect their relationship to that experience. For instance, inexperienced individuals are likely to have intense stage 0, 1, and 2 concerns (awareness, informational, and personal) about that which is new to them. As they become more involved, they become more concerned about managing the change (stage 3 concerns). As they work further with the innovation and feel more confident with it, consequence concerns begin to emerge (stage 4). As they become more intensely concerned about the consequences of their efforts, they may seek out other individuals with whom to collaborate to increase impact (stage 5) or begin to refocus, to investigate better ways to do things (stage 6).

This developmental sequence is represented in the concerns "profile" shown in Figure 2.1. At any point in time an individual will have a number of different concerns but will likely have one that is the most intense. This will be revealed on a profile as higher in relative intensity than the other concerns. Figure 2.2 shows what is called the "wave pattern" of concerns. Here, the way concerns change from the nonuser to the renewing user indicates what is most important to individuals at each stage.

Assessing Stages of Concern

There are three ways to assess Stages of Concern, and staff developers can determine which to use based on their particular needs and context.

Stages of concern questionnaire.   Data for the initial research studies supporting the development of Stages of Concern (SoC) were collected using a questionnaire (Hall et al., 1979). The most formal and precise measure of Stages of Concern, the questionnaire consists of 35 items, each with a Likert scale (not true of me now . . . very true of me now) on which respondents indicate their present degree of concern about the topic described in the item. There are five items for each of the seven Stages of Concern. A sample item representing stage 5 collaboration is: "I would like to coordinate my efforts with others to maximize the innovation's effects."

The questionnaire takes about 15 minutes to administer and can be scored either by hand, using percentile tables, or by computer. The questionnaire is psychometrically rigorous and reliable enough to provide both meaningful research data and information for planning change

FIGURE 2.2 Hypothesized Development of Stages of Concern

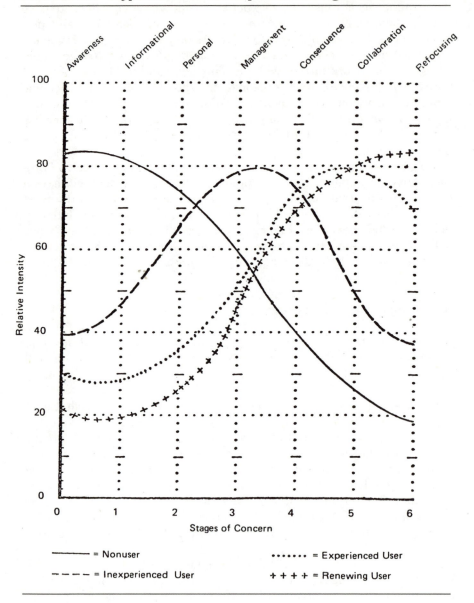

strategies. SoC Questionnaire data can be interpreted in two ways. The first and simplest is by noting the stage that received the highest percentile score. This indicates the kinds of concerns that are most intense for the individual at that particular point in time. A more complex interpretation of SoC Questionnaire data is possible by examining the "profile" of scores, that is, the percentile score for every stage for a respondent. The scores must be viewed as relative, with the highest and second-highest scores indicating areas of greatest concern and the lower scores as areas of least concern. Analysis of a concerns profile allows the staff developer to assess the relative value of different activities to an individual.

The SoC Questionnaire has some obvious advantages and disadvantages. Its psychometric value makes it appropriate for research and more vigorous evaluation studies. It is more efficient than the open-ended statement (described below) with large numbers of people, and it provides more precise information on the basis of a larger quantity of data. It indicates what concerns are important to individuals or groups and readily allows for comparison of groups across time. However, in contrast to the open-ended statement, it does not say what specific issues those concerns are about. For this reason, where possible, it is best to use both forms together, perhaps with the statement added at the end of the SoC Questionnaire, especially in instances where concerns data are being collected to plan as well as to monitor implementation.

Open-ended statement.   One of the methods most frequently used by staff developers involves asking for a written response to the question: "When you think about [the innovation], what are you concerned about?" The response is then scored for concerns based on the definitions shown in Figure 2.1. (A manual by Newlove and Hall, 1976, gives instructions for administering and scoring such open-ended statements.)

Figure 2.3 is an example of an open-ended statement. Here the individual who wrote the response has management (stage 3) concerns, as reflected in complaints about time, efficiency, and planning. As are all open-ended responses, this paragraph is scored by considering each sentence, scoring it according to the definitions in Figure 2.1, and then developing an overall picture of the paragraph. Care must be taken to consider the overall flavor of the responses (which often reflect preoccupation with more than one Stage of Concern) and not to focus purely on the numerical scores.

The open-ended statement can be used anytime new activities are being planned and can be used as a quick reference point to check the relevance of the activity. The staff developer can easily flip through a

FIGURE 2.3   Open-Ended Statement of Concerns (Sample)

When you think about [the innovation], what are you concerned about? (Do not say what you think others are concerned about, but only what concerns you now.) Please write in complete sentences, and please be frank.

My biggest concern is how much time it is taking me to get this new program to run smoothly. I either prepare too much or not enough material for the day's lesson. The kids have so many questions and always seem to be lined up in front of my desk! I wonder how long it will take to make it work.

---

stack of responses to get a feeling for the total group and to spot problem areas. Statements also have the benefit of reporting on specific issues important to users. For instance, individuals with management concerns may describe how they are unable to get the material to work for them; others with early consequence concerns may indicate that not all students are responding well and that they are considering ways to reach more of them. As a result, open-ended statements give two kinds of information— that of concerns in general and that of concerns about specific issues. Both can be examined for a group or for individuals in determining next steps.

Conversational assessment.   The "one-legged interview," the simplest and most informal method of collecting concerns data, simply involves talking about the innovation. The staff developer asks leading questions, listens for clues in informal discussions, evaluates requests for information and help. This is called a "one-legged interview" because it is brief enough to be done while standing on one leg (or taking a stroll down the hall). Individuals are asked to talk about what they are doing with the innovation and how they are using it, much in the manner of "management by wandering around." Questions about their perception of the innovation's strengths and weaknesses, typical problems, and response to recent training or help all provide information that can be considered within the concerns framework.

What the one-legged interview may lack in scientific rigor, it makes up in ease of use, cost-effectiveness, and rapport with clients. The method is unobtrusive and does not typically generate misleading information. If used frequently enough it can also be a major source of support to users, who often feel adrift in dealing with the change alone. This kind of assessment can be used to confirm or update more formal data and is most valuable to the experienced staff developer who wants to keep in close contact with the progress of change.

Implications of Concerns for Staff Development

The data collected in the research studies on concerns have a variety of implications for the staff developer. First, it is clear that, before they begin using an innovation, people have their most intense concerns on stages 0, 1, and 2. They are most preoccupied with getting general descriptive information about the change (stage 1) and thinking about how it will affect them personally (stage 2). They are not as concerned, relatively speaking, about the impact of the innovation on students (low intensity of stages 4, 5, 6). This suggests that staff development for nonusers should address those initial information needs and personal concerns, perhaps by providing an overview of the innovation with attention given to personal experience with it, that is, in the nature of "testimonials" by individuals who have used it and who can talk about what that is like.

Nonusers or early users can also benefit from a show of support by supervisors and discussion of where their current skills are applicable, where new skill will be developed, and the amount of time it will take from their current schedule to put the innovation into place. At this stage the primary concerns of individuals will normally be focused on themselves and their initial use. They are naturally somewhat concerned about the implications of the innovation for students, but they are *more* concerned about what the innovation means to them. A lot of discussion of the benefits for students might help sell the innovation but will not likely help in *use* of the innovation. Hence the often-heard statement "you should do this because it's good for the students" does not address the concerns of the typical nonuser. In fact, such a statement may exacerbate personal and informational concerns instead of helping individuals move toward using the innovation well and seeing those benefits for themselves.

How can one put knowledge of concerns to use? The diagnostic and prescriptive powers of the concerns concept are obvious. The staff developer who gathers individual concerns data possesses valuable information with which to plan relevant and effective staff development activities. Guesswork is removed from the planning process. "Gut feelings" about training needs are replaced by a reliable yardstick. The SoC profiles can provide both individual and group data that can be used in various ways: to plan interventions, to evaluate progress, and to spot individual problems. In the next section, we present an example of an implementation effort based on concerns data.

AN EXAMPLE OF
A CONCERNS-BASED STAFF DEVELOPMENT PROGRAM

An illustration of how the concept of Stages of Concern can be employed in a staff development program comes from a collaborative effort of the Texas R&D Center and the Jefferson County (Colorado) public schools, a large suburban school district (Hall et al., 1980). In this district, teachers in the approximately 80 elementary schools were helped to implement a revision of the science curriculum for grades 3–6. Revised by teams of teachers, the science curriculum included a set of activities from several existing curricula (e.g., Elementary Science Study and Science Curriculum Improvement Study), as well as outdoor education, environmental education, decision making, and health education. The materials were combined into one large teacher's guide for each grade level. This guide was designed to address stage 3 (management) concern issues. The "how-to-do-its" of teaching were included, with detailed information about how to conduct each activity, where to locate materials and supplies, and how to order films and backup references.

The curriculum materials and the teacher's guides were developed and field-tested within the school system. The Texas R&D Center became involved after science consultants and staff developers in the district had completed field-testing and were designing plans for implementation in all 80 schools in the system.

Initially the plan was to use three released-time inservice days placed closely together early in the fall of the school year. The planned inservice activities were well designed. In general the plan was consistent with a concerns-based approach, providing teachers with model lessons, direct handling of materials, experience with student activities and science content, with experienced teachers as inservice leaders. As the collaborative effort developed with the Texas R&D Center, however, the school district's plan was adjusted to include Stages of Concern and other data collected within the school system.

Influenced by the idea of a concerns-based implementation, the first change in the plan was to extend the time between each of the three released-time inservice days. In fact, rather than completing the training before the school year started or within the first couple of months, the inservice workshops were distributed over one and a half school years. This was done because we knew that the teachers' concerns would not develop within eight weeks from high information and personal concerns to high impact concerns. Rather, at least one or two cycles of use would be required to resolve management concerns and to move toward consequence concerns. By a broad distribution of the inservice training days, more concerns could be addressed.

A second decision, made early in the collaboration, was to clarify the goal of the implementation effort. In designing the staff development program the school system had a choice of goals: to have a portion of the teachers teaching science at a high level of quality (e.g., with consequence concerns), or to have all teachers simply teaching science using the new materials. It was not possible for both goals to be accomplished with the same staff development plan, as the content would be quite different for different objectives. The school system's decision was to have all students receiving science instruction with the new materials.

We learned from the initial assessment of Stages of Concerns that informational (stage 1) concerns were highest, with some personal (stage 2) concerns. Since personal concerns were not particularly high, especially for nonusers, the emphasis was placed first on addressing informational concerns, since it was suspected that many of the personal concerns would be resolved with more information. The activity selected was a small-group "pre-inservice" meeting that lasted for one hour after school. At this meeting, which took place the semester before actual inservice activities, teachers from two schools met with one of the science consultants. They were introduced to the schedule and to the plans for the inservice days; they received their teacher's guides. A slideshow depicted how the curriculum would look as they taught it in their classroom. General questions were answered. The emphasis was on giving general descriptive information about the curriculum in anticipation of personal and management concerns.

The released-time inservice days were structured to respond to "how-to-do-it" management concerns. Teachers were to work directly with materials and discuss such topics as classroom management and material storage. To have the greatest opportunity for learning, they met in grade-level groups, focusing in each workshop on the two to three units they would teach before the next workshop.

Since there were teachers in the school system who had been involved in field-testing the curriculum and others who were already highly proficient in the teaching of science, it was predicted that although most teachers attending the inservice days would have management concerns, some would have consequence concerns. Therefore, inservice days were designed with two tracks. One track was designed for teachers with more intense management concerns, the other for teachers who had more intense consequence concerns.

The route designed for teachers with intense management concerns continued their involvement with science department staff and the inservice leaders. The content of these sessions emphasized the nitty-gritty and "how-to-do-its" of teaching the science units. The alternate route intended for teachers with consequence concerns entailed self-paced modules dealing with such areas as wait time as a teaching strategy, Piaget, learning theory, and conducting outdoor education activities. These modules were designed to allow teachers to work in a self-directed mode either individually or in small groups. Teachers were given a choice of the two options.

Stages of Concern data were gathered from the teachers before the double-tracked inservice days and then again afterwards to help us see whether they would self-select into the group designed for their Stage of Concern. As hoped, teachers with higher personal and management concerns (stage 2 and 3) stayed in the large group with the face-to-face contact and the how-to-do-it content. Those teachers who had lower personal and management concerns chose instead to engage with the more independent, consequence-oriented learning modules.

Using the concerns concept in this way, Jefferson County district staff developers were provided with an overall schema and diagnostic data for planning further staff development activities. To help even more with personal and management concerns, they chose to include on-site help for teachers in their classrooms, afterschool "comfort and caring" meetings, and sessions with principals to discuss their role in supporting classroom implementation. The teacher materials and the original training design were a good start, but the trick was to mesh these elements with the teachers at the right time and in the right ways. The key to the timing was an assessment of the state of the change process using the SoC Questionnaire. Questionnaire data gathered over time helped staff developers to monitor the impact of the change and tailor their activities to be of most help to the teachers. Evaluation of progress over a three-year period indicated a high level of implementation, with teachers' concerns about and use of the curriculum changing dramatically (Loucks & Melle, 1982).

OTHER DIMENSIONS OF THE CONCERNS MODEL

Stages of Concern is one of three dimensions of the CBAM. Stages of Concern focuses on the affective dimension—how people feel about change at different points in the process. The second CBAM dimension, Levels of Use (LoU), asks what individuals are *doing* with that information or doing in response to the introduction of an innovation (Hall & Loucks, 1977). As with Stages of Concern, Levels of Use is also developmental, describing individual behavior in response to change. The eight Levels of Use can indicate individuals who are working with an innovation well, those who are still experimenting and preparing for use, and those who are improving and adapting it based on their experience.

The third diagnostic dimension of the CBAM is Innovation Configurations (Heck, Stiegelbauer, Hall, & Loucks, 1981). This dimension describes the various operational forms of an innovation that different users choose to implement. A tool called a Practice Profile can be developed that describes an innovation from an ideal perspective, providing users, staff developers, evaluators, and others with a picture of behavioral expectations and a way to describe individual interpretations of use of an innovation (Loucks & Crandall, 1982). The Profile can be used to clarify and set goals for progress and to monitor group and individual growth. Whereas Stages of Concern and Levels of Use focus on the individual, Practice Profiles describe the innovation as it is used by individuals.

Later research on the CBAM focused on the role of change facilitators (among whom are staff developers) in providing the necessary interventions to support individuals in their use of an innovation. Six functions of *interventions* were described in this aspect of the research:

1. Supportive organizational arrangements
2. Ongoing training and information
3. Consultation and reinforcement
4. Monitoring and evaluation
5. External communication
6. Dissemination of results (Hall & Hord, 1984)

These components of a "game plan" for change have been shown to be important to the success of implementation efforts. In conjunction with Stages of Concern, Levels of Use, and Practice Profile data, the concept of interventions allows staff developers to reflect on the needs of a change effort in order to determine next steps.

The CBAM provides staff developers with diagnostic information about the status of users in working with change. With this information, decisions can be made to better support and address the needs of those individuals such that they are more satisfied and successful in their efforts. As one success builds on another, one potential outcome of the use of CBAM tools is to make the process of change easier for all involved.

USING THE CBAM
WITH INDIVIDUALS OTHER THAN TEACHERS

As our research team developed the CBAM, we knew that teachers were not the only ones who experienced a developmental progression in their concerns about and use of innovations. Even in our personal lives, we each recognized our changing concerns, knowledge, and behaviors in new relationships, new jobs, new locations. We had included college professors in the first set of research studies that validated the dimensions of the CBAM and found their experiences to be similar to those of teachers.

Late in the 1970s, after completing the initial research reported above, we learned that principals greatly influenced how teachers progressed (or did not progress) through the change process, and we hypothesized that there was something akin to Stages of Concern that drove principals to support teachers in different ways. Three different styles appeared to characterize how principals facilitated change in their schools—that of the responder, the manager, and the initiator. These styles were described and then examined in a series of research studies (Hall, Rutherford, Hord, & Huling-Austin, 1984).

At the same time we were learning about the important role of a change facilitator, that is, anyone with the responsibility for helping people implement innovations. Change facilitators had their own concerns about their role and about the changes they were supporting. We knew that knowledge of their concerns could help them get the support they needed and could help researchers and evaluators examine the facilitator's influence on implementation success. For this purpose we developed a slightly revised scale of Change Facilitator Stages of Concern and designed a Change Facilitator's Stages of Concern Questionnaire (Hall & Hord, 1987).

Elements of the CBAM have been applied to groups other than educators. Marsh and Penn (1988) measured the concerns of students. Horsley (1990) used the CBAM extensively in helping participants in Project Adventure, an experience-based ropes program similar in goals to Outward Bound, to understand and articulate their experiences in risk taking and team building. The CBAM concepts have also been used to understand change in a variety of business settings, in hospital emergency rooms, and in human service organizations.

MORE OF THE CBAM IN ACTION

CBAM tools have been used in many settings to plan staff development activities and develop supports for implementation. State educational agencies have used it to design and monitor statewide programs. For example, in 1989 the Nebraska State Department of Education initiated a statewide assessment of their Learning Strategies in Special Education program, using Practice Profile and Levels of Use interviews to assess the impact of the training offered teachers. These data were also used to plan later Learning Strategies sessions. Similar staff development program evaluations using Levels of Use and Practice Profiles have recently been implemented by state departments of education and school boards in Florida, New York, Maryland, North Carolina, and Colorado, to name a few (for one example, see Nielsen and Turner, 1985). Also at the state and federal level, CBAM tools continue to be used in the evaluation of state and federal special programs and innovations (Anderson, Stiegelbauer, Gerin-LaJoie, Partlow, & Cummins, 1990).

Local school districts have also used the CBAM to support changes in schools and teachers. In Ontario, Canada, the Scarborough Board of Education (1987) has integrated the concepts of Stages of Concern and Levels of Use into their handbook for principals as a guide to interventions in support of program change. Also in Ontario, the Durham Board of Education has adapted the Levels of Use concept as a vehicle for setting teacher goals related to specific implementation projects. Further, training in CBAM diagnostic dimensions, especially Stages of Concern, has become a regular feature of principal training as a way to develop awareness of what "leadership for change" really means (Stiegelbauer & Loucks-Horsley, 1987). Such training not only offers a way to assess progress and diagnose needs related to implementation but also provides a hands-on experience with the change process. Training in CBAM tools, combined with on-site coaching, has been used to help school-based facilitators in their roles in effective schools projects (Stiegelbauer, Buehler, & Turner, 1989).

These and other situations illustrate that the CBAM is flexible to the needs of many different settings. One specific benefit mentioned by participants in CBAM training is that a concerns-based perspective helps them see what is happening in almost a "commonsense" way, allowing them to feel more in control of what is often an ambiguous process.

THE CBAM MOVES INTO THE 1990s

If current activity is a good predictor, the CBAM will continue to be useful for the kinds of purposes illustrated in this chapter. Certainly changes in curriculum, instruction, organizational structures and procedures, roles and responsibilities all require attention to individual needs and the kinds of help and support for which the CBAM can be a useful framework. But what are some of the unique aspects of today's reform efforts that need to be considered as staff developers call on their knowledge of CBAM to do their jobs?

Scope of the Innovations

Many of today's restructuring efforts are on a different scale from innovations of the past. We used to talk about "innovation bundles," such as open classrooms, where such innovations as open space, team teaching, individualized instruction, and multi-aged grouping were all called for at once. Our advice: Think about concerns and uses for each separate innovation, knowing that people will be in different places and help and support must vary.

As if that image of staff development was not complicated enough, today's changes require not only the same magnitude of change at the classroom level, but changes at every level: in management, governance, organizational arrangements, community involvement, district and state assessment, just to name a few. And, true to form, individuals will have concerns and progress through change differently for each facet of the change.

One of the tasks of the staff developer is to acknowledge this fact, to discern which facets may generate the most intense concerns or the greatest range of concerns across participants, and pay closer attention to those. A simple open-ended statement could help identify the facets of greatest concern. Attention to different parts of the change could then be focused and phased in.

Focus of the Efforts

More and more, reform efforts in schools are taking an explicit, structured focus on student learning. School people are asking: What is our new definition of learning for our students? How can we create an environment that will help students achieve that vision? Such a focus requires a great deal of early attention—in meetings, workgroups, leadership teams—to issues of consequences. Yet we know that individuals typically do not begin with those kinds of concerns. Requiring people to suspend their questions about "what is it?" and "what does it mean for me?" is problematic, because leaving these questions unanswered often will inhibit participants' ability to engage thoughtfully in discussion of student outcomes.

This again calls for staff developers to be sensitive to issues of developing concerns and to try to address participants' lower-stage concerns even as discussion of student outcome ensues. One way is to acknowledge the dilemma and discuss it openly. Another is to make time to address information and personal needs regularly as the discussion proceeds (e.g., "If we believe students need good adult models, what might that mean for us individually?").

A staff development colleague, Sarah Caldwell (personal communication, December, 1989), suggested another strategy that proved effective in her work with school-based planning teams. One team decided they needed a Nitty-Gritty Committee. When the team's vision-building activities left them off in the stratosphere, with participants getting frustrated because of all the apparent impediments (usually logistical) to achieving the vision, the problems were relegated to the Nitty-Gritty Committee to come up with some alternative solutions. After this worked to calm the frustrations a couple of times, the committee became a standard feature of the management structure.

Collaborative Nature of the Reforms

More and more, schools and districts are designing shared leadership structures to ensure ownership and responsibility among the staff and community for the education delivered to young people. Taking a CBAM perspective, one might wonder whether that is "forcing" people to a collaborative stage of concern before other, lower-stage concerns are resolved. In one way, this is true. We are expecting people to work closely together to restructure their current practice in ways that benefit students before they make their own sense of things and "get their house in order." This is difficult for most people. There is, however, another way of looking at it.

Collaboration is, in fact, an innovation in and of itself. If staff developers see it as such, they can predict the kinds of concerns that will emerge and plan to address them in many of the ways illustrated earlier. Helping people understand what shared leadership is and can be, what mechanisms schools and districts have used to make it successful, and what it will mean for participants personally in terms of new roles and relationships—discussion and information on these topics are highly appropriate at the onset of the change. Trying out and reflecting back on the new roles and shared leadership strategies while working on a new design for the school are logical and "concerns-sensitive" ways to proceed.

SOME FINAL THOUGHTS

At the beginning of this chapter we discussed the importance of the individual dimension of change in the larger context of reform. While the CBAM is valuable to the repertoire of the staff developer, it is not, and has never pretended to be, a comprehensive model for change. As a result of our involvement in subsequent research on change in schools, most particularly the Study of Dissemination Efforts Supporting School Improvement (Crandall & Loucks, 1983), we have come to think of change as involving four primary ingredients: *people, processes, practices,* and *policies* (Loucks-Horsley, 1989). More recently, our observations of major reform efforts have prompted us to add at least two more ingredients to the list: *power* and *philosophy.*

The CBAM can be seen as the keystone of the first two ingredients in its ability to illuminate what happens to *people* in the *process* of change. Further, a concerns perspective can help us understand how the other four ingredients affect individuals and suggest some ways of framing them and focusing their impact. The CBAM provides a valuable framework for the individual dimension of change and should continue to complement our understandings of change as an organizational phenomenon.

REFERENCES

Anderson, S., Stiegelbauer, S., Gerin-LaJoie, D., Partlow, H., & Cummins, A. (1990). *Project excellence: Evaluation of a student-centered secondary school.* Toronto: Ontario Ministry of Education.

Cohen, M. (1982). Effective schools: Accumulating research findings. *American Education, 18*(1), 13–16.

Crandall, D. P., & Loucks, S. F. (1983). *A roadmap for school improvement.* Executive Summary of *People, policies, and practices: Examining the chain of school improvement.* Andover, MA: NETWORK.

Edmonds, R. (1979). Effective schools for the urban poor. *Educational Leadership, 37,* 15–27.

Fullan, M. G., with Stiegelbauer, S. (1990a). *The new meaning of educational change* (2nd ed.). New York: Teachers College Press.

Fullan, M. G. (1990b). Staff development, innovation, and institutional development. In B. Joyce (Ed.), *Changing school culture through staff development,* 1990 Yearbook of the Association for Supervision and Curriculum Development (pp. 3–25). Alexandria, VA: ASCD.

Fuller, F. F. (1969). Concerns of teachers: A developmental conceptualization. *American Educational Research Journal, 6*(2), 207–226.

Goodlad, J. (1984). *A place called school: Prospects for the future*. New York: McGraw-Hill.

Hall, G. E., George, A., Griffin, T., Hord, S., Loucks, S. F., Melle, M., Metzdorf, J., Pratt, H., & Winters, S. (1980). *Making change happen: A case study of school district implementation*. Austin: University of Texas Research and Development Center for Teacher Education. (ERIC Document Reproduction Service No. ED 250 162)

Hall, G. E., George, A., & Rutherford, W. L. (1979). *Measuring stages of concern about the innovation: A manual for use of the SoC questionnaire*. Austin: University of Texas Research and Development Center for Teacher Education. (ERIC Document Reproduction Service No. ED 147 342)

Hall, G. E., & Hord, S. M. (1984). A framework for analyzing what change facilitators do: The intervention taxonomy. *Knowledge: Creation, Diffusion, Utilization, 5*(3), 275–307.

Hall, G. E., & Hord, S. M. (1987). *Change in schools: Facilitating the process*. Albany, NY: State University of New York Press.

Hall, G. E., & Loucks, S. F. (1977). A developmental model for determining whether the treatment is actually implemented. *American Educational Research Journal, 14*(3), 263–276.

Hall, G. E., & Loucks, S. F. (1978). Teacher concerns as a basis for facilitating and personalizing staff development. *Teachers College Record, 80*(1), 36–53.

Hall, G. E., Rutherford, W. L., Hord, S. M., & Huling-Austin, L. L. (1984). Effects of three principal styles on school improvement. *Educational Leadership, 41*(5), 22–29.

Hall, G. E., Wallace, R. C., & Dossett, W. A. (1973). A developmental conceptualization of the adopting process within educational institutions. Austin: University of Texas Research and Development Center for Teacher Education. (ERIC Document Reproduction Service No. ED 095 126)

Heck, S., Stiegelbauer, S. M., Hall, G. E., & Loucks, S. F. (1981). *Measuring innovation configurations: Procedures and applications*. Austin: University of Texas Research and Development Center for Teacher Education. (ERIC Document Reproduction Service No. ED 204 147)

Horsley, D. L. (1990, March). *Leadership for change through experiential education*. Action Lab presented at the annual meeting of the Association for Supervision and Curriculum Development, San Antonio.

Loucks, S. F., & Crandall, D. P. (1982). *The practice profile: An all-purpose tool for program communication, staff development, evaluation, and improvement*. Andover, MA: NETWORK.

Loucks, S. F., & Melle, M. (1982). Evaluation of staff development: How do you know if it took? *Journal of Staff Development, 3*(1), 102–117.

Loucks-Horsley, S. (1989). Managing change: An integral part of staff development. In S. Caldwell (Ed.), *Staff development: A handbook of effective practices* (pp. 114–125). Oxford, OH: National Staff Development Council.

Marsh, D. D., & Penn, D. M. (1988). Engaging students in innovative instruction:

An application of the stages of concern framework to studying student
    engagement. *Journal of Classroom Interaction, 23*(1), 8–14.
Newlove, B. W., & Hall, G. E. (1976). *A manual for assessing open-ended
    statements of concern about an innovation.* Austin: University of Texas
    Research and Development Center for Teacher Education. (ERIC Document
    Reproduction Service No. ED 144 207)
Nielsen, L. A., & Turner, S. D. (1985, April). *Staff development program evalua-*
    tion: Interview techniques to measure skill application. Paper presented at
    the annual meeting of the American Educational Research Association,
    Chicago.
Rosenholtz, S. (1989). *Teachers' workplace.* New York: Longman.
Scarborough Board of Education. (1987). *Three steps towards success: The*
    principal's handbook for curriculum implementation. Scarborough, Ontario:
    Program Development.
Schmuck, R. A., & Miles, M. B. (1971). *Organization development in schools.* La
    Jolla, CA: University Associates.
Schmuck, R. A., Runkel, P. J., Arends, J. H., & Arends, R. I. (1977). *The second*
    handbook of organizational development in schools. Eugene, OR: Center
    for Educational Policy and Management.
Sizer, T. (1984). *Horace's compromise: The dilemma of the American high*
    school. Boston: Houghton Mifflin.
Stiegelbauer, S., Buehler, G., & Turner, S. (1989). Facilitating process: Integrating
    concerns-based approaches into implementing an effective schools model.
    The Council Journal, 7(1), 64–102.
Stiegelbauer, S., & Loucks-Horsley, S. (1987, April). *Putting research to work:*
    Utilizing field-based research on implementation to develop a training pro-
    gram for principals. Paper presented at the annual meeting of the American
    Educational Research Association, Washington, DC.

③ Adult Development
Insights on Staff Development

Sharon Nodie Oja

Developmental age and stage theories provide a powerful set of concepts for understanding adults' motivation, personal life choices, and principles for personal and professional effectiveness. A developmental perspective on adulthood can be helpful in the design and conduct of staff training programs. It can provide a comprehensive theoretical framework on which to base one's work in these fields. It is also relevant for individuals with interest in general management and supervision; it provides knowledge for self-development and also for better understanding of the people one works with, supervises, and leads.

Learning about adult development will help one

1. Gain an understanding of selected theories and research from the literature on adult learning and development in order to better recognize the individual needs of different adults who are teachers and administrators in educational settings
2. Examine one's own developmental learning experiences in a structured fashion and compare and contrast them with selected theories in order to gain self-insight
3. Apply the theories and research in order to more adequately understand and be sensitive to the experiences of other adults in a variety of contexts: career development, personality development, staff development, supervisional administration, and so forth
4. Use critical judgment in applying the principles of adult development and learning to the design of staff development activities (and intervention strategies) to be used in a variety of staff development settings and learning environments with adults

This chapter reviews the knowledge base in adult development, including developmental tasks and periods of the life cycle; stages of intellectual, ego, and moral development; transition periods in adult life; and the dynamics of growth and transformation. The chapter also focuses on design elements important in planning for adult development in educational settings.

PATTERNS OF ADULT DEVELOPMENT

Two primary patterns in adult development can be identified. The first pattern is formed by age-related life-cycle issues and career motivations that help describe "why" adults at certain ages choose certain personal or professional activities in their career. The second pattern is formed by developmental stages of thinking and problem solving that help describe "how" adults behave and think while involved in staff development activities. Teachers who are in the same school, of relatively the same age, and with the same years of experience may think and solve problems quite differently from one another. Stage theory helps one understand these differences in problem solving.

Age Theories

Patterns in adults' age-related transitions, suggested by the life age/cycle theorists such as Levinson, Gould, Sheehy, Havighurst, Neugarten, and Erikson, help describe problems, dilemmas, career tasks, and personal issues we face in our lives.

Review of age patterns.   Age theories suggest a pattern of adult tasks beginning with the transition from adolescence to adulthood during the late teens and early 20's and moving into the 20's for a period of provisional adulthood and initial commitments. At this time the adult is concerned with exploring new options in the world in order to form an initial perspective of oneself as an adult. Daniel Levinson (1986) calls this "forming a life structure." It is this life structure that continues to be redefined and transformed as the tasks of adulthood are undertaken. As part of this initial life structure, the new adult makes initial commitments to a job and career, gets hired, adjusts to work, changes jobs, quits (or gets fired), deals with unemployment, moves, establishes a significant love relationship, marries (or decides not to get married), decides whether to raise children, buys a house, and so forth.

In the late 20's or early 30's a transition "age-30 crisis" of examination and questioning results in a change or reaffirmation of initial commitments. In this transition the adult asks, "What is life all about?" In confronting this question, the adult reexamines the initial life structure and the commitments made in the previous phase. This transition may result in restabilization or trigger a change in career and in personal relationships. The adult may go back to school, get divorced, get married (or remarried), change jobs, or change occupations.

The 30's are a period of "settling down." Having dealt with the issues of the age-30 crisis, the adult settles down in the early 30's, reaffirming commitments and often choosing a career as the most highly valued investment of one's time and energy. Children are in school; mother (if she was at home) probably returns to work or school. Setting long-term goals both for work-related and family-related activities becomes important to adults in this phase. Career-related goals become even more important in the late 30's and early 40's when the adult is concerned with becoming one's own person. Promotions are crucial markers of success. While work relationships are important, the adult seeks to break away from advisors and mentors in order to become more independent in work.

A "midlife transition" involving another round of major questioning about priorities and values occurs in one's early 40's with the realization that time is finite and success and achievement have limitations. This results in a "restabilization period" (around age 45) with further investment in personal relationships. Transitions in the 50's are followed in the 60's by restabilization often marked by pleasingly mild and gentle reactions to life's experiences and/or a vigorous sense of flourishing.

At each of these different ages, the adult is trying to create a better fit between the life structure one has defined and the reality of life's challenges. Age-related phases do not fit completely for all adults. Age alone is not totally predictive of the dilemmas adults face. Life ages, however, can be helpful to staff developers who want to recognize and understand the nature of the dilemmas that may face adults with whom they work.

A variety of researchers explicate the age-related phases of development that can be used in the planning of staff development activities. This information on age theory is readily accessible. It begins to differentiate among adults in terms of their reasons at different phases in their careers or at different ages in their life as to why they might take on certain kinds of staff development activities. (See, e.g., Burke, Christensen, & Fessler, 1984; Fessler, 1985; Krupp, 1987; Oja, 1989.)

Perspectives on the life course and life structure. Basic concepts from the age theorists important to adult development include life age, life structure, developmental task, adaptation, transition, trigger, age-norms, life cycle, and marker events. The concept of structure building and structure changing (Levinson, 1986) is particularly important to a conception of life periods in adulthood. In a psychosocial perspective, adult growth is the evolution of a life structure over time through (mostly conscious) choices. Adaptation occurs through periods of stability and transition, each with characteristic concerns. There are a number of extensive reviews of life-age and life-cycle theories (see, e.g., Chickering & Havighurst, 1981; Wortley & Amatea, 1982).

A sociological perspective of the life cycle by Bernice Neugarten and Gunther Hagestad (1976; Hagestad & Neugarten, 1985) is most concerned with the social clock and the concept of age norms by which persons judge whether they are "on time or off time." "On-time" crises—for instance, the death of a parent aged 70—are usually mentally anticipated and rehearsed, and the transition is accomplished without shattering the continuity of the life cycle. Examples of "off-time" crises would be the death of a parent who is in his or her late 40's or the sudden death of a child in an accident. Sociological changes (political, technological, economic, and demographic) can result in life-cycle changes. In this perspective the life course is a progression through successive social roles and status expectations in which an "age status system" describes how laws link rights and responsibilities to chronological age.

Neugarten and other developmental-task researchers rely on interviews for their data on how adults at specific ages deal with the tasks of adulthood. The interviews focus attention on the issues that are of major concern to the individual, that is, what one selects as important marker events in one's past and present, what one hopes to do in the future, what one predicts will occur, what strategies one uses to cope with life events, and what meanings one attaches to time, life, and death. These researchers use the person as the reporting and predicting agent. They gather systematic and repeated self-reports in addition to other types of questionnaire data to combine a phenomenological and objective perspective. Limitations to the generalization of this work revolve around issues of socioeconomic status, gender, race, history, and marital status of participants in the studies from which the theories were developed.

Research from age theorists suggests that the negotiation of certain life tasks may indeed have a significant impact on the functioning of the individual. Staff developers need to recognize the legitimacy of these age-related tasks and issues in their work. They need to investigate how the staff development programs they design can respond to and provide for teachers' continuing needs to

1. Confront off-time events
2. Rework life-cycle issues of identity, intimacy, generativity, and integrity (Erikson, 1959)
3. Negotiate life-structure transitions
4. Balance continual periods of transition and stability

Stage Theories

Developmental stage theories can help a staff developer understand "how" people at the same age can confront developmental issues in different ways. Each stage is a complete whole, a frame of reference through which adults at that stage interpret the events of their lives and their work. Cognitive-developmental stages are not defined by age; in fact, adults at many different ages can be viewing their lives from the same stage of development.

Rather than focusing on the tasks each individual faces in the course of his or her lifetime, stage theorists focus on underlying patterns of thought and problem solving that play a central role in determining an individual's approach to the world. Stage theorists posit more global, holistic determinants of experience than those highlighted by the life age/cycle theorists. Stage theorists such as Piaget, Kohlberg, Loevinger, Selman, and Hunt maintain that human development, personality, and character are the result of orderly changes in underlying cognitive and emotional structures. Development involves progression through an invariant sequence of hierarchically organized stages. Each new stage incorporates and transforms the structures of the previous stages and paves the way for the next stage. Each stage provides a qualitatively different frame of reference through which one interacts with and acts upon the world. The sequence of development progresses from simpler to more complex and through differentiated modes of thought and functioning. The higher stages of development are said to represent more adequate modes of functioning in the sense that they include adopting multiple points of view, more empathic role taking, and more adequate problem solving.

Ego development. Jane Loevinger developed a model of ego development that I have found very adaptable to staff development. According to Loevinger (1976), the essence of the ego is the search for coherent meanings in an experience; she describes the ego as providing the frame of reference that structures one's world and within which one perceives the world. This definition differs from other definitions in that ego development is seen as a sequence of steps along a continuum of differentiation and complexity. Each ego stage is more complex than the last, and none can be skipped in the course of development. Ego development is not tied to chronological age. Different individuals may stabilize at certain ego stages and, consequently, not develop beyond those stages. The stage names represent characteristics that are most predominant at that stage, although these same characteristics may be present, to a greater or lesser degree, at all stages. However, in order to adequately define a stage, the total pattern of characteristics must be present. For example, an individual who evidences impulsiveness is only designated to be operating from the impulsive stage if the whole pattern of characteristics of that stage is demonstrable. A brief summary of each stage is provided here.

At the *impulsive stage*, the person uses bodily impulses to maintain the formation of a separate identity. When the impulses dominate behavior, control is effected through external constraint and immediate rewards and punishments. Persons at this stage are strongly dependent and demanding; others are valued according to what they can "give to" the individual. Value judgments are in terms of absolutes, that is, people are either good or bad. The present predominates, with little sense of past or future. Aggressive behavior and temper tantrums exemplify the intense, impulsive reactions of this stage, and an individual's problems are attributed to others rather than one's self or the circumstances of one's situation.

At the *self-protective stage*, persons control their impulsiveness and anticipate rewards and punishments. Rules are recognized at this stage and used for one's own advantage. The main rule is "don't get caught." Blame is placed on other individuals or the circumstances when satisfaction is not achieved. People at this stage maintain manipulative and exploitive relationships and thus tend to be opportunistic, deceptive, and preoccupied with control and advantage.

People at the *conformist stage* place strong trust for their welfare in the family group, the peer group, or in socially approved norms. Rules are obeyed simply because they are group-accepted rules. Belonging is of utmost importance. Feelings of disapproval and shame are crucial issues at this stage. Individuals here are peer-dominated, easily directed by others, fearful of being noticed as different, and always conscious of the expectations of others. Behavior is viewed in terms of external actions and concrete events rather than inner motives and feelings. Personal emotions are expressed in clichés, stereotypes, and moralistic judgments. A person at this stage is preoccupied with appearance, social acceptance, and reputation.

At the *self-aware transition* between the prior conformist stage and the subsequent conscientious stage, there is an increase in self-awareness and a beginning appreciation and understanding of multiple possibilities, alternatives, and options in problem-solving situations. Growing awareness of inner emotions enhances the capacity for introspection (crucial at subsequent stages), although at this stage feelings continue to be expressed in vague or global terms. Growing self-confidence and self-evaluated standards at this stage begin to replace group standards as guidelines for behavior. This level may be the most predominant ego level for adults in the United States.

At the *conscientious stage* a person is capable of self-criticism. This combines with long-term self-evaluated goals and ideals and a sense of responsibility to form the major elements of the adult conscience, all evident at this stage. Rules are internalized; guilt is the consequence of breaking inner rules. Exceptions and contingencies in rules are recognized in direct relation to a growing awareness of the subtleties of individual differences. Behavior is seen in terms of feelings, patterns, and motives rather than simple actions. Achievement, especially when measured by self-chosen standards, is crucial. Persons at this stage are preoccupied with obligations, privileges, rights, ideals, traits, and achievement, all defined more by inner personal standards and less by the need for external recognition and acceptance.

It is the individualistic level and the autonomous and integrated stages, however, that incorporate the postconventional stages of moral reasoning and the more complex and postabstract stages of intellectual development. The individualistic transition level and the autonomous stage have the following characteristics.

At the *individualistic level* one's sense of individuality is of utmost concern, especially as it is coupled with heightened awareness of emotional dependence on others. A person at this more complex level can tolerate paradoxical and contradictory relationships between events in contrast to earlier stages where individuals attempt to eliminate paradoxes by reducing them to polar opposites. There is also greater complexity in conceptualizing interpersonal interactions. Interpersonal relationships are highly valued in contrast to the cherishing of ideals and achievements at the conscientious stage previous to this one. This is also a transition level to the autonomous stage.

The distinguishing characteristic at the *autonomous stage* is the individual's capacity to tolerate and cope with the inner conflict arising from conflicting perceptions, needs, ideals, and duties. A person at this stage is able to unite ideas that appear as ambiguous or incompatible options to persons at prior stages. In particular, at this stage the individual acknowledges other persons' needs for autonomy to make their own choices and solutions and to learn from their own mistakes. At the same time, the autonomous person realizes the limitations of autonomy; consequently, mutual interdependence is highly valued in interpersonal relationships.

Self-fulfillment, differing perceptions of one's role, and issues of justice are added to the concerns about individuality and achievement issues of prior stages.

The *integrated stage* is the hardest to describe because cases are rare (Cook-Greuter, 1990). In addition to the characteristics of the autonomous stage, there is evidence of consolidation of a sense of identity, as in Maslow's self-actualizing person. A person at this stage has the capacity to reconcile conflicting demands, to renounce the unattainable, and to truly cherish individuality and interdependence.

I find Jane Loevinger's work to be helpful as an umbrella for overall adult development, under which are subsumed the individual strands of moral development, intellectual development, and interpersonal development. Stage change and the dynamics of transition from stage to stage are described well by Robert Kegan. He uses the same paradigm and the same progression of stages as Loevinger, but he names the ego stages differently. His stage names reflect sets of perceptions about oneself in relation to others and the balance one achieves at each stage: the imperial balance, the interpersonal balance, the institutional balance, and the interindividual balance. His stage concepts are helpful in distinguishing the different ego stages. Through the use of poignant case study examples, Kegan (1982) describes the elements of growth and loss at each stage, the balance achieved at each new stage, and the transformation to the next stage. A good summary of his work, including the diagrams used to distinguish the different stages, can be found in *Promoting Adult Development in Schools* by Sarah Levine (1989), a book I highly recommend as one begins to investigate progressions in stages of development.

Moral development.   Lawrence Kohlberg (1981, 1984) has identified stages of moral development representing different reasoning processes that people employ in dealing with dilemmas. He developed a moral judgment interview, and James Rest (1986) developed an objective questionnaire to determine stage of moral judgment. The Kohlberg framework of moral reasoning includes six stages divided into preconventional, conventional, and postconventional levels of moral judgment. This model has been called a "morality of justice."

At the preconventional level, the individual is obedient to a superior power, a person with prestige and authority, in order to avoid trouble and punishment (stage 1, *punishment and obedience*), or else the individual is concerned with satisfying his or her own needs first and foremost and values others according to what they can do for the individual at this stage, thus making relationships one-way only (stage 2, *instrumental purpose and exchange*).

At the conventional level, the individual is concerned about conforming to group norms, being a "nice person" in order to be accepted, and helping others; in this sense there is a two-way relationship in which people are reciprocally good to each other (stage 3, *mutual interpersonal expectations, relationships, and conformity*). In the next stage at the conventional level, the individual is concerned with maintaining and preserving order in society, doing one's duty, maintaining rules, and showing respect for earned authorities (stage 4, *social systems and conscience maintenance*).

At the postconventional level, the individual agrees that what the whole of society decides is what is right and that standards can be changed by mutual agreement based on the greatest good for all (stage 5, *prior rights and social contract*), or else the individual's conscience is the basis of a decision as to what is right, and ethical principles that apply to all humans—such as justice, equality, and dignity—are the basis of decision making (stage 6, *universal ethical principles*).

Recent research investigating women's development by Carol Gilligan (Gilligan, 1982; Gilligan, Ward, & Taylor, 1988) has identified a different voice of morality called *response and care*. In Gilligan's model of moral reasoning, individuals spiral through a three-level evolution of care and responsibility to themselves and others. In the first level, the individual's primary concern is for *one's own survival in the face of powerlessness*. In the movement to the second level, the individual seeks *goodness in caring for others* and values *self-sacrifice as the highest virtue*. In the transition to the third level, the individual recognizes *oneself as a legitimate object of care*, and this insight becomes the framework for an *ethic of care*.

Gilligan and colleagues (1988) describe the two moral voices of *justice* and *care* as two different frameworks for problem solving.

> From the perspective of someone seeking or loving *justice*, relationships are organized in terms of equality, symbolized by the balancing of scales. Moral concerns focus on problems of oppressions, problems stemming from inequality, and the moral ideal is one of reciprocity or equal respect. From the perspective of someone seeking or valuing *care*, relationship connotes responsiveness or engagement, a focus on problems of detachment, on disconnection or abandonment or indifference, and the moral ideal is one of attention and response. (p. xvii; emphasis added)

By adopting one or the other moral voice, people focus attention on different types of concern. The research on these two moral voices suggests that adults do raise both justice and care concerns in describing moral conflicts, but that they tend to focus their attention on *either* justice or care concerns, elaborating one set of concerns and minimally representing the other. In particular, women tended to focus on care, while men tended to focus on justice (Lyons, 1983). This tendency to focus on one voice or perspective means that loss of the other perspective is a liability that both men and women share. Gilligan suggests that moral maturity can be defined by the ability to see in at least two ways and to speak in at least two languages, the voice of justice and the voice of care. Questions then can be asked in our educational settings: Under what circumstances do some educators seek justice solutions as preferable, while others prefer care solutions? How can educators help one another recognize and understand both moral voices?

The justice and care orientations to moral development represent different ways of organizing a moral problem, reasoning about it, and making choices for action. Nel Noddings (1984) discusses the ethic of care in relation to teachers and asks whether teaching by its very nature becomes an ethic of care. Do educators in our schools reflect more the voice of care in solving problems?

Intellectual development. Progressions in intellectual development include the evolution in cognitive development from adolescence to adulthood discussed by Jean Piaget and William Perry, stages of conceptual development and a matching model teaching process by David Hunt, and recent case studies of women's intellectual development by Mary Belenky, Blythe Clinchy, Nancy Goldberger, and Jill Tarule.

Piaget (1972) did not identify specific adult cognitive stages, but he did postulate continuing cognitive development through adulthood in two ways: (1) at first, the transition from concrete operations into the stage of formal abstract thought is evidenced by the ability to reason, to view a situation from a variety of perspectives, to use alternative problem-solving solutions, and so forth; (2) later, the stabilization of formal abstract thought is evidenced by increasing application of abstract thinking processes to progressively more complex issues in life and work, religion, politics, management, interpersonal relationships, and so forth.

David Hunt's (1975) work defined conceptual level by degree of abstractness (ability to separate, integrate, and/or discriminate many conflicting conditions) as well as by degree of interpersonal maturity (increasing self-responsibility). Concrete thinking is characterized by less self-delineation, greater tendency toward extremes, and less flexibility in problem solving. Concrete thinking also tends to be accompanied by absolutism, categorical thinking, and by a greater belief in external causality and the "oughtness of rules." Concrete thinkers tend to seek a simple and highly structured environment and seem less capable of adapting to a changing environment than a person at a higher conceptual level. The more abstract thinker, on the other hand, is able to consider alternatives and is consequently able to integrate facts of the world in terms of their interrelatedness. Furthermore, abstract conceptual structure is associated with creativity, greater tolerance for stress, greater flexibility, and a wider array of coping behaviors. A less structured environment is usually required by the more abstract thinker, who usually prefers tasks with greater complexity (see reviews in Hunt, 1981; Miller, 1981).

Recent investigations support the fact that cognitive development is not completed in adolescence. Many college students—estimates from 33 to 75%—are unable to solve tasks requiring abstract thinking. Research among adults suggests that even if abstract thinking levels have been attained, they may not be retained across the lifespan (see studies cited in Long, McCrary, & Ackerman, 1979).

Significant cognitive development can take place during adulthood. Among those who have attained abstract operations in a narrow sphere, we should be able to observe a broadening of perspectives as these abstract thought processes are applied to other spheres of life. This recent research in cognitive development has several implications for staff development. Any program that assumes that adults have attained abstract operations in all aspects of their thinking is likely to encounter problems. Thus efforts need to be made to aid adults in the transition from concrete to abstract modes of thought in new areas of learning. And in some contexts an appropriate educational goal would be to foster development beyond abstract operations to a stage of problem finding (Arlin, 1975) or to foster cognitive development of a different sort, such as dialectical thought (Basseches, 1984).

William Perry (1970) describes intellectual development evolving as different ways of seeing the world, knowledge, education, values, and oneself. His longitudinal data give vivid descriptions of the emotional turmoil connected with intellectual growth. Through extended excerpts of the individual's own words and thinking, Perry identifies four main positions and five transitions of intellectual growth.

Dualism is the first position. Meaning is divided into polarities: good versus bad, right versus wrong, we versus they. Right answers exist somewhere for every problem, and authorities know them. Right answers are to be memorized by hard work. Knowledge is quantitative. Dualism gives way to multiplicity as one comes to understand that authorities may not have all the right answers. In *multiplicity*, diversity of opinion and values is recognized as legitimate in certain areas such as the humanities, which seem to be more a matter of opinion and taste than fact. No judgments can be made among these differences, so "everyone has a right to his own opinion; none can be called wrong." The transition to relativism begins as one's personal opinion is challenged by the need for evidence and the basis for one's opinion.

In the position of *relativism*, diversity of opinion, values, and judgment is derived from coherent sources, evidence, logic, systems, and patterns that can be analyzed and compared. Some opinions may be found worthless, while there will remain matters about which reasonable people will continue to reasonably disagree. Knowledge becomes a qualitative, dependent on the contexts in which events take place and the framework that one uses to understand the event. It is within the ability for relativist thought that the transition to the final position of commitment in relativism takes place. *Commitment* is the affirmation, choice, or decision made in one's career, values, politics, or personal relationship within the context of questioning as defined by relativism. As one cycles through these intellectual positions in response to new experiences and learning, personal identity is affirmed (Perry, 1981). Perry's account of intellectual development is helpful in understanding the growth of reflective judgment (King, 1977; Kitchener & King, 1979), reasoning in action (Argyris, 1982), and the teacher's ability to be a reflective practitioner (Grimmett & Erickson, 1988; Schön, 1983).

Another approach to intellectual development is found in *Women's Ways of Knowing* (Belenky, Clinchy, Goldberger, & Tarule, 1986). This study documents the ways of knowing that women have learned to cultivate and value, ways that are powerful but have been neglected or denigrated by the more dominant traditional intellectual development theories. Belenky and colleagues use voice as a metaphor that applies to all aspects of women's experience and development. This is in comparison to sight, so commonly used and associated with traditional intellectual development. Sight stands alone as an understanding of information and the ability to grasp meanings. Voice represents the intertwined development of a sense of voice, mind, and self.

Analyzing interview data from 135 women, Belenky and colleagues describe five different perspectives from which women in their study view reality and draw conclusions. The first one is *silence*. This individual is unaware of herself as a knower. She is subservient to authority and feels powerless. She knows no other way. There are no words that suggest knowledge of an inner voice or awareness of mental acts. There is neither a comprehension of dialogue within oneself nor a sense of introspection. The individual at this position is dependent on others for her identity and is unable to structure her self-concept in any other way.

The *received knower* is capable of receiving knowledge from authorities but believes it is beyond her capacity to develop or to create her own knowledge. Individuals at this position are good followers and obedient workers. Feelings of low self-esteem and lack of originality prevail. The received knower accumulates facts, and the words of others become her own.

The *subjective knower* begins to listen to her own inner voice, and as it comes alive, this individual becomes her own authority and perceives her gut feelings as infallible. The trust in an outside authority is lost, and her own experiences become the primary source of her truth. This individual must begin to listen to others as well as herself. She will in time develop a public voice.

The voice of reason emerges in the *procedural knower*. This voice of reason permeates one's attitudes about authority, the world, and oneself. Reason coupled with intuition and feeling predominates. Two categories evolve at this position, separate and connected knowing. The separate way of knowing functions under standard rules and conventions of rational thought, much like that described in Perry's model. The separate procedural knower is more concerned with principles and critical thinking procedures. In the connected way of knowing, knowledge and reason are gained through personal experience and relationships. The connected procedural knower is also concerned with caring, empathy, and patience.

The *constructed knower* is able to integrate voice, mind, and self. The individual at this position is aware that truth is based in the context in which it is embedded; thus her frame of reference is important and directs her knowledge and understanding. Constructed knowers are able to weave together reason and emotion, the objective and the subjective. In this fifth position of ways of knowing, speaking, and listening are used equally in active dialogue with others, in situations in which knowledge is constructed by persons who experience themselves as equals. In constructed knowledge, women "find a place for reason and intuition and the expertise of others" (Belenky et al., p. 133).

Throughout the interviews from *Women's Ways of Knowing* the importance of "connected education" is demonstrated. Connected education describes an educational environment in which individuals value personal individual experience; nurture each other's thoughts to maturity; construct truth through consensus, not conflict; bridge private and shared experience; accord respect for one another's unique perspectives; and base authority on cooperation, not subordination. Connected education concepts, when used as guidelines for group process in staff development settings, may create more effective committees, task forces, and working groups.

Interpersonal development.   Robert Selman's (1980) stages of interpersonal development are helpful in thinking about group interactions and processes, including group formation, cohesion, norms/rules, decision making, and leadership. He defines four stages of interpersonal development.

In the first stage of *unilateral relations*, group members do what the leader says with no awareness of possible agreements or converging interests among members. In the second stage of *bilateral partnerships*, group members believe that they are supposed to like one another and that teamwork occurs through the exchange of favors based on equal treatment of all members. In the next stage of *homogeneous community*, members organize the group as a shared community regardless of their specific relationships to one another. At this stage the group works together and is held together by consensus on common goals and expectations. A group member operating at this level of interpersonal development feels an obligation to go along with the group because of a perception that the group requires the uniformity of all its members. Limitations at this stage occur when group members become rigid in their focus on homogeneity of values and are unable to see or accept different values. At the fourth stage of *pluralistic organization*, the group is perceived as a multifaceted system that can incorporate and coordinate the individual differences of its members. Individual diversity among group members is not suppressed, but rather united behind common goals. At this stage of interpersonal development the individual compromises in order to integrate the diversity of interests and goals of all group members.

DESIGN PRINCIPLES FOR ADULT DEVELOPMENT

Key concepts in the design of significant learning and developmental growth environments include stages of development as a transformation of capacities, supports for role transitions, and supports for development within a stage and for stage change. Also important is the concept of developmental match, that is, a career or new learning situation slightly more complex and demanding than the person's routine levels of response. This new career choice offers some challenge. Some people first choose a "contemporaneous match" for initial support and then move to incorporate more elements of complexity for a "developmental match."

Four Focus Points in Developmental Growth Settings

Four focus points are essential in thinking about the developmental possibilities in the schools. I first discussed them in an earlier work (Oja, 1980) and now review them here.

1. Practical application followed by reflection. Cycles of experiences applying new learning, followed by examination of and reflection on those experiences, will promote development. Regular systematic reflection in seminars and conferences following an active experience serves to facilitate the cognitive restructuring process needed to integrate new learnings with old patterns of thought. In addition, systematic reflection serves as a support to individuals who are confronting old assumptions and ways of doing things. As old assumptions about teaching conflict with new learnings, teachers realize the need for additional, alternate roles for themselves so they can more adequately deal with new situations in the classroom and school. As new behaviors and curricula are tried out, teachers can get feedback and support from colleagues through the ongoing seminar.

2. Peer supervision and advising. Continual, consistent, on-site peer supervision and advising of teachers by colleagues and staff developers are important for teacher development. For example, staff developers (and others) can model interpersonal communication and group process skills in activities aimed at developing group cohesion and collegiality among teachers and staff. Once new skills are learned, the staff developer can shift to the role of supervisor in helping participants evaluate their own skill effectiveness. Videotapes can be used to encourage participants to move from excessive self-criticism and negative self-evaluations to realistic self-assessment within the context of the classroom and school environment.

When teachers apply new skills in their classrooms, they need support. Weekly seminars can be used to encourage participants to supportively supervise one another. In addition, staff members can offer to team up with participants in designing, teaching, and evaluating curricula. Teachers can be encouraged to work in teams whenever possible for further support, mutual feedback, and ongoing peer supervision.

This model of support/challenge and action/reflection can stimulate adult development in the areas of ego maturity, cognitive complexity, and moral reasoning.

3. More complex role taking. Teachers can be encouraged and empowered to take on more complex roles and responsibilities in their school programs and staff development activities. Significant role-taking opportunities are essential to adult development. Role taking is defined as the ability to take into account the perspective of others, to understand a situation from another person's point of view, and to act "as if" by assuming the role of another.

Viewing role taking as a major means for personal and social development, adults can utilize two different types of role-taking activities. First, to develop the ability to accurately understand another's point of view, one can initiate interpersonal communication skills training. Individuals can be helped to listen to another person and then to communicate back to that person an accurate statement of the feelings and the content of the message. Second, to develop their confidence and ability to take on more complex roles in the classroom, school, and district, teachers can be encouraged to actively try out new roles, such as group process observer, group discussion leader, peer teaching supervisor, peer supervisor, cooperating teacher, resource person and negotiator of individualized instruction, and action researcher.

4. Supportive environment. The introduction of new concepts causes a period of cognitive conflict and disequilibrium. In this challenging period, the adult learner is likely to feel anxiety and frustration. If the anxiety and frustration are overwhelming, the learner will not be able to resolve the conflict but rather will retreat to the stability and comfort of old assumptions and patterns of thinking. Consequently, rather than learning, one will more likely become rigidly entrenched in those comfortable old ways of thinking. Psychological and personal support is therefore essential to developmental growth. As new learning is taking place, personal support should be available so that a learner feels understanding, empathy, and warm personal regard from others. This can happen in a supportive seminar with colleagues and in one-to-one conferences with empathetic staff members.

In addition to these four focus points in the design elements for adult development, a further consideration of supports and challenges at different stages of adult development can inform knowledge of one's own development and interaction with others. The following section on supports and challenges provides a number of suggestions for ways to address the potential for growth and change of adults at different stages of development.

Supports and Challenges for Stage Development

Challenges and supports to new learning differ at each stage. What is a challenge at one stage may well feel like a support to a person operating at a subsequent stage. For example, self-reflection in journal writing may be a challenge to the teacher operating from the conformist ego stage who is unused to expressing himself or herself. On the other hand, journal writing can be a support to the teacher in the autonomous stage who uses writing as a routine form of introspection and self-evaluation.

Table 3.1 summarizes concepts of support and challenge at different stages of ego development in relation to different kinds of staff development activities. An adult who exhibits characteristics of the self-protective stage may be preoccupied with control and advantage. The challenge in developing to the conformist stage is to identify one's own welfare with that of the positive interests of a group. The self-protective adult needs opportunities and a social environment in which to develop trust.

The challenges in new learning to the conformist adult are developing empathy for others, clarity of "self," and a sense of personal achievement. The overall goals in the development of persons at the conformist stage are toward gaining more inner-directedness and self-confidence, toward speaking out for oneself, toward setting realistic goals and taking realistic risks, toward broadening one's perspectives, toward conceptualizing at higher levels, and toward more adequate problem-solving and reflective thinking. Programs that can provide the context for development from the conformist stage to the conscientious stage include conflict management; assertiveness training; achievement training; responsible role taking in which the new role is significant, important, and of high quality; identity training to increase inner-directedness; survival training using wilderness training experiences; and programs with self-evaluation and self-supervision to encourage self-reflection. These programs all encourage agency, inner-directedness, and self-confidence. In education we would additionally teach a variety of different models of teaching, which seem to fit different conditions in the classroom, and encourage teachers to actively practice these roles and learn to discriminate their appropriateness. All of these are challenges to the conformist adult, but within reach if a supportive environment is designed to include the four focus points in developmental growth settings (e.g., see Oja & Sprinthall, 1978).

At the conscientious stage a person is fairly inner-directed, self-confident, with a sense of agency and achievement. The major elements of the adult conscience are in evidence at this stage, that is, long-term, self-evaluated goals and ideals, differentiated self-criticism, and a sense of responsibility. The conscientious person is future oriented, able to delay gratification, prone to follow rules, and inclined to internalize rules that are chosen, not simply accepted as group sanctions. Exceptions and contingencies are recognized; for example, the individual at this stage, though less likely to feel guilty about breaking a rule, is more likely to feel guilty about hurting another person while conforming to the rules. A

TABLE 3.1 Matching Supports and Challenges to Teacher Stages of Development

DEVELOPMENTAL STAGE[1]	STAGE CHARACTERISTICS	APPROPRIATE SUPPORTS	APPROPRIATE CHALLENGES
Self-protective	Fearful Rigid Dependent Distrustful Manipulative Authoritan	Demonstrate trust; mutual respect Set short-term goals Interact often Model/guide openness	Role playing Journals Value activities Constructive feedback Social activities
Conformist	Rule oriented Conventional Concern with status, social acceptance, belonging	Focus observations Share many options Encourage visitations and workshop attendance Interact socially	Reflection exercises Role taking Assertiveness training Problem-solving projects Graduate courses
Conscientious	Responsible Goal oriented Self-critical Efficient Inner standards	Facilitate sharing of district resources Structure new roles Videotape performance Model empathic behavior	Peer supervision Conflict resolution training Intern/aide supervision Action research projects Curriculum development
Autonomous	Flexible Concern with self-fulfillment Creative Interdependent Deals with complexity Sees/uses many options and alternatives	Provide many options for growth Develop flextime options Facilitate networking Encourage self-growth Differentiate roles Share power	Mentoring Assuming leadership/power roles Create new programs and policies Group supervision Becoming a change agent

Note. Developed by M. C. Ham and S. N. Oja.
1. From Loevinger (1976).

person's own standards determine the aspiration for achievement that is prevalent at this stage. Behavior patterns, traits, and motives in oneself and others are perceived at this stage. The dedicated, highly stable professional who is sometimes resistant to change can be found here. At this stage concern with achievement and obligations may interfere with one's ability to experience empathy or mutuality in interpersonal relationships with those who appear different from oneself. Consequently, a challenge to many conscientious adults in our schools is to develop their ability to empathize with, experience mutuality in interpersonal relationships with, and resolve conflicts with other faculty, staff, students, or parents. Collaborative action research as a school-based, problem-solving context can stimulate growth of adults at the conscientious stages. (See Oja & Pine, 1983, 1987. For additional reviews of teachers as researchers and action research examples, see Cochran-Smith & Lytle, 1990; Kyle & Hovda, 1987).

Adults at the autonomous stage are more tolerant of ambiguity and more confident in confronting conflict. Development at the autonomous stage is characterized by inner-directedness with empathy for others; mutuality in interpersonal relationships; ability to see multiple points of view and synthesize them; more understanding of rules and reasons behind rules, and therefore more selectivity in priorities; ability to maintain broader perspectives; ability to cope with inner conflict and conflicting needs and duties; and awareness of psychological causality and development. Teachers at the autonomous stage are confident in using many models of teaching to meet the many perceived variations in the cognitive, social, and psychological needs of students. In our schools we also find adults at the autonomous stage who are able to use many models of supervision to meet the many perceived variations in the learning needs of other adults in supervisory situations or beginning teachers in mentoring situations and induction programs (see Thies-Sprinthall, 1984; Thies-Sprinthall & Sprinthall, 1987).

The challenge to the autonomous adult is to maintain control of his or her own destiny in the school environment, to learn more on one's own, and to use his or her complex problem-solving and reflective thinking skills in new situations where others listen. People in transition to the autonomous stage can be supported and encouraged to assume leadership positions with responsibility for creating new programs and initiating restructuring efforts (see Oja, 1988; Oja & Ham, 1988). Leadership issues are quite interesting to investigate using the developmental stage perspective (see Bradford & Cohen, 1984; Kegan & Lahey, 1984; Torbert, 1987).

An adult's perceptions are filtered through his or her own developmental stages and built on experiences in classrooms and schools; each perception is characteristic of the person's internal system of management and problem solving and provides guidelines for relationships and interaction. In talking with other adults in the schools, it is important to recognize that one's perceptions of school and classroom issues are filtered through one's own developmental stage lens. Gaps in communication can result from these different lenses. As we look to adult development in our schools, we need to be aware of the implications regarding the needs, learning environments, and resulting personal and professional issues common to adults at various stages of development. We need to be cautious and refrain from "labeling" ourselves or others. Adult experiences are rich and diverse, and care needs to be exercised in using stages as labels because doing so often results in negative and simplistic judgments that ignore ever-present possibilities for growth and change. We need to use the knowledge base of adult development in positive, supportive, nonjudgmental ways to better understand aspects of life transitions and interactions with colleagues and to address the complexity of change strategy issues in the restructuring of our schools and planning for more effective staff development options.

IMPLICATIONS FOR STAFF DEVELOPMENT

What is the value of adult development theory for staff development? It can be an enormously powerful tool. Knowledge of the theory helps one to recognize and deal more effectively with individual differences. The value in knowing the progressions in adult development and these approximate sets of individual differences or worldviews will help one to be less dogmatic about any one solution's being appropriate for everybody.

In a review of 200 journal articles and documents added to the ERIC data base from 1981 to 1988, with the descriptors of inservice education, staff development, and professional development, one finds that few explicitly address adult development as one of the goals of staff development programs. Perhaps adult development is an implicit goal included under the goals of personal/professional development of teachers. Many of the staff development activities and programs described do say that teachers' personal goals for their own development are important for staff development. This attention to teachers' personal needs and goals is definitely an improvement over the fairly rigid inservice activities mandated by districts and states in the 1970s. If the 1980s saw improved inservice education through staff development activities that tried to address teachers' self-defined needs and goals for personal/professional development, then perhaps the 1990s ought to be a time of making adult development an explicit goal and finding ways to document developmental growth as part of our evaluation of staff development activities.

A review of more than 400 articles from 23 professional journals and 507 doctoral dissertations between 1977 and 1984 found that the research methodologies were heavily based on descriptive surveys of the desired content and procedures for the delivery of staff development and inservice and that the skills sought most frequently were knowledge-level skills (Daresh, 1985). Suggestions for the future included the need to carry out continuous review and modification of a theoretical conceptualization of effective staff development. Adult development theory can be used as a theoretical basis for the practical implementation of staff development. Case studies describe characteristics of adult development in real-life, action contexts in education.

Adults at different developmental stages exhibit different patterns in their attitudes toward decision making and change, perception of group organization and process, and perception of leadership, supervision, and evaluation. The adult development knowledge base suggests supports and challenges to further enable individual development. The adult development knowledge base is helpful in mentoring, teacher induction, and supervision of student teachers. Knowledge of adult development helps one to better facilitate day-to-day interactions with colleagues in staff meetings and committee organizations. Knowledge of adult stages of development also helps one to understand why certain liaisons or conflicts develop between people who are operating at similar or different stages of adult development.

Adult development perspectives encourage us to listen to people's voices and watch people's lives. Adults can become actively engaged in their own development and work toward greater involvement in the direction of professional staff development activities and reform of their school structures and working environments.

REFERENCES

Arlin, P. K. (1975). Cognitive development in adulthood: A fifth stage? *Developmental Psychology*, 5, 602–605.

Argyris, C. (1982). *Reasoning, learning, and action: Individual and organizational*. San Francisco: Jossey-Bass.

Basseches, M. (1984). *Dialectical thinking and adult development*. Norwood, NJ: Ablex.

Belenky, M. F., Clinchy, B. M., Goldberger, N., & Tarule, J. (1986). *Women's ways of knowing: The development of self, voice, and mind.* New York: Basic Books.

Bradford, D. L., & Cohen, A. R. (1984). *Managing for excellence.* New York: Wiley.

Burke, P. J., Christensen, J. C., & Fessler, R. (1984). *Teacher career stages: Implications for staff development.* Bloomington, IN: Phi Delta Kappan Educational Foundation.

Chickering, A. W., & Havighurst, R. J. (1981). The life cycle. In A. W. Chickering and Associates, *The modern American college* (pp. 16–50). San Francisco: Jossey-Bass.

Cochran-Smith, M., & Lytle, S. L. (1990). Research on teaching and teacher research: The issues that divide. *Educational Researcher, 19*(2), 2–11.

Cook-Greuter, S. (1990). Maps for living: Ego-development theory from symbiosis to conscious universal embeddedness. In M. M. Commons, C. Armon, L. Kohlberg, F. A. Richards, T. A. Grotzer, & J. D. Sinnott (Eds.), *Adult development: Vol. 2. Models and methods in the study of adolescent and adult thought* (pp. 79–104). New York: Praeger.

Daresh, J. C. (1985). *Research trends in staff development and inservice education.* Paper presented at the annual meeting of the Mid-western Educational Research Association, Chicago. (ERIC Document Reproduction Service No. ED 292 180)

Erikson, E. H. (1959). *Identity and the life cycle.* New York: International Universities Press.

Fessler, R. (1985). A model for teacher professional growth and development. In P. J. Burke and R. G. Heideman (Eds.), *Career-long education* (pp. 181–193). Springfield, IL: Thomas.

Gilligan, C. (1982). *In a different voice.* Cambridge, MA: Harvard University Press.

Gilligan, C., Ward, J. V., Taylor, J. M., with Bardige, B. (1988). *Mapping the moral domain.* Cambridge, MA: Harvard University Press.

Grimmett, P., & Erickson, G. (1988). *Reflection in teacher education.* New York: Teachers College Press.

Hagestad, G. O., & Neugarten, B. L. (1985). Age and the life course. In R. H. Binstock and E. Shanas (Eds.), *Handbook of aging and the social sciences* (2nd ed.) (pp. 35–61). New York: Van Nostrand Reinhold.

Hunt, D. E. (1975). The B-P-E paradigm for theory, research and practice. *Canadian Psychological Review, 16,* 185–197.

Hunt, D. E. (1981). Teachers' adaptation: Reading and flexing to students. In B. Joyce, C. Brown, L. Peck (Eds.), *Flexibility in teaching* (pp. 59–71). New York: Longman.

Kegan, R. (1982). *The evolving self.* Cambridge, MA: Harvard University Press.

Kegan, R., & Lahey, L. L. (1984). Adult leadership and adult development: A constructivist view. In B. Kellerman (Ed.), *Leadership: Multidisciplinary perspectives* (pp. 199–230). Englewood Cliffs, NJ: Prentice-Hall.

King, P. (1977). *The development of reflective judgment and formal operational thinking in adolescents and young adults.* Unpublished doctoral dissertation, University of Minnesota, Minneapolis.

Kitchener, K. S., & King, P. M. (1979). *Intellectual development beyond adolescence: Reflective judgment, formal operations, and verbal reasoning.* Unpublished manuscript, University of Minnesota, Minneapolis.

Kohlberg, L. (1981). *The philosophy of moral development.* New York: Harper & Row.

Kohlberg, L. (1984). *The psychology of moral development.* New York: Harper & Row.

Krupp, J. A. (1987). Understanding and motivating personnel in the second half of life. *Journal of Education, 169*(1), 20–46.

Kyle, D. K., & Hovda, R. A. (Eds.). (1987). The potential and practice of action research, parts 1 & 2 [Special issue]. *Peabody Journal of Education, 64*(2,3).

Levine, S. (1989). *Promoting adult development in schools.* Boston: Allyn & Bacon.

Levinson, D. J. (1986). Conception of adult development. *American Psychologist, 4*(1), 3–13.

Levinson, D. J., Darrow, C., Klein, E. B., Levinson, M., & McKee, B. (1978). *The seasons of a man's life.* New York: Knopf.

Loevinger, J. (1976). *Ego development: Conceptions and theories.* San Francisco: Jossey-Bass.

Long, H. B., McCrary, K., & Ackerman, S. (1979). Adult cognition: Piagetian-based research findings. *Adult Education, 30*, 3–18.

Lyons, N. (1983). Two perspectives: On self, relationship and morality. *Harvard Educational Review, 53*(2), 125–145.

Miller, A. (1981). Conceptual matching models and interactional research in education. *Review of Education Research, 51*, 33–84.

Neugarten, B. L., & Hagestad, G. O. (1976). Age and the life course. In R. H. Binstock and E. Shanas (Eds.), *Handbook of aging and the social sciences* (pp. 35–55). New York: Van Nostrand Reinhold.

Noddings, N. (1984). *Caring: A feminine approach to ethics and moral education.* Berkeley: University of California Press.

Oja, S. N. (1980). Adult development is implicit in staff development. *Journal of Staff Development, 1*, 7–56.

Oja, S. N. (1988). *Program assessment report: A collaborative approach to leadership in supervision.* Part B of the Final Report to the U.S. Department of Education, Office of Educational Research and Improvement. Durham, NH: University of New Hampshire Collaborative Research Projects.

Oja, S. N. (1989). Teachers: Ages and stages of development. In M. L. Holly & C. S. McLoughlin (Eds.), *Perspectives on teacher professional development* (pp. 7–56). London: Falmer.

Oja, S. N., & Ham, M. C. (1988). *Project portrayal* and *Practice profile.* Part A and C of Final Report to U.S. Department of Education, Office of Educational Research and Improvement. Durham, NH: University of New Hampshire Collaborative Research Projects.

Oja, S. N., & Pine, G. J. (1983). *A two year study of teachers' stages of development in relation to collaborative action research in schools.* Final Report to the National Institute of Education. Durham, NH: Collaborative Research Projects. (ERIC Document Reproduction Service No. ED 248 227)

Oja, S. N., & Pine, G. J. (1987). Collaborative action research: Teachers' stages of development and school contexts. *Peabody Journal of Education, 64*(1), 96–115.

Oja, S. N., & Sprinthall, N. A. (1978). Psychological and moral development for teachers. In N. A. Sprinthall and R. A. Mosher (Eds.), *Value development as the aim of education* (pp. 117–134). Schenectady, NY: Character Research Press.

Perry, W. (1970). *Forms of intellectual and ethical development in college years.* New York: Holt, Rinehart & Winston.

Perry, W. (1981). Cognitive and ethical growth: The making of meaning. In A. W. Chickering and Associates, *The modern American college* (pp. 76–116). San Francisco: Jossey-Bass.

Piaget, J. (1972). Intellectual evolution from adolescence to adulthood. *Human Development, 15,* 1–12.

Rest, J. (1986). *Moral development: Advances in research and theory.* New York: Praeger.

Schön, D. (1983). *The reflective practitioner: How professionals think in action.* New York: Basic Books.

Selman, R. L. (1980). *The growth of interpersonal understanding.* New York: Academic.

Thies-Sprinthall, L. (1984). Promoting developmental growth of supervising teachers: Theory, research, progress, and implications. *Journal of Teacher Education, 35*(3), 53–60.

Thies-Sprinthall, L., & Sprinthall, N. A. (1987). Experienced teachers: Agents for revitalization and renewal as mentors and teacher educators. *Journal of Teacher Education, 169*(1), 65–75.

Torbert, W. R. (1987). *Managing the corporate dream.* Homewood, IL: Dow Jones-Irwin.

Wortley, D., & Amatea, E. (1982). Mapping adult life changes: A conceptual framework for organizing adult development theory. In *Personnel and Guidance Journal, 60,* 476–482.

4 Enabling Professional Development
What Have We Learned?

Milbrey Wallin McLaughlin

In late 1970s, we claimed that staff development was "education's ne-glected stepchild" (McLaughlin & Marsh, 1978, p. 69). This generalization no longer holds. Staff development has moved from a position of disregard in policy circles to become a taken-for-granted component of almost all education reform initiatives.[1] It seems that hardly a state-level reform effort exists that does not include a staff development component. For example, an inventory of staff development opportunities available to California teachers yielded a bewildering bundle of hundreds of state, local, and regional initiatives at an annual taxpayer cost of $1,360 per teacher and $1,800 per administrator. This is approximately 1.8% of the state's $366 million education funding for 1986 (Little et al., 1987). In addition to these direct expenditures, Little and colleagues found that approximately one of every five hours a teacher spends in staff develop-ment activities is volunteer time, which, when calculated on the basis of the average teacher's salary, is worth $502 per teacher per year. Likewise, almost all national reform proposals assume "high-quality" staff develop-ment as requisite to positive change in America's classrooms (Smylie, 1988).

Staff development's transformation from policy afterthought to pol-icy requirement represents a response on the part of the policy system to complaints of the sort that motivated the 1978 charge of neglect. Yet all of this attention and support has not fundamentally modified another 1978 complaint: Staff development efforts generally are not designed in ways

This chapter reports research undertaken by the Center for Research on the Context of Secondary School Teaching, Stanford University. This research and my time for prepara-tion of this chapter are supported by the Office of Educational Research and Improvement, U.S. Department of Education (OERI Grant Number G0087C0235).

that enable teachers' professional development. Teachers evaluate staff development efforts in much the same critical terms they did more than a decade ago—as activities planned and developed far from the school site, with insufficient relevance to their classroom practices and inadequate follow-up to permit integration of new ideas and methods into professional activities (Guskey, 1986; Little et al., 1987; Smylie, 1988). For example, while virtually all of the teachers responding to a comprehensive assessment of staff development efforts in California participated in conferences and workshops, only 1 in 6 thought these activities had any positive impact on their classroom practices (Little et al., 1987).

Our 1978 article used findings from the (then recently completed) Rand Change Agent Study[2] to examine the issue of "effective" staff development as a problem of planned change and improvement of teaching practices. In the more than ten years that have passed since the completion of that article, additional research and analyses have accumulated about staff development, planned educational change, and the factors that support or inhibit teachers' professional growth. This chapter "revisits" the 1978 analysis in light of his more recent information, experience, and thinking to examine staff development practices and policies. What factors enable and sustain teachers' professional development?

THE RAND FINDINGS

The Rand Change Agent Study examined staff development in the context of broader change efforts associated with various types of federally funded projects.[3] The study used "outcome" measures that corresponded to anticipated results of inservice education efforts and other programs of professional development. These outcomes included change in teacher practices, pupil growth, and teachers' continued use of project methods and materials following the termination of special project funding. The study also examined the influence of many process variables considered in staff development programs, such as teacher commitment to and involvement with project objectives, staff reward structures, skills training and follow-up, the role of principal and district leadership, and effects of various aspects of school climate on teachers' growth and the maintenance of changed practices. In the view of study respondents, "staff development" and "successful change" were synonymous.

The Change Agent Study identified four broad factors as crucial to the successful implementation and continuation of local planned change efforts and to staff development activities: *institutional motivation, project implementation, institutional leadership*, and certain *teacher characteristics*.

Institutional Motivation

Institutional motivation, or the reasons for participating in the project, had important implications for teachers' commitment and willingness to spend the effort and energy required for successful project implementation. Some districts adopted a "change agent" project as a response to high-priority, locally identified needs. Others were moved to initiate projects for other reasons—an opportunity to bring new dollars into the district, a way to relieve community pressures on the district to "do something" about disappointing student outcomes, school board interest in being "up-to-date."

Teachers' motivation for participation showed an analogous range. Teachers took part in change agent projects because they saw them as important opportunities for professional growth and exposure to new ideas, or because they were told to, or because colleagues pressured them into it, or because attractive "perks" such as extra money or time off were attached to participation.

The Change Agent Study found that a high level of initial teacher commitment had the most consistently positive relationship to all outcomes. However, we also saw that teacher commitment was not a "given" but was affected by district choices and activities. Three choices were especially critical influences on teachers' commitment and motivation: *the motivation of district managers, project planning strategies, and the scope of proposed change agent project.*

Motivation of district managers was a "signal" to teachers about how seriously to take a project and its goals. Even teachers with initial interest in a project participated only in a pro forma fashion in the face of apparent district indifference. They assumed their efforts would be neither rewarded nor supported in the long run.

The project planning strategies chosen by the district influenced teachers' commitment and motivation in two ways. The extent to which they were or were not included in decisions about project strategies and activities determined their sense of "ownership." Planning that was solely top-down alienated teachers. But planning that was totally bottom-up was no more successful in the long run because it did not include district leaders to a significant degree and so did not engender their substantive commitment and support. District-level ownership is important too!

District planning strategies that were successful in motivating and sustaining teachers' commitment and support were broad-based and involved actors from all levels of the system. Evidence from the Change Agent Study shows that *who* originated a project did not matter. What did matter was *how* project planning was carried out.

A third factor that influenced teacher enthusiasm and interest in meaningful involvement in a project was scope of project change. Somewhat counterintuitively, complex and ambitious projects were more likely to elicit teachers' excitement and active participation than were routine or limited efforts. The most potent rewards for teachers' substantive involvement in the change agent project was intrinsic—belief that they would grow professionally and their students would benefit.[4]

Project Implementation

Project implementation strategies, or local choices about how to put project methods and goals into practice, also had critical consequences for the outcomes of planned change efforts and for teachers' professional development. Most important were those local choices that determined the ways in which staff would be assisted in acquiring the new skills and information necessary to implementation—staff-development strategies.

Implementation strategies that fostered teacher learning and change had two complementary components: staff training activities and training support activities. Well-conducted staff training and support activities improved project implementation, fostered student gains, and enhanced the continuation of project methods and objectives after special funding ended. These training and support activities, by themselves, accounted for a substantial portion of observed variation in project success and continuation.

This in itself is not surprising. More interesting and important from the perspective of policy are the quite different functions played by these two elements of staff development. By themselves, skill training activities had strong, positive effects on percent of project goals achieved and on student performance. However, skill-specific training had only a small, nonsignificant effect on teacher change and on the continuation of project methods and materials.

In other words, skill-specific training influenced student gains and project implementation *only in the short run*. Skill-specific training had only transient effects because, used alone, it did not support teachers' assimilation and integration of project methods. Once the supports of the funded project operation were removed, teachers stopped using project methods because they had never really learned them in the first place. Staff support activities were necessary to sustain the gains of how-to-do-it training.

Projects used a number of activities in support of project implementation activities, most particularly classroom assistance by local resource personnel, outside consultants, project meetings, and teacher participation in project meetings. Taken together, these activities (when they were seen as useful by school staff) had a major, positive effect—as did staff training—on project outcomes. But in contrast to skill-specific training, these support activities also generated strong positive and direct effects on longer-term project outcomes—teacher change and continuation of project methods and materials. Staff support activities not only reinforced the contribution of training, they made their own important contribution to project implementation and continuation.

Concrete assistance from individuals skilled in project methods was indispensable as teachers attempted to put plans into classroom practice. For this reason, local consultants generally were judged more useful than outside consultants because they were available on an as-needed basis and because they were more likely to provide technical assistance in concrete, situational terms. External consultants, by and large, were often seen by teachers participating in change agent projects as "too abstract to be useful" and providing "a lot of generalizations and worthless theory."

Good consultants also assisted teachers in learning how to solve problems on their own. Ironically, some otherwise effective consultants unintentionally diminished project outcomes because they preempted staff learning opportunities and prevented teachers from learning to implement project strategies for themselves.

We interpreted the negative effects of external consultants as a result of both too little and too much help from consultants. Subsequent research has shown, however, that these conclusions were too skeptical about the role of external consultants in supporting local change efforts and professional development. We were a captive of our sample. By and large, the packaged programs and outside consultants we observed in the mid-1970s were ineffective. But as the NETWORK's succeeding DESSI study (Crandall & Associates, 1982)[5] and other, subsequent research has shown, externally developed programs and external consultants can be extraordinarily effective in stimulating and supporting professional growth and planned change efforts. We understand now that it is not so much the "externalness" of outside practices and experts that inhibits their effectiveness, but how they interact with the local setting.

Frequent project meetings that focused on substantive issues were another important source of support for teacher change and project continuation. These meetings provided a forum for development of clarity about project methods and objectives as well as for collegial assistance and problem solving. Project meetings were also important to successful implementation and long-term continuation because they provided an opportunity for teachers' expertise to inform project decisions and to engender the teachers' sense of "ownership." The meetings, combined with concrete assistance from consultants, were critical strategies enabling teachers to integrate project practices into the classroom, to make them "theirs."

Institutional Leadership

Institutional leadership proved to be a third important element in the successful implementation and continuation of a local change agent project. Not surprisingly, the Rand Change Agent Study found that the more effective the project director (as rated by teachers), the higher the percentage of project goals achieved and the greater the student improvement reported as a result of the project.

However, we also saw that project leadership played a short-term and circumscribed role in the outcomes of local change agent projects. Other components of district leadership were important to the longer-term project consequences. Ironically, the effectiveness of the project director had no significant relationship to project continuation or long-term teacher change.

The support and interest of central office staff were important to teacher willingness to work hard and undertake the changes in practices and beliefs assumed by the project. Principals' support also affected project implementation, but to a lesser degree. A strong project director could overcome the indifference—but typically not the active disapproval—of a principal. Few of the projects in which principals were perceived as unfavorably inclined toward the project scored well on any of the study's outcome measures. The projects with neutral or indifferent principals that scored as highly as those with supportive principals typically focused on strategies such as individualized instruction, which could be undertaken when classroom doors closed and allowed effective project directors to compensate for lukewarm principal support.

However, the attitude of the building principal was even more critical to the long-term significance of project investments and activities. The support of the principal was directly related to the likelihood that teachers would continue the project in part or in its entirety after special funding was withdrawn. The principal gives sometimes subtle but nonetheless strong messages about the legitimacy of project operations in the school—a message that teachers cannot help but receive and interpret in terms of their professional self-interest.

We also found that the *school climate* was as important as the principal as an influence on project methods and objectives once federal funding ended. The Rand data indicate that good working relationships among teachers enhanced project implementation and promoted continuation of project methods. Good working relationships and teacher participation in project decisions were correlated: The development of one fostered the development of the other.

Teacher Characteristics

Teacher characteristics—the attitudes, abilities, and experience teachers bring to a project—comprised the fourth general factor the Rand Change Agent Study found had a major influence on the outcome of change agent projects. The study collected information on several teacher attributes cited most often as significant influences on student performance and the outcomes of innovative projects: age, educational background, verbal ability, years of experience, and sense of efficacy.

The most powerful individual teacher attribute was teachers' sense of efficacy—a belief that the teacher can help even the most difficult or unmotivated students. This factor displayed a strong, positive relationship to all project outcomes. Teachers' attitudes about their own professional competence had a fundamental and critical influence on what happened as a result of planned change efforts and how effective they were, broadly considered.

To what extent is teachers' sense of efficacy simply a "given," or can it be influenced by project design choices? The Rand Study examined this question by looking at the relationship between teachers' sense of efficacy and other factors measured in the study. We found that sense of efficacy was not related to years of experience or verbal ability, the other teacher characteristics that had significant effects on project outcomes. However, teachers' sense of efficacy was associated with project design. Teachers with a high sense of efficacy tended to be part of projects that placed heavy emphasis on staff development and teacher participation. Projects that involved teachers in project decision making, that provided timely and ongoing assistance in the classroom, and that had frequent staff meetings were more likely to have teachers with a high sense of efficacy than were projects that had narrowly defined goals, that had little teacher participation, or that relied heavily on the use of outside consultants for implementation.

An obvious question here is whether low-efficacy and high-efficacy teachers "selected into" different projects. Though such self-selection undoubtedly did occur to some extent, the Rand Study's fieldwork suggested that project training support activities did function to enhance teachers' sense of efficacy. They provided timely assistance to teachers and a forum in which teachers could talk through project strategies in terms of their own classrooms and thus feel confident in using a new idea. They promoted collegial encouragement and development of ownership of the project. They furnished opportunities for teachers to adapt project methods to their students and their classroom realities. In short, the Rand Change Agent Study confirmed much of the conventional wisdom about the importance of teachers' characteristics to the outcomes of a planned change effort. But the Change Agent Study also suggested ways in which project design and district leadership can influence these important factors.

NEW UNDERSTANDINGS

Two complementary strands of research undertaken since the Rand Study elaborate these conclusions and generate new understandings about professional development. While the general conception of staff development suggested by the Change Agent Study—a site-based activity supportive of teachers' efforts to identify and integrate new classroom practices—remains valid, focused examinations of *staff development practices* and current research on *teaching and learning* extend and amplify the findings of the Rand Study in critical ways.

Teaching and Learning as Co-Constructed Practice

In little more than a decade, research on teaching has moved from the relative simplicity of a process-product paradigm that relates specific teaching behaviors to specific student achievement measures (see, for example, Brookover, Beady, Flood, Schweitzer, & Wisenbaker, 1979; Brophy & Evertson, 1974; Gage, 1978; Gage & Giaconia, 1981) to much more variegated notions of teaching and learning (see, for example, Brown, 1989; Shulman, 1987). Research on teaching has shifted from focus on isolated pedagogical behavior to consider the teaching process in terms of relationships between content and pedagogy and to examine student-teacher interactions. Current notions of "good" teaching and "effective achievement" consequently are much more complex and differ in important respects from past, simpler conceptualizations.

Process-product researchers focused on *generic* rather than subject-specific teaching skills; recent developments in research on teaching emphasize that content matters. In particular, the notion of pedagogical content knowledge places strategies for effective teaching at the intersection of subject-area content knowledge and pedagogical skills (see, e.g., Greeno, n.d.; Shulman, 1987; Stodolsky, 1988). Good teaching practice in high school algebra, for example, entails choosing materials and techniques appropriate for teaching and learning quadratic equations as well as anticipating common student errors and assessing understandings. These skills and the knowledge base that supports them are different from the skills and knowledge necessary to teach literary analysis and guide students' learning about it. However, good teaching practice in all content areas must take into account the skills, understandings, knowledge, and attitudes of the particular learners for whom a lesson is planned.

This view of teaching and learning describes teaching and learning as *co-constructed* by teachers and students in a particular classroom around a particular instructional goal on a daily basis. Consequently, "instruction" as observed in a classroom at any point in time reflects a teacher's response to many elements in the school and classroom setting—students, competing demands, instructional goals, norms and expectations, to highlight just a few. Teaching practice is *embedded* in what John Seeley Brown (1989) calls the "nowness" of the teaching context and is co-produced by teachers and students. This "reason in action" (Sockett, 1987) generates practice in the inconstant, dynamic setting of the classroom and comprises an important explanation for the variation in an individual's teaching practice over time or across classrooms.

It also treats teachers' knowledge as situated and embodied in the school context. Professional development opportunities are only one element in this noisy, active organizational setting. This observation helps explain the disappointingly low level of project continuation that the Rand Study documented for the change agent sample. Narrowly focused special projects such as those the Rand project studied are incompatible with the daily realities confronting teachers and administrators. The single-focus assumptions implicit in special projects conflict with the context of teachers' decision making and construction of practice. Further, as Fullan, Bennett, and Rolheiser-Bennett (1989) explain, the demands of special projects can actually diminish overall instructional effectiveness because "the innovation becomes the focus, rather than the holistic, organic classroom and school life . . . innovations become ends in themselves, and paradoxically, turn out to be diversions from the more basic goals of improvement" (pp. 3–4).

This view of practice as situational and constructed on a daily basis also highlights the ongoing, site- and subject-specific nature of teachers' staff development concerns. Yet most staff development efforts implicitly conceive of professional development needs as bounded and short term. To this point, Little and colleagues (1987) found that most state, regional, or local staff development efforts in California exhibit this episodic character. Further, team-oriented staff development activities—designs that recognize collective and interdependent action at the site level—were the exception.

For all of these reasons, "decontextualized" or "disembodied" and discrete professional development activities can be of only limited assistance to teachers as they confront the "nowness" of their classrooms and seek ways to improve their classroom practices. Professional development activities consistent with this view of teaching treat knowledge as situated and as embodied in the teaching context. Research on the school-level factors that influence teachers' attitudes and practices reinforces this conclusion.

Site-Level Influences on Teachers' Professional Development

Research on the context of teaching and on staff development efforts in a variety of settings moves beyond the Rand Study's focus on special projects to consider staff development in the broader context of teachers' everyday realities (e.g., Little et al., 1987; Newmann, Onosko, & Stevenson, 1988; Smylie, 1988). The Center for Research on the Context of Secondary School Teaching (CRC) at Stanford University is conducting a three-year study of teachers' workplaces and factors that affect teaching and learning in a variety of settings. Data collected at 16 diverse secondary schools in two states include survey responses, interviews, and observations. Teachers' professional growth and opportunity for professional development are a central focus of this line of research. This research and experience extends many of the central conclusions of the Rand Change Agent Study and highlights the limitations of its analysis.

The Rand Study's charge was to examine the operation and contributions of special, federally funded projects. This special-project lens illuminated the importance of school-level factors, but it did not fully capture their collective, organizational significance. Work underway under the auspices of CRC and teacher-based examinations of staff development such as that carried out in California by Little and colleagues (1987) document the need to *consider professional development in schoolwide institutional terms*. This line of research highlights a number of site-level factors as critical to the development, support, and benefit of teachers' professional development. Among the most important are

Values and norms for professional development
School-level goals for instructional practice
School-level leadership

Values and norms for professional development. The values and norms operating at the school level create the critical context for teachers'

interest in and involvement with professional development. Is the school one in which problem solving (as opposed to problem hiding) and risk taking (as opposed to perpetuation of "safe" practice) are encouraged and supported? (See McLaughlin & Yee, 1988.) Does the school frame the achievement and success of students as solely an individual teacher responsibility or as a collective responsibility of the school faculty? (See Rosenholtz, 1989.) These *norms, values and attitudes* comprise a school-level "press" for staff development and establish expectations, supports, and rewards for teachers' professional growth and reflection. For example, Little and colleagues (1987) found that

> Consistent supporters [of staff development] are more likely to receive encouragement from their peers and their administrators for their participation and more often receive encouragement and assistance in evaluating the classroom utility of what they have learned [than are those teachers who are critical of staff development activities]. (p. 83)

It is difficult for individual teachers to sustain interest in their professional development if it is not valued and encouraged within their school workplace.

School-level goals for instructional practice. Schools vary significantly in the priorities teachers express for their classroom practices. For example, the CRC's survey asked teachers to rank eight general educational goals in terms of their classroom priorities (Center for Research on the Context of Secondary School Teaching, 1989). Teachers' average rankings of their educational goals provide a "goal profile" for a school. Contours of these goal profiles reveal important qualitative differences among high schools in the CRC sample and illustrate the substantive ways in which teaching jobs differ across educational settings. The site-specific goals that motivate and shape teachers' classroom practices provide another important context for professional development. A school is not a school is not a school! CRC field research found that, as a consequence of these school-level differences in instructional goals, teachers teaching the same subject at the same grade level in the same district express fundamentally different staff development interests and needs.

For example, a tenth-grade biology teacher working in a school serving primarily the college-bound children of university professors is eager for staff development activities that extend his laboratory repertoire and suggest new challenges for his students. A little more than two miles away, a teacher teaching nominally the same course—tenth-grade biology—is frustrated by her inability to locate appropriate materials and activities for her students, most of whom are limited-English-speaking and academically unmotivated. In contrast to her colleague down the street, she frames her staff development needs in terms of urgent need for assistance and support in working with this very different student group. Both teachers feel that staff development activities and resources provided by the district fail to meet their needs.

This site-specific perspective on staff development needs corresponds with the advice teachers have given consistently to planners and policy makers: Effective professional development efforts cannot be "generic"; they must be subject-specific and teacher-specific. Yet despite the documented importance of site-level planning for and implementation of staff development, most of the dollars and decisions associated with staff development remain centralized at the district level. For example, California teachers had a role in planning or leading *less than 10%* of all participant hours spent in staff development (see Little et al., 1987).

Little and colleagues' review of staff development activities concludes that most staff development activities are not designed in ways that can promote teachers' professional growth. Instead, centralized staff development attaches priority to separate, structured staff development activities that have little relevance to disparate groups of teachers who teach different subjects to different students at different grade levels and that "lend themselves to workshop-style presentations for large groups of teachers" (p. 69). In addition to administrative efficiency, this centralized, undifferentiated staff development also serves political ends. As a teacher comments:

> That was their easy fix because if you have people who are incompetent they say "how come I have to take the course? You say that I'm incompetent?" And the district didn't want to take that kind of pressure so they just run everybody through it. (RA02101:837–855)[6]

For these and other bureaucratic reasons, centralized staff development persists as the model of choice even though all we know about effective professional development activities and the enhancement of teachers' practice counsels against this centralized, generic strategy.

School-level leadership. CRC's research on the context of secondary school teaching and other research focused on the school as a workplace highlight not only the site-specific nature of professional development concerns, but also the multiple and critical ways in which many of the most important conditions and supports for staff development *are within the control of school leaders.*

School principals and high school department chairs are primarily responsible for establishing the norms, values, and expectations essential to consequential professional development. This normative climate is not self-creating or self-sustaining; it requires school leaders to reinforce and encourage it. One way leaders accomplish this is by establishing professional growth and problem solving as a priority for the school, and by making it "safe" for teachers to critically examine their practice and take risks.

Another way in which leadership plays an essential role is through the establishment and maintenance of the structure necessary for ongoing professional development. These structures involve ways for teachers to receive feedback about their performance and information about their students, to communicate with colleagues, and to move outside their classrooms to address issues and objectives as part of a faculty.

However, the ways in which site-level leadership creates these structures and opportunities varies by school. Within the CRC sample of schools, we have observed many different ways in which collegial interaction has been cultivated and supported. At a school confronted with the challenges of a rapidly changing student body where more than half of the students have limited English proficiency, the principal has generated an extraordinarily high level of energy, professional engagement, and collaboration through the initiation of school-level planning committees representing all academic areas as well as subject-specific concerns and has commandeered all available staff development resources for the school faculty to allocate as they see fit.[7] Teachers in this school are excited about the possibilities for growth and change as a consequence of the challenges presented by their changing student clinetele. This math teacher's assessment is typical:

> [The principal] is allowing teachers to grow and to have an input [into] changes [the school needs to make]. For example, the curriculum council, the school planning teams [have generated an] attitude that . . . now there is an opportunity to do great things, rather than [just complain about] the problems. [And change is evident.] . . . One of the good old boys on the staff said to me "maybe I need to change". We now realize that we have to change ways of presenting materials and strategies [if we are going to be effective with today's students]. (ES06901:182–207)

Another teacher at the same school stressed how his involvement on the school's planning committee had "re-motivated" him: "Maybe I was getting stagnant. It was so easy to stay back for years and not participate" (ES04001:98-108).

The attitudes and excitement of this faculty contrast starkly with those of teachers in another school facing similar challenges as a consequence of shifting student demographics. Teachers in this second school feel isolated in their efforts to develop effective responses to the students in their classrooms, feel demoralized and helpless.

These teachers *are* isolated. There is no structure for school-level communication and little or no support from school leadership for problem solving. Not surprisingly, the topic of professional development or growth seldom came up in our conversations except in a negative way.

These two schools provide dramatic illustration of the power of school-level choices and activities. Both schools operate within similar objective realities. They are approximately the same size, have a comparable resource base, and face similar challenges in terms of rapidly changing student demographics and an ethnically diverse student body. Yet these two schools comprise critically different contexts for teachers. One reflects the energy and excitement of a faculty working together to rethink their curriculum and plan strategies for responding to their changing student population. The other is a demoralized, discouraged setting where teachers look back to the "good old days" and feel ineffectual with the students who sit in their classrooms today. The primary difference between these two settings lies in school leadership and the structures established (or not) to support school-level collegiality and professional development.

We also saw that leadership of this type is not limited to the principal's office. At a third school where size makes school-level faculty meetings impractical, the department chairs have taken on the role of supporting collaboration and establishing expectations for reflection and experimentation, with the active, express support of school administration. An English teacher describes the climate of mutual support and collaboration in his department:

> It is standard, everyday practice that teachers are handing other teachers sample lessons that they've done or an assignment that they have tried and when it worked [why or if not] how they would do it differently. Or a new teacher joins the staff and instantly they're paired up with a couple of buddies who are teaching the same schedule . . . file drawers and computer disks and everything are just made readily available. And that, to me, is the only way this school knows how to function. It is quite different from the three other schools that I've taught at where it seemed

like teachers did their own thing and you didn't really dare share
. . . your one good idea [because] somebody else [might claim
ownership]. (OV04301:260–286)

The principal supports these department level activities in a variety
of ways. Last year, for example, he instituted a strategy whereby teachers
could put in for a "sub day" and "get out to see what they're doing outside
your department, inside your department, anywhere" (OV07701:401–
410). Teachers also report that he makes a point of finding out what they
are doing in the area of professional development and encouraging them
in any way he can—finding relevant contacts, funds, or additional opportunities. He is seen as a "manager of opportunities" and broker for the
professional life of his faculty. Teachers report that he has "high expectations" for their professional competence and development, expectations
that are communicated through attention to professional opportunities
and to formal and informal evaluation of classroom activities.

School-level leadership, in short, affects for better or worse the
organizational conditions that enable teachers' learning and professional
growth: Principals and department heads play a critical role in establishing the norms and expectations for professional growth, developing and
maintaining the organizational structures that can stimulate and support
it, and brokering the diverse opportunities for professional motivation
and learning.

Organizational settings so designed maximize staff development resources of any variety because learning can be integrated into ongoing
practices and shared with colleagues. Such a school is the organizational
equivalent of the "reflective practitioner" (Schön, 1983). It has the motivation and the means to examine practices on an ongoing basis, generate
feedback, and pursue strategies for improvement. It is a place where
teachers see professional growth as an expectation and collegial encouragement as unquestioned. It is a setting where it is safe to examine
practice critically and take risks with new instructional strategies.

A school-level perspective on professional development reveals the
vulnerability of staff development efforts to the complex and mutually
reinforcing conditions that operate at the school level to support or
inhibit teachers' professional development objectives and activities. Staff
development efforts are likely to have short-term and isolated benefits at
best in the absence of school-level norms for continuous professional
growth; organizational structures that provide teachers information
about students, their own practices, and practices in other classrooms;
norms of collective problem solving; and a shared mission (Fullan et al.,

1989; McLaughlin & Yee, 1988). These are the school-level factors that enable teachers to function as learners on a continuous, not episodic, basis (Rosenholtz, 1989). But schools do not function in a vacuum; they too are influenced by the context in which they are embedded.

Supports for Site-Level Professional Development

District role in supporting staff development. This emphasis on the crucial role of the school site in fostering and promoting staff development does not mean that the district is irrelevant to the outcomes of staff development efforts, or that all district-level resources should be decentralized to the school level, as some site-based management plans demand.

However, it does call for reconsideration of the district's role. If the school is the setting that provides the motivation and support necessary for ongoing professional growth, integration of new methods into existing practice, and professional problem solving, and if the centralized models presently in place are by most accounts disappointing and ineffective, what is an effective role for the district?

In theory, the district's role should be one that enables site-level leadership and teachers to identify, address, support, and sustain professional development activities. However, few districts appear to have developed staff development activities that teachers believe fulfill that function (see, e.g., Little et al., 1987). CRC respondents in diverse settings complained that district offerings were, with few exceptions, "intellectually thin," off-mark, and insufficient in terms of follow-through.

District efforts that received high marks from teachers had two common features: they were *concrete* and they were *intensive*. Teachers in three very different districts particularly mentioned district-sponsored activities on writing and on cooperative learning as especially helpful. This teacher's description of staff development activities he found especially helpful illustrates these points:

> The Writing Seminar was very valuable to me. Very practical suggestions. Some things I could implement in my classroom immediately. The district's three-day workshop on cooperative learning also was very valuable. . . . This was a three-day intensive workshop that actually spent time showing the process, having us go through the process, and then being required . . . to go back into the classroom and do it. And this seems to be . . . what makes all the difference. There are a lot of these seminars that are put on [where] you tend to take out a lot of information but nothing

really practical that you are going to implement because while you have all this stuff you never quite get the chance to process it. And then you fall back on the old ways of doing things, the familiar. (OV10601:458–491)

But equally as important as the specific staff development offerings provided by the district are the norms, values, and expectations communicated at the district level about teachers' professional development. One district in our CRC sample, Oak Valley,[8] pays deliberate attention to these often symbolic concerns and the messages about teachers' professionalism inherent in district-sponsored staff development activities. The district frames staff development activities primarily in terms of a diverse "menu" from which teachers can select activities. The opportunities for any given year are identified by a professional development committee composed of district teachers. Professional development in this district consequently is seen as planned by teachers, for teachers. And teacher attendance is voluntary: "We get to pick and choose. We are not told what we have to go to or what we need to stay away from" (OV03401:327–331). District leadership joins site-level leadership and the professional organizations in taking responsibility for managing teachers' professional development—notifying teachers of available activities or opportunities, actively seeking out appropriate activities or sources of special funding, and tailoring resources specifically for their faculty. The district is broker and stimulator of professional development opportunities.

Oak Valley district administrators stress the importance of professional vitality and professionalism in numerous ways. One mentioned most often by teachers is the evening meeting at the local country club where teachers are treated to dinner and given a sample of the professional development opportunities available to them. Both teachers and district officials saw this event as an important opportunity to "celebrate the professionalism" of teachers and to convey district priorities for and expectations about teachers' ongoing professional growth. For example:

There are a lot of things happening districtwide that end up having an impact back on the school. Number one, I think the staff development program offered by the district is really top notch. Maybe not all the teachers here—if they have only taught in Oak Valley—don't really appreciate that. But when you go other places [to other districts or to conferences] and they hear about the variety of programs we are offered, and then the way you're treated —that you get to go to a nice place and have a presentation and then you're treated to a meal afterwards—[then you really appre-

ciate what's here in Oak Valley]. [This makes] the people who
take part in the staff development programs far more interested in
being better teachers. (OV04301:110–140)

Oak Valley explicitly places teachers at the center of staff development
policies and frames the district's role in terms of enabling and managing
opportunities.

Teacher networks.   Focusing on staff development by teachers and
for teachers also points up the need to look beyond the formal policy
structure and traditional arrangements for channels that can promote
professional growth and stimulate teacher learning. If teachers' interests
and motivations lie at the heart of successful efforts to enhance classroom practices, then the professional networks that engage teachers
comprise promising vehicles for change. The reported success of such
teacher groups as the Bay Area Writing Project, the Puget Sound Educational Consortium, or the Urban Math Collaborative suggests that
professional development activities rooted in the natural networks of
teachers—in their professional associations—may be more effective
than strategies that adhere solely to a delivery structure outlined by the
formal policy system (see, e.g., Puget Sound Educational Consortium,
1989). As Oak Valley's experience demonstrates, staff development
policies that engage the natural networks of teachers can support development efforts in a more sustained fashion. Further, since teachers
rather than policies are responsible for integrating new practices with
traditional routines, it is possible to acknowledge the systemic nature of
professional development needs and the constructed, fluid quality of
classroom practice.

ENABLING PROFESSIONAL DEVELOPMENT

Taken together, the earlier Rand Study findings and the new understandings derived from more recent examinations of teaching and staff development suggest a strategic reframing of policies to stimulate and support
professional development. Many staff development policies are conceived in terms of removing or buffering the *constraints* to teachers'
professional growth and effective practice—inadequate materials, insufficient information, lack of appropriate teacher preparation, missing
teacher voice in staff development decisions, to cite a few. However, an
important lesson from the Rand Study, the CRC work, and other expe-

rience is that removing constraints or obstacles to professional growth does not ensure more effective practice or professional vitality. A teacher with new information about how to do better in the classroom does not necessarily apply or sustain it. This body of research shows that neither teachers' sense of efficacy nor classroom practices are significantly enhanced by these decontextualized "inputs."

Other and often substantively different factors are required to *enable* improvement and professional development. The factors that the Rand Change Agent Study found to be associated with effective planned change efforts, effective staff development, and teachers' positive sense of efficacy all function to enable teachers' efforts to change—such as ongoing assistance, structures that promote collegiality, concrete training and follow-through, and principal support and encouragement. And the school and district factors that have been seen to enable professional development—managing multiple, diverse opportunities; creating and supporting norms and expectations for professional growth; developing and nurturing structures for communication, collegiality, and feedback; defining a central role for teachers—are not amenable to direct policy "fixes" because they do not operate consistently or singly across settings.

A focus on enabling professional development *within existing constraints* denotes a fundamentally different policy perspective than that which has guided past practice. It highlights the conditional, mutually reinforcing, and contextual nature of factors that support professional development. It underscores the embedded nature of the education system and how the policies at one level—state, district, or school—can enable (or constrain) the efforts of actors at the next.

Thinking of professional development as a problem of enabling teachers' learning and continued professional vitality focuses attention on the organizational conditions of individual development and the critical consequences of school-level choices. Explanations of why—within the same district—some schools are "dead" and others are charged with energy and excitement lie in site-level strategies to engage teachers in learning and development *in the context* of their particular classroom settings. These site-level strategies are reinforced and enhanced by district-level or teacher-based policies that acknowledge the need for site- or teacher-specific professional development opportunities, convey high expectations and support for teachers' professionalism, and exploit the strengths of teachers' networks and professional affiliations. These are the factors that enable and sustain teachers' professional growth and feelings of efficacy in the classroom.

NOTES

1. I use the terms *staff development* and *professional development* interchangeably. Staff development reflected the language of the 1970s; professional development captures better the objectives and conceptualizations of the 1990s.

2. From 1973 through 1978, the Rand Corporation carried out, under the sponsorship of the United States Office of Education, a national study of federally funded programs intended to introduce and support innovative practices in the public schools. Rand's four-year, two-phase study examined a sample of 293 local projects funded by four federal programs (Title III of the Elementary and Secondary Education Act [ESEA], Title VII of ESEA, innovative programs funded by the 1968 Vocational Education Act, and Right-to-Read). Findings of the study were reported in eight volumes under the general title *Federal Programs Supporting Educational Change*. A summary analysis of the study is contained in Berman and McLaughlin (1978).

3. This section draws substantially from McLaughlin and Marsh (1978). Readers interested in more details of the analysis summarized in this section should consult the original article or Berman and McLaughlin (1978).

4. Certain "extrinsic rewards," we found, actually were negatively related to project outcomes. In particular, teachers who received extra pay for training (about 60% of the sample) were *less* likely than others to report a high percentage of project goals achieved. These teachers also reported less improvement in student performance, especially academic performance, than did other teachers in the study. A number of project directors commented that although teachers appreciated the extra pay, the pay alone did not induce teachers to learn new skills in the absence of professional motivation. To this point, a teacher remarked, "I'll go [to the training session], and I'll collect my $30, but I don't have to listen."

5. The DESSI study examined a national sample of the next generation of change agent projects. In their design and strategies of support, these projects incorporated many of the lessons from the antecedent planned change efforts that comprised the Rand sample.

6. Here and elsewhere, quotations from respondents are identified by their file code and the interview lines from which the text is taken. These interviews are part of a public-use file that will be made available to interested researchers at the end of the CRC's grant period.

7. This school's relatively high ranking of inservice activities as "helpful" was puzzling to us because other schools in the same district had uniformly rated district staff development activities as not helpful. When we asked teachers in this school to help us understand this anomalous survey outcome, they said they gave positive scores to their inservice because they "did it themselves" and organized it all at the school level.

8. "Oak Valley" is a pseudonym. The identities of districts participating in the CRC research are confidential.

REFERENCES

Berman, P., & McLaughlin, M. W. (1978). *Federal programs supporting educational change: Volume 8. Implementing and sustaining innovations.* Santa Monica: Rand Corporation (R-1589-HEW/8).

Brookover, W., Beady, C., Flood, P., Schweitzer, J., & Wisenbaker, J. (1979). *School systems and student achievement: Schools can make a difference.* New York: Praeger.

Brophy, J., & Evertson, C. (1974). *Process-product correlations in the Texas Teacher Effectiveness Study: Final report.* Austin: University of Texas, R&D Center for Teacher Education.

Brown, J. S. (1989). Remarks at a Stanford Center for Organizational Research Seminar, January 13, 1989.

Center for Research on the Context of Secondary School Teaching. (1989). *CRC report to field sites.* Stanford, CA: School of Education, Stanford University.

Crandall, D., & Associates. (1982). *People, policies and practices: Examining the chain of school improvement* (Vols. 1–10). Andover, MA: NETWORK.

Fullan, M. G., Bennett, B., & Rolheiser-Bennett, C. (1989, April). *Linking classrooms and school improvement.* Paper presented at the annual meeting of the American Educational Research Association, San Francisco.

Gage, N. (1978). *The scientific basis for the art of teaching.* New York: Teachers College Press.

Gage, N., & Giaconia, J. (1981). Teaching practices and student achievement: Causal connections. *New York University Education Quarterly, 12*(3), 2–9.

Greeno, J. (n.d.). *The situated activities of learning and knowing mathematics.* Unpublished manuscript, Stanford University and the Institute for Research on Learning, Stanford, CA.

Guskey, T. (1986). Staff development and the process of teacher change. *Educational Researcher, 15*(5), 5–12.

Little, J. W., Gerritz, W. H., Stern, D. S., Guthrie, J. W., Kirst, M. W., & Marsh, D. D. (1987). *Staff development in California.* Joint Publication of the Far West Laboratory for Educational Research and Development (San Francisco) and Policy Analysis for California Education (University of California at Berkeley, School of Education).

McLaughlin, M. W., & Marsh, D. D. (1978). Staff development and school change. *Teachers College Record, 80*(1), 69–94.

McLaughlin, M. W., & Yee, S. M. (1988). School as a place to have a career. In A. Lieberman (Ed.), *Building a professional culture in schools* (pp. 23–44). New York: Teachers College Press.

Newmann, F. M., Onosko, J., & Stevenson, R. B. (1988). *Staff development for higher order thinking: A synthesis of practical wisdom.* Madison: National Center on Effective Secondary Schools, University of Wisconsin.

Puget Sound Educational Consortium. (1989). *Teacher leadership: Vol. 2. Contributions to improved practice.* Seattle: University of Washington.

Rosenholtz, S. (1989). *The school workplace.* New York: Longman.

Schön, D. A. (1983). *The reflective practitioner.* New York: Basic Books.

Shulman, L. (1987). Knowledge and teaching: Foundations of the new reform. *Harvard Educational Review, 57*(1), 1–22.

Smylie, M. (1988). The enhancement function of staff development: Organizational and psychological antecedents to individual teacher change. *American Educational Research Journal, 25*(5), 1–30.

Sockett, H. (1987). Has Shulman got the strategy right? *Harvard Educational Review, 57,* 208–219.

Stodolsky, S. (1988). *The subject matters.* Chicago: University of Chicago Press.

5 Stretching the Limits of Our Vision
Staff Development and the Transformation of Schools

Myrna Cooper

The occasion of this paper provides a much-needed opportunity to revisit the issues my co-author Maurice Leiter and I raised in "How Teacher Unionists View In-Service Education" in the first edition of this book. Here I want to offer an assessment of what has been accomplished in staff development and, most significantly, to provide some understanding of what role staff development can now play in testing the limits of reform and restructure in schooling.

TEACHER-CENTERED STAFF DEVELOPMENT

The earlier chapters said what had to be said at the time. The condition of inservice education in the 1970s made it very clear that alternative approaches to inservice were necessary. The case for peer-driven (or teacher-centered) staff development under the sponsorship or with the collaboration of teacher organizations was an option whose time was at hand, and its coming to the fore paralleled the general growth of the union movement in the public sector, especially in schooling.

It was not difficult to make a convincing argument for channeling staff development through those in whom teachers placed their trust, particularly when the traditional top-down inservice models had been found to increase rather than decrease teachers' sense of alienation and powerlessness. Management-generated solutions imposed without regard to the need or will of those for whom they were fashioned lacked both justification and credibility. Thus a shift to more democratic inservice mechanisms gradually grew to fill the vacuum that we found.

The obstacles that peer-driven staff development sought to overcome were familiar at that time. Teachers were isolated professionally. They were cut off from those who judged them and unable to interact with those who shared their concerns. The knowledge base for good practice, which was growing in the researchers' universe, continued to be unavailable to the mainstream of practitioners. The teachers' insatiable need for variety of repertoire and versatility in technique was unmet. Time for training, reflection, and experiment was virtually nonexistent. Preparation for entry into teaching was mechanical and impractical. New teachers were poorly supported, clumsily supervised, and essentially left to themselves. The trial by fire of the new teacher was the ironic forerunner of the burnt-out veteran later on.

The public outcry against incompetents occupied the political arena. Teachers faced a daily reality of having no voice but that of acquiescence, no option but that of conformity, no professional freedom except when the classroom door was shut and students and teachers were alone together. The drive to "get out of the classroom" into administrative roles was the sole solution available to teachers within their stagnant and repetitive environment.

Absent incentives to learn and to grow, other than the most mundane and reflexive, rewarded more for form than substance and rewarded poorly to boot, the teacher of this last decade had little cause for being happy over his or her career choice.

Such were the circumstances of teaching and teacher development at the time. Perhaps we should have been more suspicious of the acceptance that gradually developed (not without difficulty—then and to this day) for making peer models and peer organizations the engine of the effort to make the professional lives of teachers dynamic rather than static and to make teaching a truly developmental pursuit. Had we paid greater heed to organizational behavior (if we knew then what we know now), we would have realized that institutions change only when faced with extremities, such as replacement, extinction, or evisceration. In this instance, the institution of public education changed just enough to maintain itself in the face of criticism from without and dissension within. In doing so, much of the scrutiny and accountability was shifted from the managers of education to the representatives of teachers.

Nevertheless, this corporate divestiture proved beneficial to practitioners. Carried forward in such conceptual forms as teacher centers, the practice of staff development has become integral to the introduction and support of teachers, policies, programs, curricula, and strategies.

Over the years, many of the things staff developers set as goals have been achieved. Peer-driven staff development is widely accepted and largely preferred, even by systems and researchers. That staff development is important is no longer a quibble. That teachers are deserving of respect and increased authority to determine educational and organizational priorities is daily affirmed, even as part of the national political agenda.

The importance of bringing research closer to practice and the importance of practitioners' collaborating in research has been established. Teachers' sense of isolation and burn-out has been addressed and frequently overcome. Consciousness has been raised, hope rekindled, avenues of communication opened. People have become excited about the possible and have been taught the *art* of the possible, and, in so doing, enormous range to the repertoire of teaching and to the understanding of adult learning has been provided. The factory system that we found has been made better than could have been hoped.

Sound models of staff development service delivery to individuals have been established. New and respected ways of developing and presenting courses have been created, and the establishment has been convinced that teachers can and should teach other teachers. Staff development has been redefined as a continuous and incremental process built on a practitioner's existing skills. Beginners who might otherwise have left in despair have been supported and sustained, and veterans who had lost their focus, revitalized.

Recognition has been given to the scholarship and accomplishments of practitioners, not only as classroom workers, but in other professional dimensions. Experimentation and collaboration have been encouraged and rewarded. Teacher organizations have been assisted in rethinking their own sense of their constituents' concerns and priorities, and, in turn, staff development has benefited from the political support of the teacher organizations in funding their work, empowering the practitioner, and restructuring the schools.

A set of new and vital roles for trainers has emerged: change agent, facilitator, mentor. In short, the way schools perceive both staff development and teachers has been recast.

What was accomplished in a decade of intense activity can now be viewed as a stage in the continuing evolution of staff development. But before such work can be extended, the rectitude and value of peer-driven staff development in our schools had to be established.

STAFF DEVELOPMENT:
RE-CREATING SCHOOL ENVIRONMENTS

What has been found, however, is that trying to change the way teachers teach is not the most powerful way of changing the system unless the changes enable the individual to challenge the normative environment. This will require new forms of development powerful enough to equip people to confront the political, economic, and social forces that shape the nature of schooling.

Thus, even though right, the rightness did not carry far enough. Some extension or revaluation of assumptions was necessary. The system proved more resilient in resistance than reformation. It could be squeezed, it could be bent, but it always reassumed its shape.

Part of what staff development has to do now is teach people how to re-create environments and how to think about the structures and functions that are right for children.

The present commitment to the individual development of teachers within the *unreconstructed* system and the need to enable practitioners to challenge the system's assumptions inevitably create both tension and dilemma. They place staff development at a crossroad. For as the accomplishments in staff development infuse the system, developers are more and more in danger of becoming media of the system's priorities and are forced to make difficult choices when their historic mission appears jeopardized. Normally, the staff developer who practices within the tradition of teacher centers has a clear sense of fidelity to the individual teacher's growth. The possibility of becoming a functionary within an organizational hierarchy goes against the grain. Such a staff developer would not seek to adapt the teacher to the system, but rather strive to find a balance between individual need and system need.

As the recognition grows that a sole emphasis on the mechanical skills and strategies of instruction is insufficient, staff developers turn to the exploration of teacher value and belief systems to increase the likelihood of effecting change. Yet the system tends to reject this approach.

How should staff developers treat the compartmentalization of interventions when the interventions are carried out within an environment whose implicit value system contradicts the intervention? Perhaps the difficulty of implementing cooperative learning is illustrative of the tensions between the micro-intervention and the macro-environment. To a large extent, increasing identification with systemwide solutions and programs tends to weaken the staff developer's credibility.

The issue is not whether such choices and practices are good or bad. Some have been valuable and may have new value in an authentic reconceptualization of schooling. The real question is whether the staff developer is not losing an opportunity to be a critical pivot, seeing the system through its transformation and the practitioner through a period of growth in challenging and altering the system.

TURNING VISIONS INTO NEW PRACTICES

As teacher center developers began to formulate methods to assist teams within schools to learn the skills to participate in restructuring and related school-based management activities, they discovered certain limits to the conceptual environment in which these teams were obliged to function.

As part of these efforts, team members were asked to examine their systems and challenge them to create a vision of what schools should be like as learning environments, and how young people should be activated. They generally agreed on what *should* be and how it differed from the existing system. The schools they envisioned are caring, nurturing places that reflect a sense of community where people are actively engaged in a diversity of learning experiences.

Such visions emphasized continuity of contact between child and teacher, teacher-parent interaction, a strong family service component, and provision for all needs of children, including food, clothing, and health care. Team members sensed the importance of having schools that value and respect their children and give the youngsters space and opportunity to grow and endless ways to learn.

Yet when these same perceptive and visionary people were asked to map the steps from what exists to what they envisioned, their responses tended to be conceptually similar to what already exists, albeit a better version of what we have. They relied on what was familiar.

As a result, we came to hypothesize that asking questions differently or asking different questions would prompt people to see problems differently and entertain solutions thought forbidden or inconceivable.

Take so basic a problem as lunchroom organization. To the question "What is the best way to organize a school lunchroom?" came conventional answers dealing with rules, order, enforcement, silence, lines, procedures. Suppose, instead, we had asked people to examine their vision, and out of that vision invent an environment that signifies what they believe children should experience and learn in such a setting. Quickly we see that responses will no longer address structure.

If people believe that a lunchroom ought to involve social learning, be an experience in community full of personal vitality and language and energy, have a relaxed atmosphere in which people can get to know *each* other and many *others*, perhaps not unlike what we expect of any social experience or a large family gathering, they will alter its environment to convey that meaning.

The questions change the possibilities. Whereas, before, we answered the *organizational* question with solutions of control and repression, we now answer by enabling or facilitating means. We have progressed from closed assumptive thinking to open reconceptualization.

Consider the classroom in the same vein. Are not silent classrooms preferred every time? But is not the silent classroom a vestige of a view of children no longer held, that they are empty vessels who bring no knowledge base with them? And does not a silent classroom suggest that we do not value language, communication, and opportunities for interaction? Can we allow ourselves to espouse occasional forays into strategies of interaction in an environment that values the sound of silence over the chatter of the living young?

Perhaps we also need to ask people to reflect on what made a difference for them in their own schooling or in their young lives. Was it the teacher who read to them eagerly and imaginatively? Was it the teacher who respected their creative efforts? Was it the teacher who encouraged them, who was always busy with them and who trusted them to be busy, too, and to encourage each other? We need to re-create what mattered for all of us to understand what matters to these children. Above all, we must question everything.

To do this, we must reach for a vocabulary of conception and change and for ways of looking at schools that will really break with the past.

RETHINKING THE ROLE OF A STAFF DEVELOPER

As staff developers we, too, are rethinking the roles we play within the system, and the language and the cues we use to impart skills and probe beliefs. We, too, must craft for *ourselves* a sense of this other world of schooling. We, too, have tended to apply a normative model of schooling and of our function within the system. Before we can rightly challenge others to reconceptualize, we must challenge ourselves. We cannot ultimately abide the contradiction of service to institutional norms while we seek to encourage personal and professional revaluation.

For such staff developers pointing toward a new century and new views of schooling, a shift from the delivery of *mechanical* and technical skills to the development of ways to build the *conceptual* skills of practitioners has become necessary. This is the bridging step that the profession must take in order to be able to look at schooling free of the conventions of the past that still govern the present. This constitutes a basic redirection of focus for developers, a fresh way of viewing their own role, and a bold new view of the possibility of using the potential of practitioners to decouple learning from the obsession with efficiency that has kept it married to the mechanical.

We are, after all, not building a machine, but a family, not building a production plant, but an adventureland, and we are surely more interested in intellectual and personal growth than in the superficial measurement of outputs.

To escape the model of the factory, we need to escape questions learned in the factory. In the first assault of developers and practitioners on the practices of the past, we confronted the assembly-line mentality of the pre-Dewey era. In recent years, reinforced by a more liberal and wholesome view of children, we turned to the workers on the line. Impressed by the Japanese, we seemed to understand how to make stakeholders of their factory workers, we began thinking of team approaches such as quality circles and of the general virtues of collaboration.

And so we modernized the factory floor and have come a good way toward democratizing it—but it is still a factory, still rational, linear, and outcome-driven. Before that model can be replaced, its assumptions must be challenged, learners and learning viewed differently, and questions about production and procedure replaced by questions of belief and meaning.

Certainly, staff developers have found that skills and strategies are important, necessary but not sufficient. Moreover, concentration on skill and strategy tends to gravitate to a framework of causally driven assessment, and to factory-manufactured thinking. Staff developers have found that it is essential to change the way people work (teach) by extending and honing their skill repertoire and by altering how people plan and deliver instruction. However, such change is simply not enough without helping people reconceptualize their task and their mission and understand how that reconceptualization affects what the environment of learning comes to signify.

MOVING FROM PARTICIPATION
TO TRANSFORMATION

If people can be brought beyond the mechanical to the visionary and brought there by necessarily developing a whole new set of relating and doing skills, then the system may finally open up (or relent). Then the shaping of learning environments that stretch the limits of our vision can begin, and people will commence to describe the heretofore unnameable.

As yet, the characteristics of the dream become reality are not known. The border of the permissible has not been crossed; the leap of innovation to transformation not yet made.

Dewey's dream was similar. He thought democratic schools would, by modeling a new species of social relationships, banish inequity and exploitation from the society at large. People would learn to *be* different, to *relate* differently, to *respect* difference, and the school would generate the critical mass for social change.

Why has it not happened? In part, at least, it has not happened precisely because the focus of change has been efficiencies—political, educational, and operational. Staff developers have worked within this system and accomplished much, just as those who, earlier, sought to apply Dewey's liberating vision accomplished much in building respect for the individuality and integrity of children and for new ways to experience learning. But always the norms and language of the old system have determined the limits of change.

There are many clear terms to describe the present state of schooling. Everyone knows what is meant by the factory model, by a rational causal system that deals in input and output, by productivity and efficiency. Everyone understands the tradition of bureaucracy and the virtues of hierarchy. Everyone comprehends what order means, or education for work, or democratic values.

Lacking is a metaphor to clearly express a vision of a reconceptualized educational system whose values and assumptions are truly liberating, free of cant and conformity. The absence of such a vocabulary makes it difficult to help people articulate their felt sense of mission. Lacking, too, is concreteness. The transformed school, unlike the present conception of schooling, is inaccessible to scrutiny. The description of what will succeed today's system exists only haltingly and fragmentarily.

As yet, we have only incomplete notions of how to reconceive what people are capable of, how to rethink the roles they fill and the relationships they play out. It is as if a spirit had been seen and photographed, and we clung to a hazy image of what it was like although we could not develop it on film. It dances in the mind but cannot yet be embodied.

Many of the process and implementation skills now being utilized by the staff developers in the New York City Teacher Centers Consortium in building effective teams to participate in school-based management and shared decision making can help to make the transition from participation to transformation.

These skills are directed to creating expertise among practitioners in collaboration, consensus building, communication among and within groups, self-study, decision making, and problem solving, and in developing mission and vision statements and the action plans necessary to achieve them. In short, these tools help practitioners communicate, develop, plan, and fulfill their vision.

One cannot empower without these tools for empowerment. Nor can one empower without sufficiently developing the techniques and mechanisms for raising value, belief, or ideological issues. In fact, it is wrongly held that such matters are irrelevant to teachers' professional activities. It is assumed that staff development is value-free and concerned solely with increasing the efficiency of teachers and schools.

To carry this out, staff developers must now formulate the next generation of "tool making" so that practitioners can think (conceive) differently about environments, social, economic, and political constraints, themselves, and others—especially children. We will go beyond the initial stages of process and confidence building to apply the new tools to the basic questions of teaching and learning.

However they have tinkered, how often they have labored, educators sense, still, that schools are working for an ever-narrowing strand of children and gratifying fewer and fewer career faculty. Reform lies in eschewing efficiency, in altering assumptions. It lies in a meaningful empowerment of practitioners who will use responsibility, authority, knowledge, and collaboration to make schools humane places for learning.

⑥ Revisiting the Social Realities of Teaching

Ann Lieberman & Lynne Miller

When we first wrote about the social realities of teaching (Lieberman & Miller, 1978, 1984), we approached our writing as fieldworkers, eager to capture the perspectives of teachers as they went about their work in elementary and secondary schools. Recognizing that we knew a great deal about teachers and their world, we readily admitted that there was a great deal more to know. Now, over a decade later, we want to revisit our initial understandings, deepen our earlier insights, and make more meaningful connections between what we know about the social realities of teaching and the practice of professional development. Our intention here is to reconsider meanings from "the field," understandings about teachers' views of their professional lives. We believe that in seeing schools from the teachers' perspective, we can uncover their potential for improving the conditions of teaching and learning.

THE NATURE OF TEACHING

Our earlier work led us to identify a set of phenomena we called "social system understandings" about the nature of teaching. These understandings provided a basis for formulating some generalizations about the way a teacher learns the job, becomes a teacher, and forges a professional identity. Drawing on a rich and varied literature (Jackson, 1990; Lortie, 1975; McPherson, 1972; Smith & Geoffrey, 1968; Waller, 1952) and reflection on our own experiences, we formulated these eight understandings (Lieberman & Miller, 1978, 1984).

Style Is Personalized

Teachers are faced with a central contradiction in their work, a contradiction that makes it incumbent upon each one of them to develop a style that is individual and personal. Stated simply, the contradiction is this: Teachers have to deal with a group of students and teach them something and, at the same time, deal with each child as an individual. The teachers, then, have two missions: One is universal and cognitive, and the other is particular and affective. The cognitive mission demands a repertoire of skills in moving a group and making sure that knowledge builds, extends, and is learned. The affective mission requires that teachers somehow make friends with their students, motivate them, arouse their interest, and engage them on a personal level. In order to deal with this contradiction, teachers develop all kinds of strategies and then meld them together into a style that is highly personal, if not plain idiosyncratic. This style, forged in the dailiness of work and developed by trial and error, becomes one's professional identity and, as such, is often militantly protected and defended.

Rewards Are Derived from Students

The greatest satisfaction for a teacher is the feeling of being rewarded by one's students. In fact, most of the time the students are the only source of rewards for teachers. Isolated in their own classrooms, teachers receive feedback for their efforts from the words, expressions, behaviors, and suggestions of the students. By doing well on a test, sharing a confidence, performing a task, indicating an interest, and reporting the effects of a teacher's influence, students let teachers know that they are doing a good job and are appreciated. Unlike other professionals, who look to colleagues and supervisors for such feedback, teachers turn to children.

Teaching and Learning Links Are Uncertain

Dan Lortie (1975) said that teaching is fraught with "endemic uncertainties." No uncertainty is greater than the one that surrounds the connection between teaching and learning. A teacher does his or her best, develops curricula, tries new approaches, works with individuals and groups, and yet never knows for sure what the effects are. One hopes the children will get it, but one is never sure. A teacher operates out of a kind of blind faith that with enough in the way of planning, rational schemes, objectives, and learning activities, some learning will take place. But a teacher also knows that some learnings happen that are significant but never planned for and that other learnings never take hold, despite the best of professional intentions.

The Knowledge Base Is Weak

Throughout their careers, teachers seek professional knowledge. In preparation, a teacher-to-be takes numerous courses in the theory and the practice of education—most of which are judged as irrelevant upon entering teaching. As a bona fide teacher, one takes even more courses to earn permanent certification. In addition there is a plethora of "staff development" offerings made available and often mandated on the district level. With some exceptions, this inservice work is given the same low grades for relevance and helpfulness as is early preprofessional preparation. The fact is that, as a profession, we have not been able to codify teaching under a variety of contingencies in a way that is satisfying to practitioners. The knowledge base in teaching is weak; there is simply no consensus (as there is in medicine and law) about what is basic to the practice of the profession.

Goals Are Vague and Conflicting

Although there has been much talk about goal specificity and accountability, it is still the case that the goals of education are vague and often in conflict. Are we out to impart basic skills or to enrich lives? Do we concentrate on the individual or concern ourselves with the development of the group? Are we teaching to minimal levels of competence, or are we working to develop a wide range of talents and possibilities? Do we most value discipline or learning, order and control or intellectual curiosity? Are we socializing students, or are we educating them? The answer to these questions and to others like them is usually, "Yes, we are doing both." The result is that individual teachers make their own translations of policy and that, in general, the profession is riddled by vagueness and conflict.

Control Norms Are Necessary

Daily, teachers attempt to gain some sense of direction, control, and movement of their classes. Teachers work hard to develop a set of norms and rules that both they and their students can live with. This happens as teachers move through a cycle of giving orders, threatening, being tested, and finally developing some standards that are accepted and move the class along. While this is being done in individual classrooms, schoolwide norms are also being tried and established. The setting of control norms is a necessary part of teaching; it satisfies the need for certainty in an otherwise ambiguous and uncertain world. It also assures teachers of their place in the organization of the school. No matter how effective teachers are in the classroom, all that is ever really known about them in the general organization of the school is whether they keep their classes in line or whether the students are in control. Control precedes instruction; this is a major shibboleth of teaching.

Professional Support Is Lacking

Seymour Sarason and his colleagues wrote that "teaching is a lonely profession" (1966), a characterization that is indeed apt. Unlike other professions, teaching does not provide for a shared culture based on the movement from knowledge to experience in the company of one's peers. Doctors, for instance, learn their profession through a graduated set of experiences, all shared with others. Not so the teacher. Once graduated from preparation programs, teachers find themselves alone in the classroom with a group of students, without a peer or supervisor in sight. The neophyte teacher is left with degree in hand, high expectations internalized, a fistful of untried methodologies, and few adults with whom to share, grow, and learn.

Teaching Is an Art

Teaching is an art, despite recurring efforts to make it scientific. Some parts of teaching may lend themselves to programming and rationalization, but in the long haul more artistry than science and technology is practiced as teachers struggle to adjust and readjust, to develop routines, and to establish patterns, only to recast what has been done in a new form to meet a new need or a new vision. Teachers are best viewed as craftsworkers; the reality of teaching is of a craft learned on the job. This understanding is perhaps our most important one. When viewed as a craft, teaching makes sense as a messy and highly personal enterprise, for it concerns itself with the making and remaking of an object until it satisfies the standards of its creator.

THE DAILINESS OF TEACHING

When we first formulated generalizations about the nature of teaching, we were aware that such codifications—no matter how grounded—often "miss the mark." While useful as guidelines for discussion, they fail to capture the flesh and blood of teaching, to call up its dailiness. We identified some themes to express that dailiness—rhythms, rules, interactions, and feelings (Lieberman & Miller, 1978, 1984).

Rhythms

A teacher's professional life is measured in terms of years of service. Each of those years is cyclical, mediated by the rhythms of days, of weeks, of months, and of seasons. Let us begin by talking about teachers' days. Days begin early, before the din of the rush hour has peaked, often before the sun has risen. Once sign-in procedures are completed, greetings exchanged with colleagues, the last sip of coffee downed in the teachers' room, and the warning bell sounded, the classroom becomes a teacher's total world. It is a world that is unique and separate from the world of other adults. For six hours a day, five days a week, teachers live in an exclusive and totally controlled environment. For the majority of the day they are bound in space and time. In most instances, teachers need the permission of the principal to leave the building during school hours. "Whoever heard of a profession where you can't even go to the bathroom when you have to?"[1]

Each day has its rhythm. For elementary teachers, the lunch hour divides the day into morning and afternoon activities, each marked by a recess and perhaps some instructional time with a specialist teacher; alternatively, they may spend an entire day in one classroom with one group of students. Teachers create routines and patterns that give the day form and meaning. "I live in my own little world in my classroom. Sometimes I think that my children and I share a secret life that is off limits to anyone else. We just go about our business, like so many peas in a pod." For secondary teachers, the daily rhythm is more externally determined. Bells ring to signal the passing of classes, in which batches of students spend some parcel of time with the teacher in a classroom. Though students may move throughout the building, high school teachers often never leave their rooms in the course of a day. For every "period" or "hour," there is a routine: taking attendance, briefly recapping yesterday's lesson, introducing today's material, winding down, and making an assignment for tomorrow. Repeated five times a day, such routines become fixed, and life becomes predictable.

---

1. All quotes are from fieldnotes 1977–1978 unless otherwise stated.

In the course of a day, activities and interactions multiply, energy fluctuates. Elementary teachers may organize activities to accommodate the ebb and flow of the students' and their own energies. There are quiet times and active times, times set aside for individual attention, large-group instruction, small-group work, and seatwork. Secondary teachers may acknowledge that they are less effective during the first and last hours and more energetic during the middle of the day. The pace and depth of instruction are altered accordingly. For both elementary and secondary teachers, the school day is punctuated by interruptions: P.A. announcements, telephone calls and messages from the office, minor crises that need attending. All these become incorporated into the pattern of the day. Without missing a step, experienced teachers pick up where they left off.

Days merge into weeks. Monday is always difficult. So is Friday, but the difficulties are softened by the promise of the weekend. Midweek is optimal for teaching. The process of review-teach-test fits neatly into the natural pace of weeks. Weeks become months, and months become seasons. And each has its rhythms. Fall is the time of promise; new beginnings always bring hope. As the seasons progress, there is a downward spiral of energy until Thanksgiving, a perfectly timed and well-deserved break from the routine. There is a resurgence of sorts between Thanksgiving and Christmas, the most harried three weeks on any calendar. The Christmas break brings relief and buoys teachers and students for the final onslaught of the semester's end. January is brief. February is not; it is by far the longest month by any emotional measure. "I always think of changing professions in February." By March, the end is within sight and energies surge until the spring break, anticipated as much as the Christmas holiday and well appreciated. Then time passes quickly. There is the last-minute rush to get everything done and to meet the promises made in September by early June. The final weeks are filled with activities—final teasting and grading, promotions, graduation, end-of-year events. And then, quite arbitrarily, one day in June it all stops. Teachers and students go their separate ways. For ten weeks, there are no routines, no shared rituals, no school. The patterns that were learned and shared rudely come to an end, only to be re-created in the fall when the cycle begins again. Such are the rhythms of teaching.

Rules

Like any profession, teaching has its rules—some codified and formal, others tacitly accepted as informal "rules of thumb." Two such rules may be simply stated: Be practical (Doyle & Ponder, 1977–78). Be private. Some further elaboration aids in understanding the effect of these simple rules of behavior for teachers.

After years of formal academic preparation, most teachers experience a common jolt when they enter teaching. Equipped with theoretical understandings, they lack the practical knowledge that they need for survival. Education courses in and of themselves are quite theoretical. To be sure, they are helpful as far as background material goes, but there is no substitute for actual practical experience. "My three-year stint of duty as a housemaster and teacher gave me a great deal of practical experience in learning more about young people and how to handle young people." Practical knowledge in schools is defined in terms of its opposites. Being practical is the opposite of being theoretical; being practical is the opposite of being idealistic. University professors are theoretical; inexperienced teachers are idealistic. New teachers in search of practical knowledge, then, must reject the university professors who trained them as well as their own tendencies to seek ideal solutions to difficult problems. Practical knowledge is lodged in the experiences and practices of teachers at work in their classrooms. It is to other teachers and to oneself that the novice must turn for practical ideas.

What makes an idea practical? First, it develops from the circumstance of the school. Second, it has immediate application. Third, it is offered by practical people. Finally, it addresses practical problems. Practical people are those who are or have recently been teachers. Practical school problems include discipline, attendance, order, and achievement. Practical ideas require little additional work or preparation; they fit into the existing rhythms of the school. Practical ideas are immediate and concrete and can be effected with the resources and structures that currently exist. "No teacher ever does what he or she thinks is best. We do the best we can in the circumstances. What you think is a good idea from the outside turns out to be impossible in the classroom." To be practical means to concentrate on products and processes, to draw on experience rather than research, to be short-range in thinking or planning.

As an opposite to idealism, practicality values adjustment, accommodation, and adaptation. Idealism is identified with youth; it does not wear well in the adult "real world" of teaching. New teachers are initiated into the practicality ethic during their first year on the job. They learn their "place" in the school organization, to keep quiet when private principles are violated by public practices, and to be politic about what they say and to whom they say it. To be practical, in this sense, is to accept the school as it is and to adapt. Striving to change the system is idealistic; striving to make do is practical. Concern for each student's well-being and optimal learning is idealistic; acceptance of limitations of student potential and teacher influence is practical. Reflective self-criticism is idealistic; expressing the belief "I do the best I can; it's just that the kids don't try" is practical. Being open to change and to outside influences is idealistic; being self-sufficient is practical. Being practical saves one from shame and doubt. It is a useful rule to follow.

The practicality rules has a corollary; that is, be private. In effect, it is practical to be private. What does being private mean? It means not sharing experiences about teaching, about classes, about students, about perceptions.

> I don't know what it's like in business or industry. It may be the same. I don't know how friendly co-workers are, how honest they are. It just seems that in teaching, teachers really are unwilling to be honest with each other, I think, to confide with each other about professional things and personal things.

By following the privacy rule, teachers forfeit the opportunity to display their successes; but they also gain. They gain the security of not having to face their failures publicly and losing face.

Being private also means staking out a territory and making it one's own. For most teachers, that territory is the individual classroom. Teachers have a sense of territoriality and an ideology that includes a belief of the inviolability of a teacher's classroom. To ensure their claim, teachers seldom invite one another into their classes. Observation is equated with evaluation, and evaluation violates one's sense of place and position in the world.

In being private, each teacher makes an individual and conscious choice to go it alone. "Me? You get to a point. I made a personal decision. I know a lot of teachers have done the same thing. You seal off the room and you deal with the students. You say, 'You and me and let's see what we can do alone.'" Most schools do not provide meaningful supervision, and most teachers do not ask for it. The very act of teaching is invisible to one's peers. "It is safer to be private. There is some safety in the tradition, even though it keeps you lonely." Loneliness and isolation are high prices to pay, but teachers willingly pay them when the alternatives are seen as exposure and censure. When asked in whom he confides about his days, one man replied with some sense of irony and sadness, "My wife."

Interactions

Given the power of classroom territoriality, it comes as no surprise that the most important and immediate interactions that teachers have are with their students. "You work with kids. That's what you do. And a school is a place that will allow you to do that." Since, as noted earlier, almost all rewards come from students, relationships with them are primary in the constellation of interactions in a school. For elementary teachers, the focus on children is a taken-for-granted phenomenon. "I'm with my children all day long. I watch them change by the moment. Some days they'll tell me all of their secrets. Other days, they withdraw into their own little shells. Whatever they do, I'm there to see and hear it, and take it all to heart." For secondary teachers, relationships with students are more fragmented and are mediated through the subject matter. "It is the subject matter and the kids. I love the subject matter and naturally you need an audience for that. The kids are the audience, and they're important to me. I can't teach my subject matter without touching the kids in some way." In either case, relationships with students are daily, direct, sometimes conflictual, but always central. "I dream about them. I have nightmares about them. I can't lose them. It is worse on vacation. When I'm in school and it's late October and I've accepted that I'm really back, then the dreams finally stop."

For most teachers, it is the personal interaction rather than instructional interaction that is most valued. This is true on the secondary level as well as on the elementary level.

"If someone told me that my job is just to teach math, I would quit. I couldn't stand to see myself as someone who teaches skills and nothing else. I have to feel that I am doing something more lasting." What is that "something more lasting"? It has to do with influencing and guiding children toward adulthood, with serving as a moral presence, with having a stake in the future.

> When you realize that what you say in the classroom—even though you think no one is listening—has an effect on your students, you realize that you are a role model, even if you don't see yourself that way. The kids take what I have to say, think about it, and make decisions based on it. I have that kind of influence . . . it's scary but it makes me feel good. It's a big responsibility.

Such involvement has its rewards both in the present and in the future.

> I like to see them when they come back, so I can see how they're doing, how they're turning out. I love to watch them grow. It's terrific. It's true with any age group—you can see the growth and development. Let's hope it continues. They're so cute. They are all

individuals and they bubble about certain things. Some of them, my God, are so brave.

We cannot overstate the importance of teacher-student interactions. When the rewards from these interactions are plentiful, teachers are energized and thrive. When the rewards from these interactions are diminished, teachers lose that part of themselves that is most self-sustaining and most central to the well-being of the profession.

If teaching is to be understood as a "lonely profession," then the source of that loneliness lies outside of the realm of children and in the interactions with other adults, especially peers. While relations with students tend to be immediate, direct, and engaging, relations with peers may be characterized as remote, oblique, and defensively protective. The rule of privacy governs peer interactions in a school. It is all right to talk about the news, the weather, and sports. It is all right to complain in general about the school and the students. However, it is not acceptable to discuss instruction and what happens in classrooms as colleagues. "If I were to go into the lounge and say, 'I've had a great class. The kids are really interesting. They were on the board, asking great questions, and they really got from me what I wanted them to,' no one would respond." "I have never heard another teacher say, 'I have a problem.' You just don't have one. You never open up to anyone about anything important." For most teachers in most schools, teaching is indeed a lonely enterprise. With so many people engaged in so common a mission in so compact a space and time, it is perhaps the greatest irony—and the greatest tragedy of teaching—that so much is carried on in self-imposed and professionally sanctioned isolation.

Our discussion of interactions is not complete until we consider the relation between teachers and principal in a building. Although face-to-face interactions with the principal may not be all that common, especially in a large urban high school, the relationship with one's principal is of paramount importance in a teacher's worklife. A principal sets a tone. "I think a principal can make or break a school in terms of—not even the day-to-day functioning—but in terms of the umbrella of attitudes and emotions." That umbrella covers a wide area. The principal has the power to make working in a school pleasant or unbearable; that is substantial indeed. A principal who makes teaching pleasant is one who trusts the staff to perform classroom duties with competence and who deals with parents and the community in a way that supports teachers' decisions and safeguards against personal attacks.

Teachers avoid "getting on the bad side" of a principal; such a position makes life unbearable. The principal has the power to make extra-duty assignments, to criticize classroom practices, to assign undesirable class schedules. More importantly, on an informal level, being disliked by the principal carries with it distinct psychological disadvantages. "If I see him in the hall and he doesn't smile or look at me, I'm upset all day. What did I do wrong? Why doesn't he like me? Will he listen to me if there's a problem? I know it shouldn't affect me, but it does."

When teachers view a principal as critical or punishing, they are less likely to take risks and try new approaches. When teachers view a principal as supporting and rewarding, they are more able to approach the principal for support in trying something new, in securing resources, in gaining permission for special undertakings.

The relationship of teacher to principal is one of gaining access to privilege. This is especially true for teachers who themselves aspire to administrative positions. The principal's recommendation about the administrative potential of teachers is taken seriously. While many teachers profess that they avoid the principal and learn to work around him or her, the importance of that office is constantly felt in the daily life of the school.

Feelings

Strong feelings accompany intense and varied interactions. The feelings of teachers about their work and their lives are complex, characterized by conflict, frustration, satisfaction, and joy.

When we characterized teacher-student interactions as the major source of rewards for teachers, we placed great emphasis on feelings of genuine satisfaction that derive from these relationships. The other side of those feelings, of living one's professional life always in the company of children, is also quite powerful for teachers. These other feelings are more negative and often come to light in the company of other adults who work outside of education.

> I had a disagreement with my mother-in-law the other day. I don't remember what it was about—taxes or something that is being voted on. Every time I started to talk, she would disagree and then tell me that I didn't live in the real world, that I spent all of my time with kids, and that I just didn't know about business and other things. I felt very angry. That kind of thing happens now and again. I feel that I do live in the real world, but people who don't teach don't think that's true.

To the rest of the world, teachers often seem to be living in a child's reality and are viewed as not being able to function as adults in an adult world. This perception leaves teachers uneasy at best, defensive at worst, almost always self-doubting, and characteristically ambivalent about their roles and their constant relationship with young people.

Feelings of self-doubt are exacerbated by the absence of a standard by which one can measure one's professional competence. The lack of peer support and interaction makes it difficult to develop a clear sense of the quality of one's own teaching. Teaching skills are evaluated by the students, whose judgment is not always trustworthy, and by oneself. "It took me ten years to feel that I was a good teacher. In fact, I would try very hard not to miss a day of school. I thought if a substitute came in and taught my classes that all the students would find out how bad I was and how good someone else was." There is a general lack of confidence, a pervasive feeling of vulnerability, a fear of being "found out." Such feelings are made worse because of the privacy ethic. There is no safe place to air one's uncertainties and to get the kind of feedback necessary to reduce the anxiety about being a good teacher, or at least an adequate one.

One way a teacher may gain some confidence is to define a sphere of control; for most, that is the classroom. It becomes essential to gain and maintain dominance if one is to survive. "When I'm in my classroom, I know I'm in control. I can teach the way I want to teach, do what I want to do." Inside the classroom, a teacher knows that all control is tenuous. It depends on a negotiated agreement between students and the teacher. If that agreement is violated, a teacher will subordinate all teaching activities to one primary goal: to regain and maintain control. Keeping a class in order is the only visible indication to one's colleagues and principal that one is, in fact, a good teacher. When one loses control, one loses everything.

Feelings about control are made more problematic by the awareness on the part of teachers that once outside the classroom, their control is severely limited. Within the formal organization of the school, teachers have little authority in making decisions that affect their environment. Teachers, then, move from a level of almost complete authority to a level of powerlessness. This being in-and-out-of-control leads to feelings of frustration and resignation to the ways things are and will always be.

The feelings that surround issues of always being with children, of professional competence, and of being in-and-out-of-control are highly charged and little acknowledged. They should not be underestimated; these feelings often block a teacher's impulse to improve his or her teaching or to influence what happens in the school.

THE PERSISTENT REALITIES OF TEACHING

Sarason (1982) cautioned that the more things change, the more they remain the same. This axiom is especially true of teaching. In fact, life in school—for most teachers—has changed little from 1978 and long before then.

Perhaps the most compelling evidence of the unchanged realities of teaching can be found in Kidder's (1989) popular study of one teacher in Holyoke, Massachusetts. Chris Zajak is portrayed as a caring and conscientious fifth-grade teacher in a challenging, yet not unrewarding, setting. She has developed, over a 15-year career, a distinct and personal style forged in the isolation of her own classroom and reinforced by the behaviors and feedback of her students. She has a repertoire of teaching strategies that work for her and that have been accumulated in isolation, without benefit of the research community or her colleagues in the field. She is aware of mandates and policies from above; yet within the boundaries of her classroom, she sets her own agenda and makes her own policy. She has control of her immediate environment and disciplines through sarcasm and wit as often as by positive reinforcement. She lives by the adage that a good teacher must develop mechanisms to control a class before she can begin to teach. Her interactions with her peers are guarded, and she shies away from discussions with other teachers about classroom issues and concerns. She accepts as given the rhythms of the school calendar, the rules of privacy and practicality, her lack of participation in decision making, the limitations of her relationships with others, and the conflicting feelings she has about her work. Chris Zajak epitomizes the social realities of teaching as we described them more than a decade ago.

It is ironic that this portrait of a teacher appeared just as research, policy, and practice in education are combining to create what may be a major social change in American schooling. Such a change challenges the very nature of teaching, the structure of schools, and the dailiness of practice. Chris Zajak represents one view of teaching, still dominant, as another view is struggling to be born.

REFORM IN THE 1990s:
RESEARCH AND PRACTICE

The emerging view of teaching has a solid grounding in research and policy; while many researchers have contributed to our emerging knowledge about teaching, the efforts of Little (1986) and Rosenholtz (1989) have been particularly useful. Taken together, their studies developed a convincing rationale for viewing teaching as collaborative work, characterized by colleagueship, openness, and trust. Little's study of staff development (1986) in six urban schools clearly points to norms of colleagueship and experimentation, supported by the active engagement and participation of the principal, as critical elements in shaping successful school improvement efforts. In settings where these norms were established, they replaced the traditions of privacy, practicality, and isolation that were highlighted in our earlier discussion of social system understandings about teaching. As teachers and administrators talked together about their work, observed one another, and involved themselves in problem-solving activities, they came to "own" issues in common, consider alternative approaches, and value one another as people engaged in a common enterprise.

Rosenholtz's study (1989) of the school as a workplace reinforced the importance of developing and supporting new norms of behavior for teachers in schools. Rosenholtz identified a group of schools she characterized as "learning enriched." These were schools that had collaborative goals, minimum uncertainty about their mission and direction, positive attitudes among teachers, and principal support for change and improvement. In these "learning-enriched" schools, teachers became accustomed to working together to define and solve common problems; they came to respect one another's knowledge and expertise and to appreciate that their concerns about teaching and learning were not idiosyncratic, but shared.

While we are intrigued by this emphasis on collegiality, we want to caution against its being accepted as a panacea for what ails schools and teaching. Huberman's (1990) recent research cautioned that teachers still view themselves as "independent artisans" who derive their satisfaction from independent classroom "tinkering" rather than from large-scale school reforms. And Hargreaves (1990), in making the distinction between individuality (which supports initiative and principled dissent) and individualism, reminds us that school reforms have to strike a balance between system-driven colleagueship and collaboration and the preservation of teacher individuality.

Policy research has identified another important balance that must be struck: the balance between policy and school context. Policy has long been viewed as an external initiative that teachers are expected to fit into their existing routines. An alternative position sees policy as "an endless dialogue rather than a series of self-sealing implemented demands" (Clune, 1990, p. 259).

The work of Fullan, Bennett, and Rolheiser-Bennett (1989) and McLaughlin (1990) supports this new perspective, which looks for the complementary and complex relationship among research, policy, and practice. In effect, teachers not only implement policy; more often than not, they critique it, undermine it, construct it, and reconstruct it.

The current research on the school as a workplace and on policy offers us an expanded perspective on teaching and on the possibility of creating a new culture in schools. The studies make a strong case that the social realities of teaching are not given but constructed—and capable of being reconstructed when the proper conditions are present.

Learning and understanding new conceptions of practice are likely to come about through collaboration among those who observe schools and those who work within them. The current movement to restructure schools is an example of such a collaboration. The movement promotes a radical rethinking and redoing of education. At the heart of the restructuring movement is a reconception of what the curriculum teaches and how it is taught. Traditional formulations of teaching as technological and managed work, as service and performance are being challenged and replaced by notions of teaching as developmental and thoughtful action and as leadership. Similarly, the traditional views of learning as straightforward and simple acquisition of facts and skills and as assimilation are being reconsidered. Notions of learning are emerging: that learning is production of knowledge, that it is complex and goes beyond facts to thinking and reasoning and learning to learn.

Those schools where restructuring efforts are in progress are inventing new ways to organize time, discipline, assessment, grouping, grading, decision making, and leadership. Teachers in these schools are struggling to learn new ways to organize their content areas and their classrooms. They are moving along from lecture and discussion as dominant modes of instruction and are depending more on inquiry-based methods, collaborative learning, metacognitive strategies, and dialogue and observation. National movements toward whole-language approaches to literacy, manipulatives in math, hands-on experiments in science, process-writing, and the Foxfire approach support teachers' efforts to do things differently and more effectively in their classrooms.

We have elsewhere identified five building blocks of restructuring (Lieberman & Miller, 1990a):

1. A rethinking of curricular and instructional efforts to promote quality and equality for all students
2. A new structure for how the school is run
3. A two-pronged focus on a rich learning environment for students and a professionally supportive work environment for adults
4. The necessity for building partnerships and networks

5. The increased and changed participation of parents and community

What is unique about the restructuring movement is its acknowledgement that teaching and learning are connected, that change in one requires change in the other.

In restructuring schools, efforts are underway to create and support conditions for teachers that allow them to accomplish new ends for students. In these schools, teachers are redefining and remaking their own professional lives; in so doing they are also redefining and remaking public schooling for the students in their charge.

IMPLICATIONS FOR STAFF DEVELOPMENT

Given the emerging demands and realities of teaching and schooling, we think it is appropriate to generate new perspectives on staff development. We offer the following as starting points for considering staff development in a different light:

• *Staff development is culture building.* Staff development activities should connect the renewal of schooling and the renewal of educators. Staff development as training and remediation is an outdated model, based on formulations of teaching and learning that are currently being challenged and replaced. More appropriate notions, designed to meet the new realities of the 1990s, need to be invented. Such inventions should support the development of collaborative cultures, where teachers assume new roles in their own development and in the education of their students.

• *Staff development is teacher inquiry into practice.* Staff development should encourage expanded notions of what it means to be a teacher and should provide opportunities for "reflective practice" (Schön, 1983). Through reflective practice, teachers use methods of disciplined inquiry and informal research to reevaluate their values and their actions. When viewed as inquiry-based action, staff development depends less on expert workshops and more on teacher-led activities, such as study groups, curriculum writing, action research, peer observation, case conferences, program evaluation, trying out new practices, teacher centers, and participation in outside events and organizations. (Lieberman & Miller, 1990b)

• *Staff development is about human development and learning for both students and teachers.* Staff development has to connect the activities it organizes and promotes for adults with learning outcomes for students. This is not to say that staff development's *only* value is in its effect on students. Staff development can have benefits for adults-as-learners that do not immediately translate into improved education for children. However, in the end, educators need to be able to assert—with some degree of certainty—that a large portion of the staff development effort affects what and how children learn. In order to do this, educators need to develop authentic ways of assessing learning, using tools that go beyond standardized tests and measures of behavioral objectives. Staff development must preserve the individuality of the teacher as an artisan or craftsperson.

• *Teaching is a craft.* No matter how school cultures are transformed, the individual teacher continues to make and remake the classroom, based on his or her own imagination, spirit, inspiration, and learning. Staff development programs must maintain a fragile balance between building cultures where collaboration and colleagueship are promoted and where individual integrity and artistry are allowed to flourish.

REFERENCES

Clune, W. H. (1990). Three views of curriculum policy in the school context: The school as policy mediator, policy critic, and policy constructor. In M. McLaughlin, J. Talbert, & N. Bascia (Eds.), *The contexts of teaching in secondary schools: Teachers' realities* (pp. 256–270). New York: Teachers College Press.

Doyle, U., & Ponder, G. (1977–78). The practicality ethic in teacher decision making. *Interchange, 8,* 3.

Fullan, M., Bennett, B., Rolheisser-Bennett, C. (1989, April). *Linking classroom and school improvement.* Paper presented at the annual meeting of the American Educational Research Association, San Francisco.

Hargreaves, A. (1990, April). *Individualism and individuality: Reinterpreting the culture of teaching.* Paper presented at the annual meeting of the American Educational Research Association, Boston.

Huberman, A. (1990, April). *The model of independent artisan in teachers' professional relations.* Paper presented at the annual meeting of the American Educational Research Association, Boston.

Jackson, P. (1990). *Life in classrooms* (reissued). New York: Teachers College Press.

Kidder, T. (1989). *Among school children.* Boston: Houghton Mifflin.

Lieberman, A., & Miller, L. (1978). The social realities of teaching. *Teachers College Record, 80,* 54–68.

Lieberman, A., & Miller, L. (1984). *Teachers, their world & their work: Implications for school improvement*. Alexandria, VA: Association for Supervision and Curriculum Development.

Lieberman, A., & Miller, L. (1990a). Restructuring schools: What matters and what works. *Phi Delta Kappan, 71,* 759–764.

Lieberman, A., & Miller, L. (1990b). Teacher development in professional practice schools. *Teachers College Record, 92,* 105–122.

Little, J. W. (1986). Seductive images and organizational realities in professional development. In A. Lieberman (Ed.), *Rethinking school improvement* (pp. 26–44). New York: Teachers College Press.

Lortie, D. (1975). *School teacher*. Chicago: University of Chicago Press.

McLaughlin, M. (1990, April). *Does teacher choice matter?* Paper presented at the annual meeting of the American Educational Research Association, Boston.

McPherson, G. (1972). *Small town teacher*. Cambridge, MA: Harvard University Press.

Rosenholtz, S. (1989). *Teachers' workplace: The social organization of schools*. New York: Longman.

Sarason, S. B. (1982). *The culture of the school and the problem of change* (2nd ed.). Boston: Allyn & Bacon.

Sarason, S. B., Levine, M., Goldenberg, I. I., Cherlin, D., & Bennett, E. (1966). *Psychology in community settings*. New York: Wiley.

Schön, D. (1983). *The reflective practitioner*. San Francisco: Jossey-Bass.

Smith, L., & Geoffrey, W. (1968). *Complexities of an urban classroom*. New York: Holt, Rinehart & Winston.

Waller, W. (1952). *The sociology of teaching*. New York: Wiley.

Part II

STAFF DEVELOPMENT AT WORK

7 Using Teacher Cases for Reflection and Enhanced Understanding

Anna E. Richert

Change happens. In the realm of teaching and learning, change can be reassuring, but it can also be troubling. Maybe it is troubling because it means teachers and teachers educators have to come to deal with change—a lot of change. Things are not fixed in teaching. Circumstances change, students change, content changes, teachers change.

The fact of change renders teachers learners. To respond appropriately to the changing circumstances of their work, teachers must learn to learn from their changing experiences in schools. But learning from experience is difficult for any learners. In spite of the fact that teachers repeatedly claim that most of what they know they learned from their experiences working in classrooms with students, research in cognitive psychology cautions us about the difficulty of learning from experience by suggesting numerous ways of misapprehending experience and thus mislearning from it (Nisbett & Ross, 1980; Nisbett & Wilson, 1977; Tversky & Kahneman, 1974).

Organizational barriers to learning from experience compound these cognitive barriers. Because learning from experience is difficult, teachers must be supported in their efforts to do so. Unfortunately, the organization of teaching as work, and the schools where that work takes place, provide little support for teacher learning (Jackson, 1968; Little, 1987; Lortie, 1975; Rosenholtz & Kyle, 1984). To learn from experience, for example, teachers must have time to think about that experience. *Having* an experience does not constitute learning about it; having an experience and then *thinking* about it to make sense of it does.

But schools are not organized with time for teachers to "make sense" of their experiences. Teachers rarely have time to think about what they do, about what "works" and what does not (and why), about who they are, what they believe, or what they hope to accomplish in their interactions with children and colleagues. Similarly, schools are not organized to allow teachers to work and think together—another criterion for teacher learning (Little, 1987; Rosenholtz & Kyle, 1984). Typically teachers are isolated from one another by separate classrooms, unrelenting schedules, and a norm of evaluation that engenders fear rather than confidence in the possibility of collaborative effort. If we were to critique schools as supportive environments for teacher learning, they would fall short along every dimension. Lee Shulman (1989) suggests that we apply what we know about learning to teaching and "do not unto teachers what we would not have (them) do unto students" (p. 166). We must create work environments for teachers that not only allow, but promote and facilitate learning if we hope to have a teaching population that can respond to change.

The idea of restricted opportunities for teacher learning raises a set of critical issues and questions for teaching and teacher education. Like other professionals, teachers need to be able to continue learning about their work if they are to meet its rapidly changing demands. Good teaching does not rest on a set of static, prescribed rules and technical strategies. Rather, shifting circumstances suggest teachers be reflective in their approach to classroom practice. Reflective teachers approach teaching as problem solving; they see teaching circumstances and conditions as problematic rather than given, and they approach each situation with an openness to both the known and the unknown. Reflective teachers have the capability of responding to changing circumstances—a skill that is essential given both the bounds of their own rationality and the limits of scientific rationality in the twentieth-century world of work.[1]

Seen as problematic rather than as given, teaching requires the perspectives of reflective teachers such as those described by Dewey (1933) more than 50 years ago. Reflective teachers, Dewey argued, engage in teaching as an intellectual rather than as a routine task. Intellectual engagement provides the basis for learning from experience. Reflective teachers adapt what they know to what they experience in a changing world; in so doing they create new meanings and consequently revised actions.

For teachers to function as reflective practitioners and thus learn from their work, they need time, opportunity, and support. One form of support, according to teachers, is help in learning how to function as reflective practitioners—help in learning how to learn, or learning how to make sense of their work in ways that are productive both for them as individuals and for the profession as a whole. Teacher education at both the inservice and preservice levels must include helping teachers learn to learn from their experiences. Programs that support teacher learning, such as those described in this volume, contribute to a changing conceptualization of teaching. As our notion of teachers' work shifts to include teacher learning as essential, we call for the teacher's voice in determining the character, process, and future of the profession.

In this chapter I will discuss teaching cases as both a representation of teacher knowledge and as a vehicle for teacher learning. I will discuss the characteristics of teaching cases that make them particularly powerful tools for teacher education. This will include examples that illustrate the characteristics I believe are most critical for enhancing reflection and teacher learning.

Following the discussion of what teaching cases are, I will shift the focus to why they should be used. In this section I will discuss the potential and possibilities of using cases to enhance teacher learning as well as teacher professionalization. Some of the questions that guide this latter discussion include: What do cases as a form of knowledge suggest? How do cases represent what teachers know? How do cases suggest ways for teachers to learn?

Over the past several years I have conducted research on the use and perceived usefulness of cases for teacher learning (Richert, 1989a, 1989b). My informants in this research were practicing teachers enrolled in a master's level graduate course entitled "Inquiry into the Teaching Process." As I discuss cases and case methods in this chapter, I will use data from my study to illustrate both the form and substance of the cases themselves. Similarly, I will cite the teachers' own words as I discuss the potential effects of case methods for teacher education and teacher development.

CASES OF TEACHING

Cases as a means for representing teachers' work are not new. For years, teachers and others associated with them—school administrators, teacher educators, staff developers, and the like—have used cases to describe what teachers do, and even to analyze and discuss *how* they do what they do and *why* they do it. Descriptions of teaching practice have long been the fodder for teacher conversations. What is new for teaching is the professional context in which cases are created and used. Currently there is considerable effort to understand both what teachers do and think, as well as what they know. Because of their tie to practice, cases offer the promise of representing the craft knowledge of teaching—or the wisdom of practice. They provide a medium for thinking about teachers' work using a language and system for understanding that is teacher defined.

While cases may or may not be written by teachers, if they are good, they describe teachers' work accurately. This tie to practice is at the heart of their power for teacher learning.

In the flurry of activity around case use in teaching, the profession has generated many kinds of cases. These cases often differ in purpose and form, but they all have several features in common. Three of those features are particularly important in our consideration of cases and teacher learning. First, while cases may include an analytical component, they are descriptive rather than analytical. Second, cases describe aspects of teaching *practice*. And third, cases are situated in a way that is significant for thinking of them as "texts" for teacher learning (Brown, Collins, & Duguid, 1989); they are about teaching particular students, in a particular setting, at a particular time, for a particular purpose.

Cases as Rich Description of Practice

Teaching cases describe teaching practice. The descriptions often include what teachers do as well as what they think and how they feel. Thinking and feeling are included most frequently—and possibly most accurately—if the case is actually written by the teacher. A case written by an elementary teacher with whom I worked recently provides an example. After building a case about her long-time intervention with a student who needed extra help because of a medical problem, she described her feelings:

> After two months I am very frustrated with this entire situation. I have handled each step of this problem as carefully, thoughtfully, and with as much pressure as I felt was appropriate, but it's not getting much better. Damon's grades are dropping, and it is awful to have to look at this suffering every day, especially when it seems unnecessary. It must be a hundred times worse to be living it than to be observing it. I don't understand the principal's motivation (Burke, 1988).

Depending on the purpose of the case, the teaching episode described is long or short and the description, cursory or comprehensive. The descriptive nature of cases suggests an opportunity to present teachers' work as it is—multifaceted and complex. Rather than presenting factors that contribute to teaching actions or decisions as isolated from one another, cases present the teaching act in all of its complexity as relational. One issue leads to another and another and another—though usually not in a linear fashion. Depending on one set of circumstances, another set is introduced.

As they describe practice, cases present events, experiences, and happenings that actually occur in school settings. They represent the reality of teaching in that they are able to capture the real stuff of classroom life. One teacher with whom I worked expressed the pervasive sentiment "I think the valuable part for me was that I really had to clarify my thoughts because it was a real problem" (TN).[2] In describing actual classroom practice, cases present the dilemmas of teaching, the tradeoffs, the uncertainties. They capture teacher actions as they exist in the uncertain context where those actions occur.

The sometimes dramatic, sometimes mundane quality of classroom events (including actions and feelings as they happen on site) provides the essential material for the case. Depending on its length, purpose, and consequent complexity, the case presents teachers and students not only in what they do but also in what they think and feel prior to, during, and after the teaching episode itself. Cases provide the potential for connecting the act of teaching with the cognitions and feelings that both motivate and explain that act. They offer a vehicle for making the tacit explicit. They give us access to teaching practice that "goes well" and that which does not.

Since cases can represent all aspects of teaching practice, they also provide the opportunity for exploring teacher thinking, feeling, and acting in areas other than instruction. In addition to cases of teaching instruction, there are cases of student learning, cases describing problematic contextual situations (administrative or staffing problems, difficulties with the school community, parents, scheduling problems, and so forth), and cases of moral or ethical decision making.[3]

A case written recently by a secondary mathematics teacher, entitled "The Dumping Ground," illustrates the point. The author describes a situation encountered frequently by urban math teachers. She also describes the frustration she felt when she experienced this "dumping-ground" phenomenon:

> When I was recently assigned two learning-disabled students (tenth-graders) in a competency math program designed for seniors, I was assured it was because "they can really learn something with you." My objection to the inclusion of these boys was met by the counselor with the proposal that all I needed to do was to give the students a daily assignment and send them to the special education room for help. The fact that this would summarily

negate the voiced purpose of this programming (that they would learn more by being in my class) was lost on the counselor. Unfortunately, I was not furnished with any of these students' testing records, which might aid my assigning them work, nor was I given any books or materials to use with them. In addition, the suggestion to send them for individualized help is untenable because problems beyond basic arithmetic are outside the range of skills of those on hand in the special education room. (McManus, 1988)

Rather than describing instruction, this teacher presents a set of contextual factors that affect her life and her teaching on a daily basis. In the discussion of this case, the author's teacher colleagues responded on several levels to the circumstances presented. First, they responded to the idea of "the dumping ground," which, they said, was common for novice teachers. An unfortunate number of the teachers had experienced over-enrolled classes that had students "dumped" into them regardless of the students' capability for doing the work. On another level the case was discussed as an example of lack of administrative support—a phenomenon experienced in different forms by a good number of the teachers in the case conference. In the discussion the teachers drew from the case ways in which administrators do not support beginning teachers. The examples from the case served as examples of a larger set of issues or conditions of teachers' work. Additionally, there was consideration of what beginning teachers might do to "stand their ground" to create conditions that are conducive to establishing a teaching-learning environment in their classrooms.

Describing episodes or factors of teaching by including their multiple dimensions of complexity honors the nature of teaching. It also offers the opportunity for coming to understand particular classroom situations. Cases allow us to "stop the action" and look carefully at what teachers do and why. With the action stopped, and the description accurate, we are able to analyze the teaching episodes presented. Furthermore, as the analysis of a particular case proceeds, we have the potential to move the analysis to a more general level by considering the theoretical question, "What is this a case of?" While talking about their work is common for beginning teachers (at least as they described it to me in an earlier study; see Richert, 1987), talking about it at a level that pushes for an analysis of classroom practice is new and empowering. "I didn't hear any new problems at all," one teacher explained. She continued, "those are all things that I've had or heard someone else talk with me about before, but it [the case conference discussion] was definitely at a different level" (TE).

Finally, the descriptive nature of cases allows the "reader" of the case to analyze it according to what he or she knows and believes about teaching and learning.[4] One teacher explained:

> I think case studies are a useful tool for teacher education and for teachers because they give you a chance to "stop the action" and watch what is happening in classrooms. They can help illuminate complex principles—like I think my experience with the learner case study did for me—and they give you a chance to see many different kinds of teaching and learning styles, contexts, and problems, solutions, and questions, without having to be in there as a part of the circus. (TD)

Just as in law, where cases are used to prepare and perpetuate "lawyerlike" thinking, cases in teaching are used to promote pedagogical thinking. Unlike law, however, there is no "right" answer for most teaching dilemmas. Teachers learn to respond to ambiguous and changing conditions by considering (often quickly) a multitude of factors simultaneously. Descriptive cases present teaching situations in their complexity. In the examination and analysis of such cases, teachers demonstrate their ability for informed decision making. The process suggests numerous paths, each equally valid depending on the purposes and expected consequences, given the teacher, the learners, and the context. One teacher explains:

> It's fascinating to soak in such a range of teaching styles, environments, and activities. There are hundreds of messages—small and large points that help me see my own teaching in a new or different light. (TG)

The Situational Nature of Cases

Another feature of cases that is important for teacher education is that they are situational. This is especially significant given the current view that learning is context dependent—or at least context sensitive. As teachers learn to reflect on their work for the purpose of making sense of it, they learn to focus part of their attention on the circumstances of schooling that enhance their students' learning. As they contemplate student learning, teachers must take into account the particularities of the case—who the students are, what they know, what content they are attempting to learn, for what purpose, and so forth.

Teaching cases are set in a context. They describe a particular time and place, a particular student or students, and particular content. Frequently the cases begin with a description of contextual factors the author deems necessary for understanding the case. "The Dumping Ground" case presented above, for example, begins with a description of the context that suggests why traditional methods have such a firm hold at the school described:

> Allentown is an island community of about 75,000, surrounded by a large metropolitan area. Although it is home to a burgeoning industrial park and a large Navy base, it is essentially a small town in operation and feeling. Its schools are largely populated by children whose parents and even grandparents roamed the same halls and had the same teachers. School faculties have sizable numbers of Allentown alumni. This old guard, mainly white and middle class, has seen the influx of various immigrant groups (Vietnamese, Korean, Filipino, Chinese, and so forth) and upscale professionals into its older homes and new developments on Bay Isle. (McManus, 1988)

There are many different contextual factors that are significant in both preparing teaching cases and in analyzing them. What the community is like, for example, provides important information about teaching and learning. The following incident, taken from a teaching case written by a kindergarten teacher in an upper-middle-class suburban public school, with students who are primarily Caucasian, represents an understanding of issues different from how they would be understood if the school were in an urban working-class community.

> This morning I put "Skip to My Lou" on the record player and asked the children to choose partners. This was the first time I directed the children into a cooperative activity. There was a scramble to choose partners, with the boys refusing to skip with the girls and vice versa. The scramble left two children without partners: Jennifer, who is blond and light skinned, and Anisa, who has dark skin and black hair. Jennifer refused to hold Anisa's hand or be her partner saying, "I don't want to touch her—she's dirty." My reaction was to give Jennifer the choice of being Anisa's partner or sitting out during the song. She chose to sit out, and I acted as Anisa's partner. (Walter, 1989)

Initially, when the teacher who wrote this case presented it to her colleagues, various perspectives emerged as to what the problem was, how it might be resolved, and toward what end—depending on the teacher's experience and consequent perspective. Given the particular setting of the case, the teachers were able to agree on a range of approaches or strategies that seemed appropriate in this instance. What also emerged from the discussion, however, was a set of questions highlighting various points of pedagogical decision making that would be different if the case were set differently. The choice of "textual" materials provides an example. Would "Skip to My Lou" work equally well with children of color? How do we find appropriate materials for different groups of children? Cooperative learning provides a second example. How much preactivity preparation is necessary for cooperative learning activities in different settings? Why? Toward what end is cooperative learning and/or heterogeneous group work used in classrooms with diverse populations? What cautions must teachers take to ensure emotional safety for different groups of children?

The content of instruction is another factor that makes the case situational. We have learned from recent research on teaching that different subject matters are learned in different ways. The pedagogy of these subject matters—or the pedagogical content—is similarly different. Currently there is an emergent case literature that focuses on instruction and learning in the different content areas.[5] As teachers prepare cases about teaching particular content, they provide material for an analysis of teaching that content to particular students for a particular purpose. A case that describes a teacher's attempt to teach the concept of scarcity to an eleventh-grade economics class, for example, would raise issues that are different from those encountered by a mathematics teacher teaching sine and cosine to an eleventh-grade geometry class. Similarly, what one needs to know to teach reading to first-graders is different from what one needs to know to teach science to the same students. By describing instruction of particular content in particular settings, cases are a representation of teacher knowledge as it is embedded in the practice of teachers' work.

WHY CASES?

The fact that cases represent teacher knowledge as it is embedded in the practice of teachers' work reflects the power of cases for teacher learning. By studying cases that describe actual situated teaching practices in all of their complexity, teachers are able to think about what they themselves do as it is mirrored in the actions, thoughts, and feelings of the teachers in the case. "I've been taken out of the small world of my specific teaching situation and problems," one teacher told me, "and allowed to view a variety of very different and creative teaching techniques and realities" (TE).

Part of the knowledge and skills necessary for excellent teaching practice is the ability to think about and assess the multiple factors of teachers' work—the ability to know what is happening and why, to assess the purposes and consequences of classroom actions, to know students, curriculum, context, pedagogy. Learning is ongoing for teachers. It is especially critical for teachers to continue learning throughout their careers, given the changing state of schools and those who inhabit them.

Cases and Teacher Reflection

Recently there has been much discussion of reflection in teaching. Reflective teachers think about their work. They think about what they are doing and why, what they might do (or ought to do) and why. Cases require teachers to reflect on practice. Case work "forces you to consciously think about teaching," one teacher noted and went on to explain:

> The cases helped me to think about what I'm doing and why. They caused me to think more carefully about issues. I have always been thoughtful about teaching, but now I'm compulsive about it and always trying to figure out what behaviors mean. (TE)

A second concluded: "We're always saying that we need time to reflect and think about things. This [case work] forced me to do that" (TC).

But having the time to think about one's work is only part of the picture. Reflection that is productive requires acquiring the knowledge, skill, and disposition of reflective practice. A teacher must learn what questions to ask, how to ask them, and what to do with that information once he or she has generated hypotheses. Disposition is also important. Some teachers enter teaching with a positive attitude toward reflective practice. Others enter the profession with an orientation that emphasizes the technical aspects of the work rather than the reflective ones. Whether or not one is reflective by nature, the skills of reflective teaching are ones that teachers can and need to learn. How to think about one's work, what to think about, how to learn from one's experiences, how to make sense of the complexity of the task at hand—all require both a positive attitude and the requisite knowledge and skill. Given the changing circumstances of their work and the lack of support for reflection in the workplace, teachers also need the opportunity to *practice* reflection in their work in classrooms.

Teachers learn to be reflective as they learn to think critically about their work and learn to see their work as problematic rather than given.

Such pedagogical thinking requires having the knowledge and skill to respond thoughtfully to school and classroom circumstances that are both distinct from one another and in a state of change. Because of both the complexity and the uncertainty of teachers' work, the issue of *focus* becomes central as teachers try to make sense of their classroom experiences. Working with cases helps teachers learn to focus. They learn what to attend to in any given situation—what is important and what can wait. Cases "help you zero in," one teacher said. "There are so many distractions that this just helps you focus in on one thing at one moment in time, and what you want out of it" (TI). And another explained, "I felt the experience was very helpful. It helped me focus, analyze, and reevaluate one current problem" (TK).

Choosing a focus helps teachers define problematic situations. "Naming and framing" problems is difficult in teaching, as it is in other professions, because of the complexity of the task, the multiplicity of goals, and the uncertain and changing technology of the work (Schön, 1983). "Getting centered" or "finding a focus" for one's thinking was mentioned frequently by the teachers in my study as an outcome of working with cases: "The cases have helped me to become more precise in my thinking and to focus my thoughts" (TA); "I have been positively influenced in preparing the cases and reflecting on my classroom by zeroing in on one specific problem and having to think about it" (TB); "I think I am dealing with one particular issue in a much more productive way because doing the case helped me define the problem" (TD).

As teachers learn to approach their work thoughtfully or reflectively, they learn not only to define problems but also to work toward solving them. In learning to solve problems, teachers learn what knowledge is needed to understand any particular situation and how to use that knowledge. As one teacher explained:

> That first session [in which I presented my case] helped me look at where I stood and what I needed to do. I couldn't resolve the problem for a lot of people, but I could resolve part of it for me, to meet my responsibility. (TI)

For another teacher, focus was the important outcome of her case presentation, but focus informed by a "detailed" examination of the issue presented:

> I felt the people in my group helped me see the problem I'm dealing with more precisely. There was an aspect of detail in the group which was helpful. People got specific. This helped pull the idea into a given structure more clearly. (TA)

Unraveling the complex web of details surrounding any aspect or act of teaching is an infinitely difficult process. Practicing with cases allows you to move back and forth between the details of the case, a consideration of their relevance, and an examination of the principles they represent. One teacher explained:

> The discussion with my colleagues quickly pointed out to me that some of the issues that I thought were problems, were really details of problems and that I was confused because I was allowing these details to obscure the real issues involved. I left the discussion with lots of ideas on how I could rewrite my case so that it addressed the main issues involved. (TD)

The "Skip to My Lou" case described earlier in the chapter provides a good example of the complexity of defining a problem, which includes a consideration of the knowledge required to frame, understand, and solve it. What knowledge might the teacher bring to bear in approaching the "Skip to My Lou" problem? If the problem is defined as one of moral education, the teacher might draw on knowledge of moral development. If, however, it is defined as having to do with curriculum and the teaching of social interactive skills, the teacher might focus attention on the choice of materials or the preparation of the students to handle those materials. Moral development and the pedagogy of social interaction are not mutually exclusive phenomena, however. In fact, knowledge of one informs understanding of the other. How to respond to classroom circumstances involving issues of moral development might easily involve knowing about social interaction patterns and problems for whatever age group one is considering. How to frame a problem as one attempts to solve it in teaching determines the knowledge one draws upon to solve that problem.

In learning to think through the complex dilemmas of everyday classroom practice, teachers must learn to make judgments that are subtle. They must learn to determine—often quickly—how to focus their attention, what knowledge to bring to bear, and ultimately how to act. Reflective practice requires knowledge and skill that is learned and relearned by teachers. Cases help teachers acquire these skills.

Cases and Teacher Learning

Cases help teachers reflect, and this leads to teacher learning. Part of this learning involves making both subtle and not-so-subtle distinctions in analyzing the various components of teaching practice. By slowing down or stopping the action, cases give teachers a chance to look at particular episodes or aspects of their work closely, carefully, and systematically. Strands of the complex web involved in any teaching act—strands defining the teacher's motivation, cognition, and/or action—can be teased apart as teachers consider a particular teaching case in order to understand and respond to it.

As students of their own practice, teachers can study a case to understand the dilemmas and tradeoffs of teaching that is well done or less well done. They can examine the motivations involved in teacher decision making as those motivations are either explicitly or implicitly presented in the case. Similarly, they can explore what knowledge the teacher in the case brought to bear and how they might understand the situation differently or in the same way. They can determine what knowledge is necessary and why, what action is appropriate and why. In short, teachers can think about and learn from the work of teaching—their own and that of their teacher colleague in the case. By examining teaching cases, teachers can reflect on practice; they can question the work, challenge it, come to understand it, and finally, and probably most importantly, learn from it.

Cases and Teacher Knowledge

In addition to understanding particular teaching situations and thus learning about teaching by reflectively examining cases of practice, teachers construct knowledge as they create and analyze cases. The processes of case work—writing, speaking, and listening—enhance reflection, which results in teacher learning. An important outcome of teacher learning is the construction of knowledge. As teachers write and talk about their work, they come to know what they know. The process is dialectical. Teachers come to know by writing and talking together, which is followed by their being able to write and talk because now they know what they want to write and talk about. The data in my study revealed this shift back and forth between the knower and the known. In some instances the teachers reported that their knowledge generated an easy writing of the case. "I can't write not knowing," one teacher said, and went on to explain:

> My learning was more in myself . . . which is what this whole experience has been—writing up the case and getting really involved with it. And in particular, deciding that I was going to write one thing and then another issue being on my mind so much that it wrote itself by the time I sat down. (TN)

For this teacher, as for others in my study, preparing the case and then discussing it with colleagues brought their knowledge to a new level of consciousness and understanding. Other teachers reported that the process of creating a case, or discussing someone else's, helped them discover new knowledge or rediscover old knowledge in new ways. Writing the case was particularly powerful in this regard. One teacher said, for example, "I learned more from the written case [than the other cases in the class] because of the discovery in the writing process" (TJ). Another teacher explained how she came to know about her teaching in a completely new way after discussing an early draft of the case with colleagues:

> When I came in [with the first draft of my case] I thought it was
> . . . neglect [neglect of the student by his parents]. But I didn't
> know. I had just kind of laid out the whole process, what had hap-
> pened, and why I was frustrated. You know, what am I supposed
> to do with all of this now [that I've presented it]? And so what
> happened in the session was to look at the series of events as a
> problem. But then, more importantly, what it really held for me. I
> mean, it was a problem for more than one person, but [I needed
> to consider] what was my responsibility. (TI)

One feature of cases that I discussed earlier in this chapter is their descriptive nature. By describing teaching events or episodes, cases capture the wisdom of practice—a wisdom far greater than we currently have theory to explain. Cases as representations of teachers' work reflect the richness and complexity of the task. As teachers analyze them, they draw on what they know, which is often a consciousness-raising process. In both defining what they know in new ways and creating new understandings, teachers construct knowledge. Cases render teachers not only "dispensers" of knowledge, but learners, and consequently "constructors" of new knowledge as well.

Cases capture the wisdom of practice and allow teachers to examine that practice (and that wisdom) analytically and systematically as well as intuitively. On a case-by-case basis, teachers can examine what other teachers do and why, what they themselves do and why. They can examine what teachers think, what they know, and what they feel as well as what they do. They can, in fact, examine the relationships between action and feeling, feeling and thinking, thinking and knowing, and so forth—relationships that are not necessarily linear, obvious, or explainable.

As cases are aggregated, furthermore, a cross-case analysis can generate new theory that reflects practice at new and more comprehensive levels.[6] Cases can be aggregated for analysis in a number of different ways—by teacher actions, by contextual situations, by content, by demonstrated teacher knowledge, and so forth. A cross-case analysis, therefore, can generate theory that takes into account a variety of different foci. "Cases provide a focal point," one teacher explained, "or a launching pad so that classroom experience is universal rather than unique to our schools and classrooms" (TB). Traditional principles of practice can be challenged and reconstructed by teachers to reflect the changing circumstances of their work. Similarly, new principles of practice can be generated that have greater explanatory power and consequently greater suggestive power for guiding practice under current school conditions. In addition to generating theory through the aggregation and analysis of many cases, an examination of the theoretical implications of any given case can be explored when the case is considered as an instance of some larger teaching phenomenon.

Cases and Colleagues

By definition, cases convene colleagues. At minimum, there are the teacher in the case and the teacher who is examining it. The reflection that occurs as a teacher examines a case is a conversation; the conversation occurs usually among colleagues, but possibly with oneself as the teacher examines and thinks through the case on his or her own. In their recent work on different ways of knowing and coming to know, Belenky, Clinchy, Goldberger, and Tarule (1986) emphasize the significance of the reflective conversation:

> In order for reflection to occur, the oral and written forms of language must pass back and forth between persons who both speak and listen or read and write—sharing, expanding, and reflecting on each other's experiences. Such interchanges lead to ways of knowing that enable individuals to enter into the social and intellectual life of their community. Without them, individuals remain isolated from others; and without the tools for representing their experiences, people also remain isolated from the self. (p. 26)

Case-inspired reflective conversations are powerful tools for teacher learning. As we have seen through the discussion so far, the case conversation provides an opportunity for teachers to articulate what they know and believe about their work; it also provides an opportunity for creating new knowledge as teachers work together to make sense of life in classrooms. As one teacher explained:

The cases helped me think about what I'm doing and why. Also to think about what's going on in education as a whole—not just in my room. I'm definitely giving much more thought to what I'm doing, and I think I'm understanding more. (TC)

Another factor about cases and colleagues is the opportunity the case process provides for expanding what one knows by pushing the limits of what that knowledge is and how one understands it. Working with others helps you think in new ways. As one teacher explained:

You're learning more tools for solving problems, and you're using someone else's toolbox. You know, maybe they have a Phillips screwdriver and you've always used a blade. It's like "Oh yeah, that works even better"—even when your system worked. (TE)

Viewing things more broadly, or with greater distance, is the outcome one teacher experienced: "I appreciate how good [my colleagues] are at seeing the whole when I'm focused on the piece" (TI). And another said: "Suggestions from those with different points of view helped my perspective and also helped to delineate some solutions" (TN). As teachers study cases together, they confront the bounds of their own rationality. Rather than limiting teachers in terms of what they are able to know, remember, or perceive, cases challenge them to expand what they think and how they think about it.

Current work on learning tells us that learning is enhanced when learners work together to construct meaning. Studying cases brings teachers together. Feeling connected with the professional world is an outcome that is not incidental according to the teachers with whom I worked. We have seen that by articulating what they know, teachers come to feel more confident. One teacher explained:

The cases have given me the chance to look at and think about, in depth, my teaching and education. I think it has also made me feel more a part of education and the profession. I feel more knowledgeable. (TC)

Another said, "My case experiences here have greatly broadened my perspective on every aspect of education." She continued:

These cases have had a great impact on my sense of self as a teacher. I feel I am able to focus and reflect on my teaching more effectively since I've done case studies. I feel much more professional. I feel I don't have to apologize for my ideas. (TA)

A third corroborated this sentiment:

The cases definitely enhanced my sense of myself as a classroom teacher. [The process] has made me question my commitment to the field—what is my role, my interests, and does the classroom enable me to use myself? (TB)

SUMMARY AND CONCLUDING THOUGHTS

Creating a classroom environment that enables the teacher to learn, as the above quote suggests, is an enormous challenge for educators and education. If we are to attract and retain talented people in teaching we must provide a culture that not only suggests ongoing teacher development but also requires and supports it. One important aspect of teacher learning is teacher reflection. Reflective teachers have learned to learn from their experiences in classrooms. Working with cases provides a structure for teaching teachers to reflect and thus enhancing teacher understanding. The descriptive nature of cases and their tie to practice render them especially powerful as a focus for teacher learning. In preparing cases and/or in studying cases written by others, teachers consider both the particular and the general of any given teaching situation. Similarly, cases require that teachers move back and forth between practice, precedent, and principle as they deliberate the details of the case to establish its meaning and significance for their learning and consequently their teaching. In the process of studying cases, teachers construct knowledge that guides their practice.

An important feature of the case process that enhances teacher learning is that they are collaborative. Cases require that teachers talk with one another. The reflective conversation of case work as it is conceptualized in this chapter challenges the bounds of rationality that typically inhibit teachers' thinking and problem solving.

Underlying the idea of case work for teacher development is the assumption that learning is a critical component of good teaching. In order to meet the demands of their work as it is in any moment, and as it becomes in the moment to follow, teachers must know how to evaluate and reevaluate the aims, purposes, and consequences of their work in classrooms. Similarly, they must know how to reflect on their work in light of those aims and purposes. Cases offer an opportunity for teacher reflection and consequently teacher learning. Though not a panacea, cases represent a vision of teaching and teacher education that honors the teachers as informed professionals who have the capability, right, and responsibility for continuous learning. In such a vision teachers are empowered to meet and negotiate change as it shapes the future of their work for the twenty-first century.

NOTES

1. For a thoughtful discussion of the effect of bounded rationality on teaching, see Shulman and Carey (1984). Schön's (1983) discussion of the limits of technical rationality is also helpful in understanding the limits of scientific rationality in an age of uncertainty and change.

2. The quotations from teachers included in this chapter are taken verbatim from the research materials in the case methods project I conducted during the 1987–1988 and 1988–1989 academic years. The quotes come either from interview transcripts or from questionnaire or freewrite written responses to questions I asked about the case method used in class. Seventeen teachers participated in the study, which is described in full in Richert (1989a, 1989b). Each teacher was given a letter "name" (T for teacher and A–Q to indicate the 17 different sets of responses). The citations quoted in this chapter are indicated by the teacher's assigned letter—for example, TN means that teacher "N" is quoted here.

3. A particularly powerful set of cases exploring an array of contextual factors inherent in multicultural settings, for example, has been developed by Judith Kleinfeld and her colleagues at the Center for Cross-Cultural Studies at the University of Alaska, Fairbanks. For a description of this work that cites the cases and describes the context in which they are used, as well as the research that studies their effectiveness, see Kleinfeld and Nordhoff (1989) and Nordhoff and Kleinfeld (1990).

4. By indicating "reader" in this context, I do not mean to imply that all cases are presented in written format. They are not. I use "reader" to indicate the person responding to the case, be the presentation written, oral, or visual (such as a videotape).

5. One source of case studies from which teaching cases focusing on content have been created is the Knowledge Growth in a Profession research project that was sponsored by the Spencer Foundation and directed by Lee Shulman at Stanford University. For a description of this research see Shulman (1987).

6. Grossman and Wilson (1987) discuss the use of cases to construct theory in the way I am suggesting here. While these authors do not present their argument with an eye toward a teacher-defined knowledge base for the profession (a direction I intend to suggest in this chapter), I found their discussion of cases and the generation of theory illuminating.

REFERENCES

Belenky, M. F., Clinchy, B. M., Goldberger, N., & Tarule, J. (1986). *Women's ways of knowing: The development of self, voice and mind*. New York: Basic Books.

Brown, J. S., Collins, A., & Duguid, P. (1989). Situated cognition and the culture of learning. *Educational Research, 18*(1), 32–42.

Burke, M. (1988, Spring). *Whose responsibility is this?* Unpublished case presented in class, Mills College, Oakland, CA.

Dewey, J. (1933). *How we think: A restatement of the relation of reflective thinking to the educative process*. Chicago: Henry Regnery.

Grossman, P., & Wilson, S. (1987, April). *Planting seeds*. Paper presented at the annual meeting of the American Educational Research Association, Washington, DC.

Jackson, P. (1968). *Life in classrooms*. New York: Holt, Rinehart & Winston.

Kleinfeld, J., & Nordhoff, K. (1989). *Getting it together in teacher education: A "problem centered" curriculum*. Unpublished manuscript, University of Alaska, Fairbanks.

Little, J. W. (1987). Teachers as colleagues. In V. Richardson-Koehler (Ed.), *Educator's handbook: A research perspective*. New York: Longman.

Lortie, D. (1975). *Schoolteacher: A sociological study*. Chicago: University of Chicago Press.

McManus, M. (1988, Spring). *The dumping ground*. Unpublished case presented in class, Mills College, Oakland, CA.

Nisbett, R. E., & Ross, L. (1980). *Human inference: Strategies and shortcomings of social judgment*. Englewood Cliffs, NJ: Prentice-Hall.

Nisbett, R. E., & Wilson, D. W. (1977). Telling more than we can know: Verbal reports on mental processes. *Psychological Review, 84*(3), 231–259.

Nordhoff, K., & Kleinfeld, J. (1990). Shaping the rhetoric of reflection for multicultural settings. In R. Clift, W. Houston, & M. Pugach (Eds.), *Encouraging reflective practice: An analysis of issues and programs* (pp. 163–185). New York: Teachers College Press.

Richert, A. E. (1987). *Reflex to reflection: Facilitating reflection in novice teachers*. Unpublished doctoral dissertation, Stanford University, Stanford, CA.

Richert, A. E. (1989a, April). *Cases written by teachers: Case method and inquiry in teacher education*. Paper presented at the annual meeting of the American Educational Research Association, San Francisco.

Richert, A. E. (1989b, April). *Preparing cases, promoting reflection: A case for case methods in teacher education*. Paper presented at the annual meeting of the American Educational Research Association, San Francisco.

Richert, A. E. (1990). Teaching teachers to reflect: A consideration of program structure. *Journal of Curriculum Studies, 22*, 509–527.

Rosenholtz, S. J., & Kyle, S. J. (1984, Winter). Teacher isolation: Barriers to professionalism. *American Educator*, pp. 10–15.

Schön, D. A. (1983). *The reflective practitioner.* New York: Basic Books.

Shulman, L. S. (1987). Knowledge and teaching: Foundations of the new reform. *Harvard Educational Review, 57*(1), 1–22.

Shulman, L. S., & Carey, N. B. (1984). Psychology and the limitations of individual rationality for the study of reasoning and civility. *Review of Education Research, 54,* 501–524.

Tversky, A., & Kahneman, D. (1974). Judgment under uncertainty: Heuristics and biases. *Science, 185,* 1124–1131.

Walter, S. (1989, Autumn). *Skip to My Lou.* Unpublished case presented in class, Mills College, Oakland, CA.

8 Action Research
The Missing Link in the Creation of Schools as Centers of Inquiry

Peter Holly

"After languishing for a few decades as a research approach, it [action research] seems to be enjoying a revival of interest" (p. 34). Writing this in 1987, Allan Glatthorn described action research as one of several peer-centered options for professional growth. In this same category Glatthorn placed professional dialogue (involving joint reflection about teaching), curriculum development (including the collaborative production of materials), peer supervision (the collegial analysis of teaching), and peer coaching (the supported acquisition and mastery of skills). In terms of experience in Britain, action research can be all these things and more. Indeed, action research may have been "languishing" in the United States (its birthplace), but it has been enjoying something of a heyday in Britain, its foster home since the 1960s. And now the prodigal is returning.

Undoubtedly, educational action research is big in the 1990s and getting bigger. Indeed, action research, as a major form of professional development, is now seen as central to the restructuring of schools. Currently, there is a great interest in both the creation of professional development schools and the enhancement of teacher professionalism as the basis of school reform and renewal; thus the burgeoning interest in action research. Significantly, Glatthorn's (1987) brief description of action research was contained in the special issue of *Educational Leadership* entitled *Collegial Learning*. His own article is called "Cooperative Professional Development," and it sits well with the Johnsons' (1987) contention (contained in the same edition) that cooperative learning in the classroom can be fostered within a context of cooperative teacher learning. It is a question of *congruence*, and the key, as Lieberman (1986) has so rightly pointed out, is *teacher collaboration* (see also Chapter 6, this volume).

The central argument contained in this chapter is that there is a missing link in many of the current discussions about teacher collaboration; and this missing link is none other than action research. Teacher collaboration is now seen as a major form of professional development. A major vehicle for this is collaborative inquiry—conducted by professionals acting as reflective practitioners. Basically, collaborative inquiry is action research conducted within the context of collegial support. Moreover, when the faculty of a school do action research collaboratively, they are creating—to borrow Robert Schaefer's (1967) apt phrase—"the school as a center of inquiry" (see Glickman, 1988).

Written almost 25 years ago, Schaefer's seminal text is now attracting the attention it has always deserved; perhaps because, now more than ever, its messages are so pertinent for the restructuring, redesign, and renewal of schooling. Schaefer, for instance, argued that his conception of the "school as a center of inquiry" rests on five basic principles. Building on Schaefer's principles, I would contend that action research is a most appropriate vehicle for

- Creating opportunities for teachers to undertake collaborative and systematic investigations into classroom processes
- Invigorating teachers by linking them with vital sources of knowledge and intellectual stimulation from outside their schools
- Providing teachers with rich, meaningful, and rewarding inservice experiences
- Enabling teachers as continuing learners in order to enable students to become continuing learners
- Encouraging teachers to investigate the organizational "properties" of their schools according to the criteria of the "learning school"

I have characterized the learning school as one that fosters learning on five levels (Holly & Southworth, 1989):

1. It facilitates and maximizes the learning of all students.
2. It enables the teachers to be continuing learners themselves.
3. It encourages the teachers to learn together and from one another in collaboration.
4. It is a learning organization that is both responsive and adaptive to internal and external pressures.
5. It is an institution in which the principal is the leading learner and is able to model learning behavior and attitudes for teachers and students alike.

Action research, at root, constitutes participative learning for teachers. Who better to analyze teaching and learning than the teachers themselves through the agency of action research? Where I would extend Schaefer's message, however, is in the promotion of action research as the vehicle not only for teacher involvement in pedagogical analysis but also for teacher action on the strength of their reflection. Teachers can be researchers *and* change agents. Teachers are the professional developers. Extending to teachers the intellectual tools of pedagogical analysis—careful observation, the patient search for relevant clues, and the continued refinement of theory—provides them with what Schaefer refers to as the capacity to discover more about the unrevealed mysteries of their craft. Action research, as a major professional development activity, has the potential to generate genuine and sustained improvements in schools.

THE GROWTH OF ACTION RESEARCH

In being able to fulfill this kind of potential, action research has come a very long way. As McKernan (1989) has so rightly pointed out, action research, as we know it today, has evolved from a complex web of scientific and social factors and has existed in various guises for many years. Moreover, each of these guises has been the result of various forces and influences, and each successive wave has left its mark on action research. While these waves or phases overlap to some extent, it is possible to delineate key periods in the development of action research.

Period One: 1900–1930

McKernan (1989) traces the roots of action research to the Science in Education Movement, which gave rise to the application of the scientific method to curriculum problems. Buckingham (1926), for example, wrote a book entitled *Research for Teachers* in which he included a chapter headed "The Teacher as Research Worker." John Dewey (1929, 1938) followed this up by pursuing the theme of the "researching teacher" and arguing that curriculum development would not be effective unless there is active participation by those directly engaged in the teaching process.

Action research gained two characteristics from this, its first period of development: its systematic, scientific approach to educational problems and its acknowledgment of the importance of teacher participation.

Period Two: The 1930s

While it is argued that John Collier, the U.S. Commissioner for Indian Affairs, invented the term *action research* in the 1930s, most commentators agree that Kurt Lewin, the social psychologist who escaped to the United States from Hitler's Germany, fully deserves the title of the founding father of action research. Building on the work of the applied anthropologists (see Eddy & Partridge, 1978) and the Chicago School of sociology, Lewin took their ideas one stage further. He not only perceived action research as a form of research that could marry the experimental approach of social science to programs of social action in response to major social problems of the day (see Lewin, 1946); he also set about democratizing social research by encouraging its "subjects" to take a central role in its formulation and execution.

Lewin's view of research as composed of action cycles—his process model—and his emphasis on achieving a "social-help" function became entwined with his interest in group relations and group dynamics. He was a co-founder of the Research Center for Group Dynamics based at the Massachusetts Institute of Technology (which was subsequently moved to the University of Michigan), and, central to the story of action research, he was deeply involved in the establishment of the London-based Tavistock Institute for Human Relations. Lewin visited Britian in 1933 and 1936 and established links with Eric Trist, who, with A. T. M. Wilson, prepared a proposal to the Rockefeller Foundation that led to the foundation of the Tavistock Institute and, with MIT, the joint compilation of the journal *Human Relations*. From its inception, the Tavistock Institute championed the cause of action research, especially within industrial settings (see Jacques, 1952). It is important to note that the educational world has never had a monopoly on action research. The Tavistock Institute, for instance, promoted the use of *action learning* (see Argyris, Putnam, & Smith, 1985; Emery, 1982; Lewin, 1951; Morgan & Ramirez, 1984; Revans, 1971, 1982; Trist, 1976, 1982), initially within collaborative workgroups—the forerunners of the much vaunted quality circles—in the newly nationalized coal-mining industry in Britain. Action learning, with its roots in the work of the Tavistock Institute, has been used to establish individual and group learning (as in the approach championed by Revans, 1982) and to generate organizational change and development, as in Argyris and Schön's (1978) approach to the development of learning systems and Trist's (1976) approach to action research. Indeed, it is important to note that the advocates and exponents of organizational development have always claimed that their work is a form of action research/action learning (Beckhard, 1969; Bennis, 1969; Schein, 1969).

Period Three: The Late 1940s and Early 1950s

Following the work of the human relations–oriented social psychologists, action research entered the educational arena in the United States, mainly through the efforts of Stephen Corey and Hilda Taba. Lewin himself had worked with groups of teachers and teacher educators, and the Horace Mann–Lincoln Institute of Teachers College, Columbia University, was quick to seize the initiative and ensure that the idea of action research was absorbed into the educational world. This institute, as Kemmis and colleagues (1982) have pointed out, was already engaged in curriculum development for social reconstruction and cooperative research with teachers, schools, and school districts. Action research now provided a dynamic for the joint programs in schools, and it became the institute's rallying cry from about 1946 to 1949, with Corey (1953) acting as its chief advocate. Indeed, Corey and his colleagues always argued that action research would succeed because practitioners would utilize the fruits of their own researchers. Yet it did not thrive beyond the early 1950s. It still had some adherents (see Shumsky, 1956, 1958), but the period 1953–1957 witnessed the beginnings of a decline of interest in action research in the United States (see Hodgkinson, 1957). It had, according to Kemmis and colleagues (1982), become all things to all people, and four factors contributed to its being under concerted attack:

1. A "retreat to the academy" by researchers (thus separating action from research)
2. An attack on its methodology (it was said to lack vigor)
3. A questioning of whether it lived up to its promises concerning improvements of school practices
4. The rise of the competitive, empire-building, and positivistic evaluation industry

According to Schaefer (1967), the research and development world turned its back on teachers, produced programmed educational packages, and, in the process, tried to bypass teachers in the quest for educational improvement. Indeed, when Sanford asked "Whatever Happened to Action Research?" (1970), he was able to argue that its decline was directly related to decisions to retain the academic theory–practice split in place through the funding of scholarly research, development, and dissemination-type innovations from regional educational laboratories. On the other side of the Atlantic, however, action research was moving forward.

Period Four: The 1960s and 1970s

During this phase action research was discovered by British educators and promoted with some relish. It first surfaced within the Educational Priority Area (EPA) movement in the 1960s (in which researchers were placed in socially disadvantaged schools to help the teachers with their action-oriented problems), and then became the theme of a major educational conference held at York University in 1970. One of the conference participants, Lawrence Stenhouse (1975), was in the act of putting together a new synthesis of ideas that later emerged in the mid-1970s in the teacher-as-reseacher movement, and the conference undoubtedly proved something of a turning point in his own thinking.

At this same conference, Robert Rapoport (1970) presented his paper that not only covered some of the dilemmas inherent in the practice of action research (as evidenced in the Tavistock experience), but also charted some of the characteristics of action research as a developing area of "applied social science." In particular, Rapoport mentioned the immediacy of the researcher's involvement in the action process, the existence of a client with a problem to be solved, and the central presence of a social scientist as a change agent.

What Stenhouse (1975) did, however, was to take these messages and collapse the various activities into one role—that of the teacher-as-(action) researcher. As a consequence, and for the first time in Britain, teachers were encouraged to see themselves as reseachers, problem solvers, curriculum developers, change agents, and social scientists—all rolled into one. Indeed, Stenhouse's colleague John Elliott (1979, 1981) embarked on a series of path-finding efforts in the 1970s, providing action research with much of the flavor that it still retains. Elliott was co-director of the Ford Teaching Project in the mid-1970s and, in 1976, founded the Classroom Action Research Network (CARN). In the early 1980s he directed another action research project, this time for the Schools Council, the national curriculum development agency based in London. This was called the Teacher-Pupil Interaction and the Quality of Learning (TIQL) Project and was based at the Cambridge Institute of Education. One of the schools in the project was Chesterton School in Cambridge, and from 1979 to 1981 I acted as this school's internal coordinator for the collaborative action research team. This was my entrée into the world of action research. Following this experience and a couple of years working at the Schools Council, in 1984 I succeeded John Elliott as Tutor in Curriculum Studies at the Cambridge Institute of Education and as coordinator of CARN. This network holds regular conferences, and since the late 1970s, many interested parties from North America have visited Britain to join in these events. It could be argued, therefore, that the activities of CARN have played a small part in the revival of interest in action research in the United States. Indeed, the editors of a recent compilation of papers on action research (Kyle & Hovda, 1989) said that, in terms of the factors that led to the resurgence of interest in the United States, the bulletins produced by CARN played a major role. (For examples of these bulletins, see Holly & Whitehead, 1984, 1986.)

Period Five: The Late 1970s and Early 1980s

Significantly, in the continuing paradigm shift that is the history of action research, the return to its homeland was accomplished by a new breed of educational pioneer, which included the likes of Betty Ward, Ann Lieberman, and Sharon Oja. Action research, it seems, received a new lease on life and the support of a long list of women sponsors.

Moreover, educational action research returned to the United States in a new guise: more a good idea than a *grande idée*, more pragmatic and less paradigmatic. It is pertinent in this context to cite Clifford Geertz's (1973) reference to Susanne Langer's thesis that certain ideas (such as action research) burst upon the intellectual landscape with tremendous resolve and enormous promise, only to be exploited, bent, and fitted to every purpose because they are heralded as cure-alls. The ideas soon become familiar, and, in the process, expectations are curbed and their excessive popularity is ended.

This thesis particularly applies to the history of action research in the United States. It exploded onto the educational scene in the 1940s, tried to prosper on a surfeit of eclecticism, lost momentum temporarily in the 1950s and 1960s, and then reappeared in a more viable, sustainable form in the 1970s and 1980s. This resurgence has taken the form of interactive teaching and research (Lieberman & Miller, 1984) and has revolved around three research projects concerning collaborative action research sponsored by the National Institute of Education: the Interactive Research and Development on Teaching (IR&DT) Study (Tikunoff, Ward, & Griffin, 1979), the Interactive Research and Development on Schooling (IR&DS) Study (Griffin, Lieberman, & Jacullo-Noto, 1983), and the Action Research on Change in Schools (ARCS) Project (Oja & Pine, 1989).

Along with an affiliated, fourth initiative (see Huling, 1982), these activities have been premised on three assumptions:

1. School-based problem-solving approaches to curriculum change are more likely to be successfully implemented than large, federally funded, central initiatives.

2. It was important, as Lieberman and Miller (1984) have pointed out, to rediscover action research and to rename it "interactive research and development."
3. Collaboration (between insiders and outsiders) is crucial.

The collaborative partnership for internal development must involve those who are internal to the situation and an array of external support agents and facilitators. Such collaboration rests on a team approach (Connelly & Ben-Peretz, 1980), with the participants taking ownership by defining "their" problems. Lieberman (1986) has emphasized that such collaborative research is a question of "working with, not working on," and Oja and Pine (1989) have listed the aspects of such endeavors. According to the experience gained in the ARCS project, they say, collaborative action research is characterized by several elements:

1. Research problems are mutually defined by teachers and researchers.
2. Academic/university researchers and teachers collaborate in seeking solutions to school-based problems.
3. Research findings are used and modified in solving school problems.
4. Teachers develop research skills and competencies (Corey, 1953, always maintained that this is the area of greatest need within action research initiatives), and researchers reeducate themselves in field-based research methodologies.
5. Teachers are more able to solve their own problems and renew themselves professionally.
6. Teachers and researchers co-author reports of their findings.

During the 1980s, Stephen Kemmis has been a powerful influence in the action research world. Kemmis, along with his colleagues at Deakin University in Australia, has charted (and contributed) to the growth of action research. The work of Kemmis (see Carr & Kemmis, 1983; Kemmis et al., 1982; McTaggart & Kemmis, 1982) has focused on a critical interpretive approach to action research and has overlaid the messages of Lewin and Corey with a layer of critical theory, largely arising from the writings of Jürgen Habermas. Kemmis's own writing is intellectually demanding, and as McKernan (1989) admits, "there is little doubt that this is intellectually sterner stuff and adds a new and vital philosophical analysis to curricular thought" (p. 14). The irony, however, is that although Kemmis aims to encourage practitioner participation in action research, the language in which he couches his messages is intimidating and exclusive. According to McKernan (1989):

> Heightening human understanding through hard critique is the "modus operandi." Rather than equipping practitioners with field research methods, the aim is to sharpen analytical-conceptual understanding and communal discourse so that participants can be emancipated through their collective understanding. The approach seems ideally suited for the academy, and one wonders whether such lofty critical discourse methodology will be taken on board by classroom teachers—other than those enrolled for a doctorate. (p. 14)

I have described similar feelings of doubt and expressed the fear that such a radical approach (and its anti-institutional messages) ends up neutralizing its own potential (Holly, 1986, 1989c). If real and lasting school improvement is the aim, the path trodden by Kemmis and his colleagues may well not be the way to achieve it.

Period Six: The Mid-1980s Onward—
The Era of Collaborative Inquiry

In Britain action research has continued to flourish and has permeated the educational system in many ways. Despite the termination in 1983 of the Schools Council—the main benefactor of action research in the late 1970s and early 1980s—the spirit of action research lives on in several different ways:

- Within the teacher groups sponsored by the School Curriculum Development Committee, the successor body to the Schools Council
- Within school-focused inservice activities, which have proliferated in recent years (see Holly, James, & Young, 1987)
- Within school-based development activities, which have been the main thrust of my own work (see Holly & Southworth, 1989)
- Within the increasingly popular work of classroom self-evaluation and classroom observation, both now seen as legitimate professional development/inservice activities (see Hopkins, 1985; Hustler, Cassidy, & Cuff, 1986)

I have argued that action research in Britain has gained everything and has lost only its name (Holly, 1989c). In 1988, for instance, the CARN

International Conference was entitled "Collaborative Inquiry for School Improvement." The guest speaker was Ann Lieberman, fresh from her work on collaborative research in the United States. In her speech, as in her article in *Educational Leadership* (1986), she was able to report on the recent endeavors in the United States in the area of collaborative inquiry. She was able to show that action research was alive and well in North America (in the form of interactive research and development in teaching) and that interest in such activities was certainly reviving. Furthermore, she gave witness to the power of collaborative inquiry and its important role in the enhancement of teacher professionalism. Given the rich experience of educational action research in Britain and the new thirst for action research in the United States, we decided to work together to establish action research/collaborative inquiry within Ann Lieberman's work in the Puget Sound Educational Consortium (PSEC) in the state of Washington. A report on this work is included later in this chapter.

Within this particular piece of collaborative inquiry there is emerging, I believe, a new and vibrant form of action research. The innovation that is now action research has not completed its odyssey, but it is certainly showing signs of maturity and integrity. Its essential spirit, is characterized by

1. A commitment to improving the processes of schooling (particularly those of the classroom) through practitioner research/reflection/considered action/monitoring
2. The belief in the centrality of teachers not only as professionals, but also as researchers, evaluators, developers, and change agents
3. The commitment to practical problem solving in schools (mainly in classrooms but not necessarily so) using self-evaluation techniques
4. The concomitant dedication to the demystification of research and evaluation in order to create the understanding that it can be *for* teachers, *by* teachers, and done *with* teachers and appropriate support agents
5. The growing awareness of the importance of team-based and, indeed, whole-staff (self-) evaluation work
6. The increasing awareness of the complexities of classroom processes and learning itself, which in Britain has been tantamount to a rediscovery of what is referred to as the Learning Level; whereas the emphasis had previously been on the effectiveness of teaching, the focus is now shifting to the excellence of learning (Holly & Southworth, 1989)

There is a growing interest in the *learning school* (akin to Schaefer's "school as a center of inquiry," 1967); that is, what a school has to be like organizationally speaking in order to foster the learning of all its students. The interest now is not in a school "unbuilt" by action research (see Holly, 1989a) but in a school built around action research.

I (Holly, 1984), along with Fullan, Bennett, and Rolheiser-Bennett (1989), have contended that it is a question of integrating and orchestrating change and development at two levels—at the classroom learning level and at the whole-school organizational level—and that there must be "systematic congruence" between these two levels (see Holly, 1989b). Action research has the potential to make this happen within the context of what I refer to as "the developing school" (Holly & Southworth, 1989). In this scenario, action research is returning to its roots, rediscovering organization development and action learning, and helping in the creation of schools as inquiring, reflective, and working communities.

Action research as collaborative inquiry, therefore, is what students and teachers do in the collaborative, inquiring school. Such homological considerations are vital. And this message is obviously getting across. For example, Myers (1989) has argued recently that school-site, teacher-research projects should be a basic requirement of the second wave of school reform. With the failure of centralized and externalized policy initiatives (see McLaughlin, 1987), Myers sees the need for teacher research at the local level to develop different programs and different patterns of organization to meet the needs of higher standards of student literacy.

The new action research is participative, both participative in learning and participative in action. It is fostered by a sense of community, is rooted in the real world, and is attuned to the rhythms of schooling. It is "built in" as opposed to "bolted on." And action researchers—the "scufflers" in new change scenarios—are putting down roots and becoming more and more interconnected with their colleagues through their attempts to initiate and sustain collaborative inquiry. This appears to be a trans-Atlantic phenomenon. Slavin (1987), for instance, has referred to "a small but growing number of elementary and secondary schools" in the United States that

> have begun to apply cooperative principles at the school as well as the classroom level, involving teachers in cooperative planning, peer coaching, and team teaching, with these activities directed toward effective implementation of cooperative learning in the classroom. Many of these schools are working toward institutionalization of cooperative principles as the focus of school renewal. . . . Students, teachers, and administrators can work

cooperatively to make the school a better place for working and learning. (pp. 8, 12)

ACTION RESEARCH IN ACTION

To understand a science, according to Geertz (1973), one should examine not what its apologists say but what its practitioners do. The focus in this section, therefore, is on the doing of action research.

There is common agreement that action research is both cyclical and serial and that, within each cycle, it is multistaged. These stages, or steps, are usually listed as follows:

1. Problem analysis—the initial formulation of the problem
2. Data collection—fact finding or, as Lewin (1946) referred to it, reconnaissance
3. Data analysis and conceptualization
4. Planning of an action program
5. Implementation of this action program
6. Evaluation—monitoring the effects of the action program and judging the quality of the changes

The first three stages—the research-in-action research—are now discussed in turn.

Problem Formulation

Lewis and Munn (1987) have produced an excellent booklet designed to help teachers formulate research questions within small-scale, school-based investigations. They encourage teachers to

• Be as clear as possible about the research project and ask such questions as, What do I/we want to investigate? Why do I/we want to investigate it? How am I/are we going to investigate it?
• Translate the area of general concern into a more focused, researchable question, while always balancing *worthwhileness* with *feasibility*. School-based research projects have to be do-able and manageable; research questions, therefore, should be as precise as possible.
• Order priorities among the aspects of a general area of concern in order to be as specific as possible.
• Secure the advantages of a team approach. Colleagues can then support one another through the ups and downs of doing research; team

members can bring different points of view to bear on the area to be researched (thereby ensuring more thorough consideration); and the results of team research may stand a better chance of being implemented in a school simply because a number of teachers have been sufficiently concerned about an area (or issue) to try to do something about it. Their advice is to find at least one colleague with whom to share the project.

• Aim to provide some systematic and reliable information that can be used as a basis for action. It is a question of providing the substance for data-based decision making. In this context, they argue that the "audience" for the research must be involved at the earliest possible juncture to formulate the research question by considering three major factors:

1. Personal/professional interest, commitment, and responsibility
2. The interests and concerns of colleagues and the school at large
3. Published material relevant to the topic to keep it natural, close to what has to be done anyway, and, above all, practical and relevant

Besides working according to a flowchart of the decision-making process, it is also advisable to incorporate such an investigative technique as *analytic discourse* (Posch, 1986). This technique is used within structured group work and aims not only to clarify a problem but also to attain a depth of understanding through a collaborative, co-learning approach built on "critical friendship." According to Posch:

> This method allows for the analysis of a problem or an issue in order to learn to understand its context, its many aspects and how they relate to each other. The task of the participant who wants an issue to be analysed is first to present briefly the issue or problem as he/she see it and then to respond to the questions of the other participants of the group as far as possible and in a manner acceptable to him/her. (pp. 1–2)

Posch emphasizes that it is the task of the participants (by their questioning) to gain as coherent and complete a view as possible of the problem. For this process three rules have proved helpful:

1. Only questions should be posed. Accounts of similar experiences should not be given. This rule should facilitate the concentration of interest on the problem and situation of the person reporting.
2. Critical remarks (even if they are disguised as questions) should not be made. This rule should help avoid any pressure on the reporting person to defend him-/herself.

3. Proposals for solutions should not be expressed. This rule should ease the danger that the quest for understanding might turn into the much easier collection of recipes.

If a group agrees on these rules, somebody should accept the responsibility of pointing out to the participants when violations occur.

Posch concludes that an analytic discourse can be a path to a deeper understanding of a problem—on the part of the person reporting and on the part of the whole group. The interrelationship of aspects can become clearer, and critical "knots" in the system, which may lead the way to solutions, can become visible.

In the early stages of teacher research a decision has to be made about whether the investigation is to be focused or exploratory and open ended. The advice of Lewis and Munn (1987) is unequivocal: Keep it focused. In addition, they contend that the criterion of feasibility should influence the other decision to be made—the selection of *appropriate* methods of data collection. Their argument is that every teacher-researcher should keep in mind various practical questions. Some of these might be

What information do I require?
Why do I need it?
When do I need it?
How do I collect it?
Where can I find it?

Data Collection

Data-collection methods for action research are largely qualitative, as opposed to quantitative, but not exclusively so. Borrowing freely from the ethnographic/participant-observation tradition, action research incorporates the use of such techniques as the compilation of logs and journals or diaries by students and teacher-researchers, documentary analysis, the construction of student profiles over time, the categorizing of activities and checklists (for example, the Flanders' Interaction Analysis Categories in Hook, 1981), questionnaires, photographic evidence, taperecordings, interview material, and videotaping. Action research also utilizes the approach known as triangulation (see Elliott, 1981; Hopkins, 1985), by means of which three different types of data sources can be juxtaposed in order to discern discrepancies, or, as in classroom research, three different sets of perceptions—those of the teacher, the students, and an external observer—can be set against one another. In order to initiate this kind of observation work in schools and classrooms, experience in Britain would suggest that the following approaches are all of some value (see Reid, Hopkins, & Holly, 1987):

1. Paired (or peer) observation
2. Open-house classrooms
3. Climate analysis
4. Shadow studies of either students or teachers, for example, the approach known as "A Day in the Life" (see Sagor's technique, discussed in Holly & Southworth, 1989)
5. The formation of teacher-researcher interest groups bound together by a mutual concern

Data Analysis

Miles and Huberman (1984) see data analysis as an interactive process that not only has various component parts (they refer to data collection, data reduction, data display, and conclusion drawing–verification) but also takes place over time. I would agree with their process view in two ways. First, analysis certainly starts early (during data collection) and is a form of "anticipatory reduction" or "focusing down" (see Parlett & Hamilton, 1977). Second, in terms of reflecting on the data, two interlinked processes may be described: data reduction and data conceptualization.

The process of data reduction/data processing is somewhat mechanical. It involves the identification of clusters of issues and patterns within the data. It includes deciphering themes, selecting, focusing, discarding, making associations, sifting, categorizing, ordering, and so forth. This process of reduction leads to the process of conceptualization. By "interrogating the data," as Sirotnik (1987) has argued, it is possible to provide:

- An *explanation*, to make sense of the emerging picture and to produce the story line of "What is going on here"
- An *understanding* or *illumination*, in terms of "Why is this happening?" which is reliant on the *interpretation* of the storyteller
- A *critique*, in terms of the underlying values and cultural factors that have some influence in this problem situation; that is, asking "What lies behind all this?"

The process of conceptualization involves the use or generation of theory. It is possible to produce a conceptual framework using one of three approaches: grounded theory, grounded in theory, and grounded with theory. The first involves teacher-researchers in producing "new" theory based on, and arising from, their data; the second involves teacher-researchers' grounding their investigation in a preordinate theory from the beginning; and the third entails teacher-researchers' grounding their emerging theories *with*, rather than *in*, those of others. While some advocates of action research contend that the first of these approaches is most conducive for action research, in my experience the third approach is equally profitable.

Miles and Huberman (1984) view *verification* as a crucial subprocess within data analysis. This constitutes, they say, the process of drawing conclusions, and it is a "strengthening process" over time. At first the noting of patterns and causal flows is somewhat skeptical, light and tentative, but gradually the explanations become increasingly grounded and substantiated (even though they encourage researchers to keep scanning the data for second thoughts). The process also involves *feedback to participants* (of the emerging interpretation) in order to obtain their reactions. The reason for this is to test for plausibility, believability, confirmability, and authenticity. Is the interpretation sufficiently sturdy, robust, and defensible? In other words, this process is very much an interactive one.

According to Miles and Huberman, *displaying the data* (using imaginative forms) also starts early and leads to *data reporting*. The latter should be both informal and formal; accessible, communicable, and "educative" (see Walker, 1985); and generative of resolve for action. While the process of reporting should never be allowed to divert the practitioner from the action imperatives arising from his or her research, reporting is important for the following reasons:

- *Politically*. Teachers need to exhibit their new professionalism.
- *Developmentally*. Teachers need to give accounts of their projected improvements and the progress made.
- *Educationally*. Teachers need to demonstrate their intentions to improve the learning opportunities of all their students, and, again, the progress made.
- *Collaboratively*. Teachers can co-produce and co-author research reports.
- *Institutionally*. Individual teachers or members of teacher groups need to disseminate their ideas to their colleagues, usually in the form of discussion papers, thus feeding into whole-school development.

Reporting, therefore, is a vital form of linkage between generating valid data, being able to learn from them, and then *wanting* to act on the strength of them. The learning and the resolve to change arising from data analysis are embodied within the process of action planning. I equated this process with strategic evaluation, the aim of which is to answer the question, How do we get there? Target setting (both short term and long term) and the identification of support and training needs are constituent parts of the process, which heralds more effective implementation (Holly, 1985).

MODELS OF ACTION RESEARCH

Although action research in practice has a cyclical and, indeed, serial orientation, there are various formulations, or models, of action research in action. Although they are not entirely discrete, two practical modes seem to dominate. It seems to be a question of either doing research and then taking action on the strength of it (i.e., research action) or taking action that is then accompanied or followed by research (i.e., action research).

In this context, it is noteworthy that as far back as the 1930s Collier spoke in terms of research-action and action-research. It seems to be a question, then, of either doing *research for action* (according to a prospective orientation) or doing *research in/of action* (which is largely a retrospective approach). It might be profitable, however, to separate out *research in action* from *research of action*, thus creating three approaches:

1. *Research for action* provides the database for action planning.
2. *Research in action* occurs within and during the implementation of new ideas and constitutes the ongoing monitoring of the changes.
3. *Research of action* is operated to evaluate the impact and effectiveness of the changes.

It is interesting to note that Lewis and Munn (1987), when discussing the purposes of teacher research, indicate three main reasons:

1. To try to find out what is actually going on, recognizing that what actually occurs is not always the same as what is thought to occur, and then to act on the strength of their "intelligence" (research for action)
2. To monitor and thus to formatively influence the direction of new developments (research in action)
3. To evaluate what is already taking place (research of action)

Research for Action

This approach remains faithful to Lewin's (1946) classic action research model and consists of the six stages outlined earlier. Research for
action, then, is front-loaded in the sense that it is research-led. It is also the
approach that is most akin to conventional, academic research. It allows
for thorough, systematic, but time-consuming investigations and may not
be wholly suitable for what Walker (1985) refers to as "school research."
This framework also emphasizes the importance of three kinds of data
collection:

1. An initial, early trawl to explore, and thus formulate, a problem
   area
2. The main period of data collection that is used to substantiate,
   confirm, or disconfirm the original hunches and thus to test the
   initial understanding of the problem
3. A later period of data collection that is used to monitor and test
   the effectiveness and effects/outcomes of the chosen action
   strategies

Research in/of Action

This approach is an alternative one, which is becoming increasingly
popular among educational action researchers in Britain and Australia. It
rests on four stages within each cycle: planning, action, observation, and
reflection, followed by replanning, more action, and so forth. This approach is action-led and the research is focused on new, as opposed to old
or previous, action. This framework, therefore, intertwines action and research by promoting the importance of both new action and the simul-
taneous observation of the effects of the action (see Holly, 1983).
Teachers seem to like this approach because it is natural and can be
directly related to changes they have to make. It is the perfect platform
for collaborative inquiry by teacher teams as part of their efforts in the
area of collaborative implementation. Planning, in this context, means
two things: planning implementation strategies and planning the appropriate research methods to "capture" these strategies in action.

Two promoters of this approach are McTaggart and Kemmis (1982);
they maintain, from their "critical" perspective, that "action research is a
dynamic process in which these four aspects are to be understood not as
static steps, complete in themselves, but rather as moments in the action
research spiral of planning, acting, observing and reflecting" (p. 10).

To sum up, there are various approaches to action research. I have concentrated here on two such approaches—research for action and research in/of action—but it is not my intention to select one as better. Certainly, teachers seem to be responding positively to the second approach for the reasons suggested above. What is important, however, is to select the approach that is appropriate for the circumstances and the task at hand. Moreover, I would contend, the two approaches are more similar than different; they are both parts of a larger design and they share certain generic processes—the building blocks for the overall design. The main difference between them, I would argue, is one of emphasis, which is largely a reflection of the chosen entry point.

CASE STUDIES

As mentioned earlier in this chapter, action research is now a major activity within schools participating in the Puget Sound Education Consortium in Washington state (Holly, 1989a). One of the emphases within the consortium is the development of teacher leadership. In this area, two understandings have emerged from the work thus far: Doing action research is a most appropriate professional activity for teacher leaders, and the role of internal school coordinator (or inquiry coordinator) of an action research team is also highly suitable for teacher leaders. As one of the teacher-group participants remarked: "Action research provides opportunities for inquiry, participation, and collaboration in research. It is what teacher leaders do" (p. 42).

Within the consortium, there are various examples of action research in progress, and I would like to describe the efforts of four teams.

Team 1.   The members of team 1, a school-based group in a rural elementary school, have been focusing on their implementation of "literature circles" as their research project. In evaluating their progress, this team commented in particular on the collaborative nature of the group (and their collaborative co-authoring of the end-of-the-year report on their work). One of the team members wrote:

The Literature Circles project is a wonderfully rewarding experience for both teacher and students. It is also a huge, overwhelming and sometimes frustrating undertaking, and there's a good chance that I would not have stuck with it if I had not had the other "guinea pig" teachers to fall back on. In a profession that all too often relies on each individual doing his or her job independently, working as a collaborative teaching team for literature circles is a refreshing change of pace and, in my opinion, also a matter of survival, maintaining sanity, and achieving success. (Holly, 1989a, p. 43)

Team 2.   Again a school-based group, this team in a middle school has been using action research as a formative evaluation. Their school has been involved in many change initiatives recently, almost to the point of overload, and the action research project is an opportunity to take stock and make some sense of all the activities. It is largely retrospective (research of action), yet it is also prospective and formative (research for action) in terms of its feeding into site-based decision making and future planning. As a team member commented:

The empowerment of teachers continues to grow through action research. As they are involved in developing curriculum, forming teams, or studying Glasser's reality therapy, they are part of a collaborative inquiry. They are continually identifying needs, planning, implementing and evaluating. As difficult as change can be, it is also an energizing force when people are involved in the decision-making process and share a vision of the future. (p. 44)

Team 3.   This team is a group of individuals from various schools who are interested in embarking on action research across their district. Because they are at the initiation stage, there is nothing to report as yet. They have to decide whether to form separate teams within their schools or, indeed, interschool teams. In addition, they will need to continue to meet as a districtwide mutual support group.

Team 4.   As an across-the-district group, team 4's members have been monitoring the introduction of a major innovation—department heads in elementary schools. Research in action has been the focus here in the form of a process evaluation. The aim has been a formative one: to feed the findings into district-level decision making, although their research report is also arousing interest in other schools and districts. Above all, however, the group members emphasized the fact that the process of action research "enabled us to build an *inside perspective* on the implementation of elementary department heads" (p. 45).

The work in the Puget Sound Educational Consortium has been extended to schools in Oregon, and the hope now is to spread throughout the Northwest with the establishment of LEARN (League for Educational Action Research in the Northwest).

CONCLUSIONS

Drawing on my experience with action research in Britain, I would like to offer the following concluding remarks.

Action research/classroom self-evaluation is well received by teachers when certain aspects are stressed, especially that teacher research is not something done *at* them or *to* them by a select band of external experts, but something done *for* them, *by* them, and *with* their colleagues. The implications of these prepositions are all-important in such school-based endeavors, for action research transfers *ownership of the change process* to the teachers. They are the researchers, the developers, the innovators, and the evaluators. The question of ownership is a vital one. The word *ownership* has two meanings: (1) belonging to, identifying with, and commitment to; *and* (2) arising from this psychological affiliation, a readiness to confess, to recognize/acknowledge something, to be self-confronting. Action research has an impact on both these levels.

The important thing about educational action research is that it "hooks" those who are centrally involved—the teachers themselves. Its participative, inclusive nature and its *meaningfulness* add up to its potential for "deep personal significance" (Shumsky, 1958, p. 152). And this can result in not only self-confrontation but also the *personalization of the change process*. Action-researching teachers have to face head-on the psychological barriers inhibiting teachers from subjecting their own practice to critical scrutiny.

> The teacher-researcher generally finds that his previous way of acting conflicts with the new way required by his action-research plan. His inner conflict is shown by his ambivalent feelings, by his inconsistent behavior, by his resistance to change, by insignificant or superficial change, or by vacillation. (Shumsky & Mukerji, 1962, p. 84)

The change process—with all its emotional undertow—is internalized and personalized to the point where the teacher action researcher becomes "hooked" on his or her change agenda. As Fullan (1985; Fullan et al., 1989) has reminded us, educational change is ultimately dependent on change in individual classrooms and in individual teachers. Despite the importance of the collaborative nature of action research, in the final analysis, change and learning are deeply personal matters. The focus for the change struggle, then, has to lie within the individual practitioner (see McLaughlin, 1987); this is where real change occurs.

Action research, then, can have a profound affect on individual teachers. Its impact can be enormous, in that it

- Gets teachers moving
- Operationalizes the axiom that "involvement generates commitment"
- Attends to practical, real-world problems and their solutions
- Provides opportunities to be collaborative
- Deals with the core concerns of teachers—to improve the teaching and learning process in the school

Action research is learning centered. It is what is done by teachers as continuous learners and is conducted by those teacher learners on behalf of themselves, their colleagues, and their student learners. While collaborative learning through collaborative inquiry is the key, action research is the process vehicle that enables all this to happen. Within schools as centers of inquiry, teachers need a process framework to structure their activities. Action research, therefore, is the missing link.

REFERENCES

Argyris, C., Putnam, R., & Smith, D. M. (1985). *Action science: Concepts, methods and skills for research and intervention.* San Francisco: Jossey-Bass.

Argyris, C., & Schön, D. A. (1978). *Organizational learning: A theory of action perspective.* Reading, MA: Addison-Wesley.

Beckhard, R. (1969). *Organization development: Strategies and models.* Reading, MA: Addison-Wesley.

Bennis, W. G. (1969). *Organization development: Its nature, origins and prospects.* Reading, MA: Addison-Wesley.

Buckingham, B. R. (1926). *Research for teachers.* New York: Silver Burdett.

Carr, W., & Kemmis, S. (1983). *Becoming critical: Knowing through action research.* Victoria, Australia: Deakin University Press.

Connelly, M., & Ben-Peretz, M. (1980). Teachers' role in the using and doing of research and development. *Journal of Curriculum Studies, 12*(2), 95–107.

Corey, S. (1953). *Action research to improve school practices.* New York: Teachers College Press.

Dewey, J. (1929). *The sources of a science of education.* New York: Horace Liveright.

Dewey, J. (1938). *Logic: The theory of inquiry.* New York: Henry Holt.

Eddy, E. M., & Partridge, W. L. (Eds.). (1978). *Applied anthropology in America.* New York: Columbia University Press.

Elliott, J. (1979). *How do teachers learn?* Unpublished manuscript, Cambridge Institute of Education, Cambridge, UK.

Elliott, J. (1981). *Action research: A framework for self-evaluation in schools.* Schools Council's TIQL Project Working Paper, Cambridge Institute of Education, Cambridge, UK.

Emery, M. (1982). Searching for new directions. In *New ways for new times*. Canberra: Australian National University.

Fullan, M. G. (1985). *The meaning of educational change*. Toronto: Ontario Institute for Studies in Education.

Fullan, M. G., Bennett, B., & Rolheiser-Bennett, C. (1989, April). *Linking classroom and school improvement*. Paper presented at the meeting of the American Educational Research Association, New Orleans.

Geertz, C. (1973). *The interpretation of cultures*. New York: Basic Books.

Glatthorn, A. A. (1987). Cooperative professional development: Peer-centered options for teacher growth. Collegial learning [Special issue]. *Educational Leadership, 45*(3), 31–35.

Glickman, C. D. (1988). *Supervision of instruction*. Boston: Allyn & Bacon.

Griffin, G. A., Lieberman, A., & Jacullo-Noto, J. (1983). *Interactive research and development on schooling* (executive summary of the final report). Austin: University of Texas, Research and Development Center for Teacher Education.

Hodgkinson, H. L. (1957). Action research—A critique. *The Journal of Educational Sociology, 31*(4), 137–153.

Holly, P. J. (1983). *On the outskirts: A case study of educational action research*. Unpublished thesis, Cambridge Institute of Education, Cambridge, UK.

Holly, P. J. (1984). The institutionalization of action research in schools. *Cambridge Journal of Education, 14*(2), 5–18.

Holly, P. J. (1985). *The developing school*. CIE/TRIST working paper, Cambridge Institute of Education, Cambridge, UK.

Holly, P. J. (1986). Action research: Third party, fire and theft? In P. J. Holly & D. Whitehead (Eds.), *Collaborative action research* (CARN Bulletin No. 7). Cambridge Institute of Education, Cambridge, UK.

Holly, P. J. (1989a). Action research: The missing link in teacher leadership and collaboration. In P. Wasley (Ed.), *Contributions to improved practice* (pp. 27–49). Seattle: University of Washington, Puget Sound Educational Consortium.

Holly, P. J. (1989b). *School-based development for flexible learning: Harnessing the power of whole school approaches*. Paper commissioned by the UK National Council for Educational Technology.

Holly, P. J. (1989c). Action research: Cul-de-sac or turnpike? In D. W. Kyle & R. A. Hovda (Eds.), The potential and practice of action research, parts 1 & 2 [Special issue]. *Peabody Journal of Education, 64*(2, 3), 71–100.

Holly, P. J., James, T., & Young, J. (1987). *The experience of TRIST: Practitioners' views of INSET and recommendations for the future*. DELTA Report TVEI/ Cambridge Institute of Education, Cambridge, UK.

Holly, P. J., & Southworth, G. W. (1989). *The developing school*. Lewes, UK: Falmer.

Holly, P. J., & Whitehead, D. (1984). *Action research in schools: Getting it into perspective* (CARN Bulletin No. 6). Cambridge, UK: Cambridge Institute of Education.

Holly, P. J., & Whitehead, D. (1986). *Collaborative action research* (CARN Bulletin No. 7). Cambridge, UK: Cambridge Institute of Education.

Hook, C. (1981). *Studying classrooms.* Victoria, Australia: Deakin University Press.

Hopkins, D. (1985). *A teacher's guide to classroom research.* Milton Keynes, UK: Open University Press.

Huling, L. L. (1982, April). *The effects on teachers of participation in an interactive research and development project.* Paper presented at the meeting of the American Educational Research Association, New York.

Hustler, D., Cassidy, T., & Cuff, T. (Eds.). (1986). *Action research in classrooms and schools.* London: Allen & Unwin.

Jacques, E. (1952). *The changing culture of a factory.* New York: Dryden.

Johnson, D. W., & Johnson, R. T. (1987). Research shows the benefits of adult cooperation. Collegial learning [Special issue]. *Educational Leadership, 45*(3), 27–30.

Kemmis, S., et al. (1982). *The action research reader.* Victoria, Australia: Deakin University Press.

Kyle, D. W., & Hovda, R. A. (Eds.). (1989). The potential and practice of action research, parts 1 & 2 [Special issue]. *Peabody Journal of Education, 64*(2, 3).

Lewin, K. (1946). Action research and minority problems. *Journal of Social Issues, 2,* 34–46.

Lewin, K. (1951). *Field theory in social science.* New York: Harper & Row.

Lewis, I., & Munn, P. (1987). *So you want to do research! A guide for teachers on how to formulate research questions.* Edinburgh: Scottish Council for Research in Education.

Lieberman, A. (1986). Collaborative research: Working with, not working on . . . *Educational Leadership, 43,* 28–32.

Lieberman, A., & Miller, L. (1984). School improvement: Themes and variations. *Teachers College Record, 86,* 4–19.

McKernan, J. (1989). Action research and curriculum development. In D. W. Kyle & R. A. Hovda (Eds.), The potential and practice of action research, parts 1 & 2 [Special issue]. *Peabody Journal of Education, 64*(2, 3), 6–19.

McLaughlin, M. W. (1987). Learning from experience: Lessons from policy implementation. *Education Evaluation and Policy Analysis, 9*(2), 171–178.

McTaggart, R., & Kemmis, S. (1982). *The action research planner.* Victoria, Australia: Deakin University Press.

Miles, M. B., & Huberman, A. M. (1984). *Qualitative data analysis: A sourcebook of new methods.* Beverly Hills, CA: Sage.

Morgan, G., & Ramirez, R. (1984). Action learning: A holographic metaphor for guiding school change. *Human Relations, 37,* 1–27.

Myers, M. (1989, April). *Teacher research: A policy perspective.* Paper presented at the meeting of the American Educational Research Association, New Orleans.

Oja, S. N., & Pine, G. J. (1989). Collaborative action research: Teachers stages of development and school contexts. In D. W. Kyle & R. A. Hovda (Eds.), The potential and practice of action research [Special issue]. *Peabody Journal of Education, 64*(2, 3), 96–115.

Parlett, M., & Hamilton, D. (1977). Evaluation as illumination. In D. Hamilton et al. (Eds.), *Beyond the numbers game*. Basingstoke, UK: Macmillan.

Posch, P. (1986). *Analytic discourse*. Unpublished manuscript, Klagenfurt University, Austria.

Rapoport, R. (1970). Three dilemmas in action research. *Human Relations, 23*, 499–513.

Reid, K., Hopkins, D., & Holly, P. J. (1987). *Towards the effective school*. Oxford: Basil Blackwell.

Revans, R. (1971). Action learning: A management development program. *Personal Review, 11*, 36–44.

Revans, R. (1982). *Action learning*. Bromley, UK: Chartwell Bratt.

Sanford, N. (1970). Whatever happened to action research? *Journal of Social Issues, 26*(4), 3–23.

Schaefer, R. J. (1967). *The school as a center of inquiry*. New York: Harper & Row.

Schein, E. H. (1969). *Process consultation*. Reading, MA: Addison-Wesley.

Schön, D. (1983). *The reflective practitioner: How professionals think in practice*. New York: Basic Books.

Shumsky, A. (1956). Co-operation in action research: A rationale. *Journal of Educational Sociology, 30*, 180–185.

Shumsky, A. (1958). The personal significance of action research. *Journal of Teacher Education, 9*, 152–155.

Shumsky, A., & Mukerji, R. (1962). From research idea to classroom practice. *Elementary School Journal, 63*, 83–86.

Sirotnik, K. A. (1987). Evaluation in the ecology of schooling: The process of school renewal. In J. I. Goodlad (Ed.), *The ecology of school renewal*. Chicago: University of Chicago Press.

Slavin, R. E. (1987). Co-operative learning and the co-operative school. Collegial learning [Special issue]. *Educational Leadership, 45*(3), 7–13.

Stenhouse, L. (1975). *An introduction to curriculum research and development*. London, UK: Heinemann.

Tikunoff, W. J., Ward, B., & Griffin, G. A. (1979). *Interactive research and development on teaching study: Final report*. San Francisco: Far West Laboratory for Educational Research and Development.

Trist, E. L. (1976). Action research and adaptive planning. In A. W. Clark (Ed.), *Experimenting with organizational life*. New York: Plenum.

Trist, E. L. (1982). The evolution of sociotechnical systems as a conceptual framework, and as an action research program. In A. H. Van de Ven & W. F. Joyce (Eds.), *Perspectives on organization design and behavior*. New York: Wiley.

Walker, R. (1985). *Doing research: A handbook for teachers*. London: Methuen.

⑨ The Practical Work of Teacher Leaders
Assumptions, Attitudes and Acrophobia

Patricia A. Wasley

Everyone seems to be interested in providing teachers with more and new opportunities to lead. The educational community is abuzz with terms that indicate this shift in focus: *lead teachers, teacher leaders, mentor teachers*. Several institutes in various parts of the country have been designed to foster teachers' leadership skills. In Pennsylvania, the legislature provided funds for the institution of teacher leadership positions.

The impetus for this new activity surrounding teacher leadership comes from the widespread recognition that previous reform attempts have been unsuccessful in institutionalizing significant change in schools. Recent reform literature has discussed the creation of lead positions for teachers as a means by which to bolster the professional development of the educational workforce and, as a result, to improve the overall quality of public education (Carnegie Foundation, 1986; Devaney, 1987; Holmes Group, 1986). Those calling for these lead positions believe they will improve several conditions that have long proved problematic in schools:

1. The flat nature of the teaching career
2. The poor learning environment schools provide for adults
3. Autonomy and isolation

These three conditions have emerged as problematic over and over again in studies undertaken in recent years. Work done by Lortie (1975) and reconfirmed by Lieberman and Miller (1984) and Darling-Hammond (1984) demonstrated that because the incentives to remain in teaching are almost nonexistent, there is a steady drain of the very best teachers from the profession. Circumstances necessary for professional growth are also sadly lacking, historically traded for a school structure that protects and ensures professional autonomy. Because most teachers work in individual classrooms with few opportunities to interact with other adults, their own learning and professional growth are stunted. Studies done by Boyer (1983), Goodlad (1984), and Sizer (1984) indicated that the autonomy and isolation in which teachers work perpetuates traditional frontal teaching, which is, unfortunately, the least effective method of instruction.

Conversely, more recent studies by Rosenholtz (1989) and Warren-Little (Little, 1986) indicate that teachers who work in collaborative, growth-oriented settings are more likely to engage in experimentation and more likely to feel professionally stimulated. These studies have fostered the hope that staff development programs that place teachers in leadership positions might build more collaborative settings and foster instructional experimentation and improvement.

Thus those calling for leadership positions for teachers hope that these positions might provide the following:

1. Stimulating career options that allow excellent teachers to grow without leaving the classroom
2. School cultures that foster learning for adults as well as for students
3. Opportunities to reduce the conditions of isolation and autonomy in which teachers have traditionally worked

I would like to argue here that the solutions to these three problematic conditions have already been put to the test in actual practice. Teachers have for some time held leadership positions of various kinds designed to provide personal growth for excellent teachers and professional development for their colleagues. Unfortunately, these roles have gone largely unnoticed and are conspicuously missing from the current discussion on teacher leadership. However, careful examination of these roles indicates that the simple creation of leadership positions is not enough. Without significant systematic contextual change, these positions have as little chance of effecting serious educational change as all their other older, dreary reform relatives.

In order to prove my point I would like to share brief "snapshots" of the practical work of three teacher leaders whom I studied during the 1987–1988 school year. These snapshots confirm that teachers are already filling a variety of leadership roles designed to address the conditions mentioned earlier that impede the improvement of public education. In addition, the snapshots illuminate what I perceive to be the disabling systemic conditions that restrict these leadership positions from achieving their true potential. It appears that leadership positions are weakened by the ways in which they are created, by the kinds of structural working conditions in which they are placed, and by the lack of communication within the educational community. My hope is that the examination of the assumptions and attitudes that undergird the professional development work lead teachers do will encourage the creation of stronger positions—positions which have greater potential to contribute to the improvement of public education.

SNAPSHOTS: TEACHER LEADERS AT WORK

In the spring of 1987–1988 school year, I spent two weeks at each of three sites in order to study the work done by teachers who currently hold leadership positions in public schools. Their fictional names are Ted Smith, Mary Jones, and Gwen Ingman. (For the complete text, see Wasley, 1989.) Each was perceived to be a leader by both administrators and teachers within his or her own district. Each held different kinds of leadership roles within his or her own teaching community. All taught half of the time, and had half-time release to fulfill their leadership responsibilities.

A brief snapshot of a typical working day in the lives of each of these teacher leaders should help to demonstrate the points I wish to make. Risking accusations of longwindedness, I have included incidents from both their work with students and their work with adults because their own teaching plays a significant part in their individual conceptions of teacher leadership. At each site, four of the lead teacher's colleagues were interviewed in order to get a sense of the teaching faculty's response to the positions. Those interviewed were selected by the lead teachers to represent a strong supporter of the position, someone who was neutral to the position, someone who did not support the position, and the local association representative. A summary of their responses to the lead teacher's position has been included in each of the snapshots. The incidents reported in the snapshots all actually occurred but may be reordered to give the reader a true sense of the complexity of the dailiness of these roles.

Ted Smith: Dewey Reconsidered

Ted Smith has been teaching for 22 years at the high school level in a rural southern community and has achieved national recognition for his work with students. His own teaching reflects John Dewey's theories of experiential education in which the student has a great deal of responsibility for decision making and participation. The successful nature of his projects with students has allowed him to form a sort of school within a school and to form an outside corporation, Talking Mountain, of which he is the president. He teaches four classes per day in the local high school, where he is the senior staff person. He holds no formal leadership position within his school, and he does not recognize himself as a teacher leader. The rest of his time is spent running the corporation, housed on a hundred acres purchased with royalties from various projects he and his students have pursued. He works with a board of directors, secures funding from outside sources, manages a large budget that supports a variety of activities, and hires the other teachers who teach with him in the school within a school. The salary paid Ted by the corporation allows him the flexibility to teach only half-time at the local school.

In an attempt to spread his very successful teaching philosophy, he has won a significant grant to support teacher outreach work throughout the country. As part of this grant, he teaches college courses in four different states for teachers who wish to experiment with his teaching methodology and supervises a large support staff that coordinates the activities of those teachers who have taken the course and wish to continue their involvement. These teachers, their coordinators, and the Talking Mountain staff together produce a magazine written by teachers and students that documents their experiments with curriculum and instruction.

Within the school, Ted is treated as any other teacher, given that he is allowed to run his own project. He grades papers, calls parents, and counsels students, just like everybody else. The principal evaluates him twice a year and expects him to attend all faculty meetings and to participate in all other regular school duties. In recent months the principal wrote Ted up for not correctly completing his state learning objectives checkoff.

Ted Smith arrived at his Talking Mountain office at 8:00 A.M., as he did each morning to meet with the corporation support staff for an hour and a half. He reviewed budgets, set schedules, arranged travel, checked on publication deadlines, and dealt with correspondence. He and Kate, his office manager, reconfirmed a schedule of two meetings for that afternoon, when he would drive to the local metropolitan area to teach a college course for teachers. One meeting was an initial visit to a foundation president, a potential funding source; the other, an interview with a possible board member for Talking Mountain. The course Ted taught walked teachers through the process of building an experiential curriculum with students. Arrangements made, Ted moved on to the local high school some ten miles down the road.

When he arrived, his second-period class was working away—spread out all over the floor, some in the makeshift darkroom that protruded into the middle of the room, some at the computers at the back of the room. These students generated a magazine four times a year, and determined their focus, researched their topics, conducted interviews, transcribed the tapes, and then wrote and edited their final articles. In addition, they did their own layout and photography work. The room, like Ted's office, was a riotous mess of stuff, with mountain artifacts hanging on the walls and from the ceiling and stacks of books and papers piled up on all available space. Betty, another Talking Mountain teacher who teamed the class with Ted, was there, busy with the students at the computers. The room buzzed with conversation and quiet industry, sounding much more like an office than a traditional classroom. Ted worked with each group as they needed help and organized the stacks of papers, books, and lesson plans on his own desk. At the end of the period, this group left and another arrived.

Ted used the time between classes to help students refocus their work, find out how they were, and troubleshoot problems with students who needed help. He talks about the necessity of creating a room that is home base for students, a place where they throw their books down, go out to do other things, and then come back to.

The next group of students were participants in a college preparatory research class. Sitting on the floor with the students, Ted helped them generate questions and organize an interview they would conduct with a local Cherokee. The atmosphere was relaxed, but they accomplished their objectives. At the end of the lesson he asked them to describe the steps they had just been through in the generation of an interview: brainstorm interest areas, formulate questions, organize the questions into categories of related topics, refine the questions, and put them into sequence.

After a five-minute break, another large class of students piled into the room. This was the beginning Talking Mountain class focused on magazine production. Two other Talking Mountain teachers joined Ted to team teach this group. After waiting for quiet, Ted had each group report where it was on its particular project and reviewed deadlines and assignments. The group then divided, some staying in Ted's room, some disappearing with each of the other two teachers. Again, Ted ranged around the room to help the students.

At the end of the class, the whole group reconvened to visit with 11 teachers from two outreach networks in neighboring states who had taken Ted's course and were experimenting with their own experience-based curriculum projects. The students talked with confidence and enthusiasm, noting that they worked far more hours in this class than they did in others because they were interested in the material. As the class disappeared with the bell, Ted organized the visiting teachers to observe other Talking Mountain classes that were in session.

The day proceeded, with only half an hour for lunch. Two women teachers sat with Ted in the cafeteria and asked him questions while he bolted a sandwich. One had taken his course, and the conversation revolved around whether it is actually possible to change traditional teaching modes. One of the women whispered to me that while she had been in the community and the school throughout Ted's career, she had never been in his room, nor did she really understand what he was doing. She noted, however, that the entire community supported him—that he had made an important contribution.

Ted's fourth class was another college preparatory English class. This group was working on different kinds of essays. Ted demonstrated one essay form and then went over the evaluation criteria with them. It was a negotiating process in that he asked them to change anything they did not understand and to suggest options for writing that they felt would be more appropriate.

When the bell rang, Frank and Tom, his co-teachers in the magazine class, hurried in so that they could confer quickly over the course and the students' progress, and determine what needed to be done. They then reviewed the individual curriculum writing projects they were involved in. Both Frank and Tom were full-time teachers at the local high school but had been hired by Ted and the Talking Mountain staff to write curriculum guides to describe the teaching process they used in a variety of disciplines. Frank was writing his about music, while Tom was writing his about producing radio shows. Both were past their deadlines and looked sheepish. Ted dashed out the door to drive a couple of hours to the city to attend his two meetings and teach his college course for teachers.

In the car, while driving, he reviewed the end of the year report of the foundation with whose president he was scheduled to meet—his eyes moving back and forth between the report and the winding mountain road. His objective was to inform the president of Talking Mountain's work in hopes that the foundation might be willing to support a new project.

During the meeting, Mr. James, a white haired southern gentleman who appeared to be in his mid-seventies, indicated that he too had done his homework, noting the many awards and grants Ted had managed to secure as a result of his work with students. He asked Ted several piercing questions about the effects of his work on students, indicated his willingness to support the work at some time, but made no commitment. The meeting concluded with a touching exchange. Ted explained his vision for public school classrooms with quiet but resounding passion. Mr. James noted his appreciation of the contribution Ted was making and reminisced over what he believed to be his greatest contribution: He had headed a collaborative, multiracial community task force that had averted racial riots in the city after Martin Luther King's death and established a precedent in the South for multiracial, nonviolent negotiations. The two men shook hands with a great deal of mutual respect.

After a brief meeting with the potential board member, Ted drove to a local university campus to meet with 40 teachers for a two-and-a-half-hour class. Bill, one of the other Talking Mountain staff, was already there, writing the evening's agenda on the board. Ted and Bill ran this class for adults in much the same way they ran their courses for high school students. They started by asking the participants to review the agenda and to make any amendments they felt would be helpful. Next, the class proceeded to discuss a brief section from John Dewey's *Experience and Education* (1938/1963). At several points, they discussed the implications of Dewey's philosophy for their own classrooms. Several of the teachers were very skeptical, given that they had detailed district curriculum guides, testing required by the state, and new state mandates to monitor basic skills.

During the second segment of the class, Ted modeled the process he uses with high school students to help them determine their curricular focus for the term. The teachers generated topics of focus in which they were interested. Ted helped them to evaluate the practicality of each, to determine what kind of work would be required. Finally, he asked them to consider each possible focus in light of the statewide goals for senior English to demonstrate how this kind of instruction can be easily blended to serve the statewide agenda.

During the final segment of the class, teachers from the previous year's course came in with several of their students to talk about their experiential project, where they hit snags, what went well. Most of the description of the projects was done by students who ranged from 10 to 15 years of age. The students appeared perfectly comfortable describing their work and the advantages of this kind of instruction to a large group of teachers. The class concluded by building the agenda for the following week and outlining the work the teachers would do in the interim. Many stayed to discuss their ideas with Ted and Bill after class or to continue the conversation with the visiting students and teachers. One woman's students had determined that they wanted to design billboards along the city's freeway. She had originally despaired, having no idea how to begin. One of the students located a number to call, and, as a result, a major advertising firm had agreed to support them in the design of two billboards. She was all at once thrilled, horrified, and amazed at her third-grade students' audacity and courage! At nearly 10:00 P.M. Ted got back in his car to drive the two hours home. Dinner never materialized.

Ted's colleagues.   While at Ted's school, I interviewed four other teachers whom Ted and I selected together. He believed that the group would demonstrate the range of attitudes toward his work, from support to indifference to disagreement. Of the four colleagues I interviewed, all perceived Ted as a leader. They perceived Ted as a leader because he had the courage to do things differently, because he brought information to them from other schools all across the country, and because he exposed them to the hundreds of visiting educators who trooped through his classroom every year. They also saw him as a leader because he was able to accomplish so much with his students. All of them had taken his course. Perhaps because he did not have a formal leadership position and because his work did not impact their classes in any way, they were most supportive of everything he did. None of them suffered higher class loads or interruptions in their own teaching, nor did they have to donate time to any of Ted's projects. All of them had voluntarily taken Ted's course, yet only one of them indicated that her teaching had changed substantially because of Ted's influence. One of the teachers indicated that she already taught that way. The other two found the class stimulating but indicated that they didn't have the time to learn a new approach, nor did they think the methodology particularly well suited to public schools as they currently exist. Three of them stressed that it was the best college class they had ever had. Clearly Ted's leadership position allowed him enormous professional growth and personal success. While it is clear that he held no formal position in the school, he frequently mentioned his own frustration that so few of his colleagues changed or were affected by his work. It is important to note that all of Ted's colleagues wanted more opportunities to exercise leadership even though they had difficulty imagining what such opportunities might look like!

Gwen Ingman: Instructional Support Teacher

Gwen Ingman is just finishing her tenth year of teaching in a rural elementary school. She had been appointed to a half-time specialist position to support other teachers in their practice of Madelaine Hunter's approach to teaching, which has been labelled Instructional Theory into Practice (ITIP). Gwen's position is formal, created by the superintendent, who sees himself as a great teacher advocate. He is proud of his doctorate, earned at Teachers College, Columbia University, and constantly looks for ways to improve the professional practice of his teachers. An avid reader of reform reports, he concurs that teachers needed to be given more responsibility for the conditions in the classroom, and so he created these specialist positions at the ratio of one teacher specialist per building, although he did so without consulting any teachers or the local education association.

Each Instructional Support Teacher (IST) is selected by the building principal. The ISTs all receive training in ITIP from Dr. Hunter, who has worked in the district for years. Mary, Gwen's principal, believes that the role is very successful in her building. She notes that she observed some very good results in teachers' classrooms as a result of Gwen's work. Mary indicated that Gwen conducts five observations per week and the consequent feedback sessions as well. While Mary has occasionally asked Gwen to work with a particular teacher, she was firm about the fact that they never discussed Gwen's interactions with the teachers. She felt that this was critical to the teachers' trust level. Mary stated that she had worked long and hard to build Gwen's credibility with the staff and that they met regularly to discuss her work.

A teaching librarian in the morning, Gwen visited other teachers' classrooms in the afternoon in order to observe, give feedback, demonstrate such techniques as teaching to objectives, anticipatory set, monitoring, adjusting, or reteaching. She felt that her IST position was designed to support better instruction and to provide teachers with more collegial opportunities. At the same time, she experienced some frustration, since she was assigned a number of other responsibilities—critical thinking curriculum coordinator, absentee principal when Mary was out of the building, assembly coordinator, school bus coordinator, end-of-the-year parent volunteer tea coordinator, peer coaching program coordinator. She also taught a college course in ITIP once each school year for teachers throughout the district; the course was required as a condition of employment. Gwen noted that she was lucky to make three observations per week and that she wished that she and Mary had time to meet more than once a month.

Gwen arrived in her office in the library at 8:00 A.M. Although classes would not start for an hour, she had a number of things to do to keep the library running smoothly, to prepare for her morning classes, and to get ready for the additional responsibilities that were part of her leadership role. She checked her "to-do" list, laminated plastic protective coverings on a few books, and talked to the library aide about all that needed to be done. She then moved to the faculty room to participate in a birthday gathering for one of the staff members before hurrying back to the library to prepare for her first class.

Gwen shared responsibility for the library with Jane, a morning kindergarten teacher. To provide the rest of the faculty with a badly needed half-hour of planning time, each class in the school came to the library for a half-hour session once a week. While Jane taught the majority of the primary classes, Gwen took the intermediate. They also divided the work of running the library. Gwen had responsibility for the audiovisual equipment, for checking new books, for coordinating the library aides. Jane was in charge of ordering new materials, shelving procedures, and the library inventory.

Gwen's first group was Jane's kindergarten class. They tiptoed in and sang a song about being quiet in the library. She spent the first ten minutes checking in books they had taken out and reviewing their plans for the day. The next ten minutes were spent looking for new books. Students who had not returned their library books were not allowed to look for new books and so sat quietly at their desks. Gwen wandered among the others, reminding them to be quiet and helping them to find good selections. The last ten minutes of the class were spent with Gwen reading the children a story they had illustrated. They held up their pictures at the right moment in the story. They clearly thought this was fun. Class over, they lined up quietly, hugged Gwen's knees, and filed out with Jane.

The next class, made up of sixth-graders, was one that Gwen worried about. They were tough students whom she found very difficult to motivate. The students filed in noisily and settled at round tables. Gwen followed the same format—ten minutes to review what they would do and to return books, ten minutes to check out a book, ten minutes to engage in a lesson. She spent a good deal of the time waiting for quiet and disciplining troublesome students. During the time allotted to checking out books, one boy went into a corner of the library, picked up the U.S. flag, and began waving it around wildly. Another group of boys and girls congregated in the reading loft to talk. Gwen roamed the room asking for quiet and moving students who were disrupting others.

She rang a bell to signal that it was time for them to move back to their seats. The lesson asked them to think about how they wanted to be remembered as a class by their elementary school. The students were uninterested and reticent about answering her questions, which required that they review material she had just told them. Gwen stopped repeatedly to ask for their attention. Everyone was drained by the time the half-hour ended. Two more classes filed in and followed much the same format as the earlier two. Then Jane came in to take her turn at teaching in the library.

At lunch, Gwen and the other teachers talked about how much more difficult teaching had become as a result of all the family problems and disruptions in students' home lives. The school secretary came in to tell Gwen that Child Protective Services (CPS) would be there in an hour about a suspected abuse case. Because Mary was out of the building, Gwen would have to be present during the hearings as the principal designee. As Gwen left the lunch table, the conversation had turned to the difficulty of keeping up with yardwork in the spring.

After lunch, Gwen hurried into a third-grade classroom so that she could fit a few classroom visits in prior to the CPS meeting. In this particular classroom, the students were playing a game in which they solved a problem and had to race up to the teacher's desk with the right answer. The students were wild, but working. The teacher then moved to a timed math quiz after calling for quiet. He yelled "Stop!" after a few minutes, and the students moaned and groaned. He then had the students take out their math books. "If you want to do this in class, you can, but you'll have to do it quietly. If you can't be quiet, you'll have to read the book by yourselves at home." At this point Gwen, who had been taking notes unobtrusively in the back of the room, put a note on his desk asking him to schedule a follow-up conference with her at his convenience. Gwen noted that he was working on his administrative credentials and was interested in working on classroom management issues.

The observation lasted approximately eight minutes. Both Mary and Gwen agreed with Madelaine Hunter that brief observations—walk-throughs—were productive for teacher growth. While Mary felt that one could gather substantial information in two to three minutes, Gwen found that she needed between ten and fifteen minutes. She tried hard to be unobtrusive in her entrances and her exits. Gwen noted that while there had been no open discussion among staff members about the focus of the observations or the ways in which feedback should be given, she generally looked for the objective of the lesson, the level of difficulty for the students, the teacher's ability to monitor and adjust the lesson, and active participation on the part of the students. Gwen wrote a brief report based on her notes and shared her observations with the teachers whom she had observed. In the case of this particular third-grade teacher, ten working days elapsed before Gwen and the teacher could find a time that worked for both of them.

Next, Gwen went to the artroom to meet with the art teacher, who had recently transferred from the community college to the elementary level. They talked for ten minutes about an art class that Gwen had observed the week before. Gwen indicated that the teacher had used her time well, that she had involved all of the students by having them hold up their hands to demonstrate that they understood what she was doing. The art teacher noted, "I have them do that so I can understand where they are, and so I can watch those kids. I promised them that if they give me a signal, I won't call them on it if it's wrong. I just want them to participate." There was no further discussion about whether this kind of active participation was productive, whether it really demonstrated any kind of understanding or not. Gwen indicated that the teacher might have extended the lesson by connecting what the children were doing to other cultures. The teacher grinned and said she had wondered whether Gwen would catch that connection. The conversation turned then to their personal lives. The teacher seemed most appreciative of Gwen's feedback.

Gwen felt that she had time for one more walkthrough. She moved toward a second-grade classroom where all of the children were down on all fours in a circle. Heads were down, bottoms up. It was difficult to locate the teacher in the midst of the group. They were studying a box turtle that was slowly lumbering across the empty space in the middle of the circle. Gwen veered away from the doorway, explaining to me that ITIP coaching worked best with direct, teacher-centered instruction, so that she would rather come back on a day when the teacher was conducting a lesson. Since she takes verbatim notes on what the teacher says and does, this kind of lesson is not as appropriate for her observations. She also noted that since they were investigating a turtle, things might get a little wild, as they do in those kinds of unstructured activities. She then hurried on to the CPS meeting.

When Gwen returned to the library, she prepared for the next day's assembly. As indicated earlier, she had a host of additional responsibilities, including assembly planning. She felt very fragmented and unable to spend as much time with the teachers as she would have liked. As the end of the day neared, she grabbed her coat and a few signs and flew out to the playground to ensure that the students got on the correct buses.

As the buses rolled out of the school grounds, teachers began filing into the library for a faculty meeting. Mary, the principal, chaired the meeting, which had been convened to discuss student awards. Mary indicated that she would like to engage in the process of building consensus on how awards should be given to students. She asked that every faculty member air his or her feelings on the subject. The staff's opinions varied. Some believed that the awards were a waste of time. Others believed that giving them was the only way they kept their students in line. One teacher indicated that such awards trivialized the learning endeavor.

After hearing everyone's comments, Mary stated that a policy was being considered that every student in the school should receive at least one award for something well done during the school year. She went on to say that there was considerable research indicating that awards do make a difference to student motivation. She then asked the teachers to vote by secret ballot on whether every student in the school should receive an award and told them that she would get back to them on this issue. The voting concluded the activity on building consensus. The staff went on to discuss guarding keys to the building, earthquake drills, and the spring fun run sponsored by the PTA.

To conclude the meeting, Gwen gave a brief report on how the peer coaching activity had gone. Earlier in the year, Mary had asked that each teacher use periods of release time for peer coaching. One period was to be used for peer observing; the second was for the debriefing session between the two peers. While the teachers had hoped to observe colleagues who taught the same grade, Mary had insisted that they would benefit from watching teachers at other grade levels. Gwen had assigned the peer coaching teams and organized the schedule. No formal evaluation of the coaching had been conducted, but Gwen had asked most people whether they found the activity useful. She shared these informal comments with the staff—most of which dealt with scheduling concerns. Because several people had suggested that they would like to do more peer observing, Gwen created a sign-up sheet/schedule that faculty could use to organize themselves further if they chose. No further follow-up was discussed.

At the end of the meeting, Gwen returned to her office to straighten things up and to prepare for the next day. She left at 5:00 P.M.

Gwen's colleagues. Gwen, too, selected four teachers in her building whom she believed represented the full spectrum of attitudes towards her position. Of the four people interviewed at Gwen's school, all were supportive of Gwen as a person. Two were supportive of her position, while two others were adamantly opposed to it.

The two who supported it believed that it gave them an opportunity to talk to someone else. One hoped that it was a way for her good ideas to be shared with other staff members. Both of them indicated that they had had some very good discussions with Gwen about teaching, although one of them indicated that those conversations were never about ITIP. One described Gwen's position in this way:

> She visits classrooms and gives feedback. I don't know what she's supposed to look at—but to give us a pat on the back. She also helps with problems. She has a great deal of confidence and

offers suggestions in a confident way. She has research to back her suggestions up. She conducts observations in a sensitive way. I never have felt like I was being spied on. I don't know if what she does enters evaluation, but I feel she'd be fair. She does inservice things at our staff meetings and teaches the ITIP classes. I liked the class [which is required of all staff in the district]. She presented ITIP in a nice way—that it is a tool. She really dealt with a less than cooperative group in an excellent way. They were a lot worse than third graders. She had a positive attitude toward her job and doesn't take negative feedback personally.

Those opposed to the position believed that it increased their class size, that it did not improve the quality of their instruction, or that it was an administrative support position. They were angry because they had not been consulted about the role and had little idea what Gwen did with her time or how the information was used. Their feelings were summarized by the following statement made by one of them: "All positions/opportunities which exist are advisory to the administration. They are very superficial and unempowered. They are not truly leadership roles."

In Gwen's case, her leadership role appeared to reduce the isolation of some of the staff. There was little indication that it significantly affected traditional classroom instruction. Gwen's colleagues hoped for greater leadership responsibility, which they envisioned in a variety of ways. Teachers might be represented on the school board. Individual teachers should be encouraged to pursue curricular areas of interest and then share new understandings with staff. Teachers should be provided with opportunities to engage in school-based decision making and in decisions about their own professional growth.

Mary Jones: Demonstration Teacher

Mary Jones teaches in an experimental project in a large middle school in the northwestern United States. At the time of the study, she was just completing the first year of the project in which she and her colleague, Barb, team taught a heterogeneous group of 57 sixth-graders. They had the students for half of the school day and were responsible for math, science, English, social studies, and drug/alcohol education. They added computer instruction when they gained access to 16 computers, which were set up midyear around the perimeter of the room. The women shared a double classroom that could be divided in two by a folding wall.

They taught their students by integrating the curriculum along thematic lines. No students were pulled out for remedial work or extra services; all specialists came to them in the classroom. Mary and Barb designed this program as a demonstration center for other teachers in their building and their district. Both had previously held full-time leadership positions as Instructional Support Teachers, experiences they had found unsatisfactory. During the course of their work as ISTs they had both found it difficult to gain access to the classrooms of the most troubled teachers. They felt that the demonstration lessons they had taught in other teachers' classrooms were treated not as instructive lessons but as catch-up time for the teachers. They felt unable to practice the full range of their instructional program in other people's classrooms. As a result, they designed this demonstration classroom as a place where other teachers could come to work collaboratively on new instructional strategies. The administration in their district and in their building were completely supportive of the project and helped them to get set up and to secure the resources they needed in order to work. However, the administration at the building had asked the women to be relatively quiet about what they were doing. No discussion was ever held to determine how teachers in the building would take advantage of the center.

Mary arrived at school at 7:00 A.M.—much earlier than usual—in order to get set up for the day prior to attending a morning grade-level team meeting. People sauntered in slowly and began to discuss the end-of-the-year field trip to the local zoo. The predominant tone was negative. Eventually, Mary, Barb, and another woman took responsibility for contacting parents, gathering slides of African animals, and organizing the day's activities at the zoo. The tone was chilly, as the staff was clearly divided between those who constantly advocated for students and those who wanted to do as little as possible. Mary left feeling indignant about the other teachers' responses and attitudes.

Students were waiting outside her room. She pulled the wall shut to work with her smaller group and turned on the overhead projector, which showed:

> Good morning!
> Write: How dialogical reasoning (both sides) is different from my
>   side reasoning.
> Which is better? Why?
> Write neatly and put your name on the paper.
> Thank you.

As the students settled in, they began to write. Mary used the time to greet students, listen to their news, and accept work. She posted a list of due dates on the board and then had the students share what they had written with other students near them. She gave them time to revise what they had written—to make their own argument stronger. She then went over the agenda for the day. The students would have an hour and a half of project time—integrated learning time.

As part of their study of immigration, students had been working on a computer simulation that followed an Irish family to the United States. In addition, they had completed family trees and traced their relatives' journeys to this country. They had prepared budgets, created family crests with LOGO, and studied the countries from which their own families came. (Several of the students were recent immigrants—from Cambodia, Iran, and Italy.) Mary reminded them of what had to be done to complete the unit, and then two boys pushed the wall back and all 57 students moved to new activities at once.

The two classrooms of children quickly mixed and paired up into groups of two and three or four. Several groups raced to the computers to make sure that they got on right away. One willowy little girl sat right down to read a Sweet Valley High book. Completely engrossed, she did not move for the rest of the project time. An interracial group of boys— two blacks, an Asian, and a white—pushed four desks together and proceeded to work on their math. One of the boys went to the cutter and sliced paper into the fractional segments they needed for their assignment. As they began their work, they sang "I'm a Little Teapot," complete with unselfconscious motions.

A minuscule girl with long, brown braids named Kittie and a tall Asian girl tried to get their computer partner, Mike, to work with them. Kittie had secured the computer and was insistent that he come and help. He ignored them until her persistence wore him down.

Two other boys worked at a computer together, trying to figure out the LOGO exercises in the package that Barb had prepared for them. They carried on a lengthy discussion consisting of one-syllable words, eyes constantly on the computer screen as they attempted to make a circle and then chart their movements.

"Try this."

"Huh!"

"Oh NO!"

"That's wrong . . ."

"Try this."

"Maybe this."

"Wow!"

Another group of students worked with the math specialist in the center of the room. Others sat on the floor in clumps, using resource books to get information for reports. The room hummed—a noisy place—while Mary and Barb moved from group to group, giving advice, answering questions, offering encouragement.

At this point seven teachers and a central office administrator from a neighboring district came in to visit. They were interested in interdisciplinary teaching and wanted to observe and ask questions. Mary and Barb sent them around the room to visit with students. After about 20 minutes of observing in different parts of the room, the visiting teachers gathered back around Mary, while Barb monitored the classroom. They had a number of questions:

> How do you use the computers, and who schedules the students on them?
>
> How do you give students instructions about what to do during project time?
>
> Where did you get the unit on immigration? Where do you get the rest of your curriculum?
>
> How does the noise level affect you?
>
> How do the specialists know when to come in? Do they ever work one-on-one? I saw them working with two or three children.
>
> What textbooks do you use?
>
> How do you evaluate student work?
>
> What happens to their math skills if you don't work out of a book?
>
> How do you communicate with parents? How do the parents feel about the program?

Mary answered their questions and gathered copies of the materials she and Barb had developed to suit their program, as well as a copy of the parent newsletter they send out once a month. At the end of the question-and-answer period, the visiting teachers were clearly more excited about the possibilities of interdisciplinary work than they were earlier. They asked to send another team of observers, to which Mary readily agreed.

In the meantime, three student teachers had arrived—two to teach lessons and one to observe. Mary and Barb called the students back together, had them switch sides in the room, and pulled the room divider shut. Mary repeated the morning's assignment with the new group of students while the student teacher prepared her lesson. A supervisor from the local university settled into the back of the room to observe. Mary took her place in the back to collect information on the students while the student teacher launched into a halting lesson. Mary took notes and, after a tricky 30-minute lesson, quickly took a cue from the student teacher to resume working with the class.

Mary reviewed the agenda with the students, peeked through the wall, and opened it up for another 40-minute project time. Mary, Barb, and the three student teachers ranged around the room and worked with students. Shortly before lunch, Mary called the entire group to order and asked the students to write for a few minutes about how they had used their project time. These reports were handed to any of the teachers as the students trooped out to lunch. The quiet was quite unsettling.

At lunch, Mary, Barb, and the student teachers sat apart from the rest of the faculty and discussed the lessons the student teachers had presented. They then discussed one child who had a great deal of emotional difficulty, wondering how best to support him. They called the principal over to indicate that they thought that the child had suicidal tendencies. They spent the rest of the time determining the best possible strategies for dealing with this student and his family.

After lunch, Mary went to another middle school in the district to meet with the vice-principal in order to plan a language arts inservice for teachers in the building. The inservice would be held during a half-day special release for the entire English department. The vice-principal hoped Mary would help these teachers move toward a process approach in writing. Mary asked a number of questions about the building's goals and about the English department before suggesting a possible outline. She devised a quick questionnaire that the vice-principal agreed to give to the teachers so that she could determine their levels of awareness. Mary was clearly looking forward to conducting the session and knew many of the teachers.

Back at the school, Mary and Barb threw student papers into their bags to be reviewed that evening before sitting down to a 20-minute private debriefing session with the student teachers, during which they shared their notes with them. Both student teachers felt negative about the lessons they had conducted. Mary said that there was no single way to teach children and that teaching was extremely complex work, requiring small steps, patience, a love of children, and a good deal of reflection. The student teachers left with some issues to ponder, but feeling that they were making progress.

Mary and Barb went out to their cars to rush to the central office to meet with their IST colleagues who had maintained the positions as originally designed. The purpose of the meeting was to enable the two women to summarize their experiences in their experimental program for the rest of the group. They talked about the benefits of their partnership. They told about the long hours they maintained in order to develop curriculum because none existed. They talked about the difficulty they had in dealing with four of the students who did not work well during the class, the demands of working with three student teachers, the work of coordinating numbers of visitors who were interested in observing—all of whom came from districts outside their own. Finally they talked about the discomfort they felt among their own staff members, only two of whom had come in to the center all year. The conversation was deep and thoughtful.

Several of the specialists noted that they did not want to go back to the classroom because it was so much work. Mary replied by saying, "If you value students, then you have to behave in these ways; you have to try to find new ways that work." It was close to 5:30 P.M. when the group dispersed. Mary and Barb hurried off to their cars to go home to eat, to plan for the next day, and to review student work.

Mary's colleagues. At Mary's school only three colleagues were interviewed because time for teachers was in short supply—it was the end of the year. All were supportive of Mary as a person. She commanded a great deal of respect from her colleagues as a talented teacher and as a good listener. While all understood that Mary and Barb were experimenting with a demonstration classroom, two were unclear as to how that affected their own classrooms. Neither had made any attempt to visit during the course of the year. The third teacher was blatantly angry. She perceived that Mary and Barb were given the lion's share of the resources and of the administrators' attention while the rest of the teachers were ignored. She was unclear about the purpose of the project and felt that the rest of the staff needed more information to understand the purpose and the benefit of the demonstration classroom. She had visited the room once and found the room to be quite chaotic.

Mary's colleagues derived little benefit from the leadership role that had been created to provide them with better support. Mary's colleagues also expressed interest in more leadership opportunities. They generally expressed an interest in smaller opportunities for a larger number of teachers rather than a single position.

INTENTIONS AND REALITIES

Given the brief descriptions of these three very different teacher leadership positions, let us return to the conditions these positions were designed to improve. Paradoxes surfaced in each. These positions were designed to

• *Provide career options that allow excellent teachers to grow while remaining in the classroom.* In all three cases, the lead teachers noted that the growth they had experienced as a result of their leadership opportunities had staved off consideration of a career change. They indicated that their own understanding of the complexity of the educational enterprise grew enormously and that their greater understanding made them better able to reach students in the classroom. At the same time, their positions created a tension of loyalties—while they enjoyed their own personal growth, they found that their leadership activities took time away from their students. All felt conflict about this tradeoff.

• *Create a more professional, growth-oriented culture in schools for the participating adults.* Ted's position was not specifically designed to influence the overall culture in his school, and it did not. On the other hand, he did provide a collaborative network for like-minded teachers to foster their growth and development. Teachers who participated in the network thoroughly enjoyed the association with other experimenting teachers and gave significant amounts of their free time in order to get together. However, one of the major topics of their discussions was the isolation they felt in their own buildings. Many found it difficult to change their instruction and their approach to the curriculum in the midst of colleagues who were uninterested. For Ted and the teachers who participated in the outreach networks, their efforts did little to improve the culture of their own school settings.

Gwen's position appears to have provided some of the teachers with a sense of a more professional culture. Two of the teachers mentioned how important it was to them to have someone to talk with. However, three of the teachers interviewed indicated that the focus of the position—ITIP—did not interest them as a vehicle for the improvement of professional practice. Two of them mentioned that the focus and the purpose of the position were unclear. They did not feel that it contributed to a stronger professional culture, and they felt resentful of the time and money spent on it. Thus the position as it was created, with a focus on ITIP, appears to have done little to create a more professional culture.

Mary's position did not appear to improve the professional culture in the school for anyone other than Mary and Barb. Given the fact that their project was in its first year, and given how long it takes to create new structures, it would be unfair to dismiss the potential of the demonstration center. The paradox here is that while the center was created to provide a more professional culture, no time or information was provided to the surrounding staff to enable them to use it.

• *Reduce the conditions of isolation and autonomy in which teachers have traditionally worked.* All of these positions reduced the isolation and the autonomy of the teachers who held the leadership roles but did little to improve these conditions for their colleagues. Both Mary and Ted worked collaboratively with other teachers who were teamed with them in their classroom. All three had the opportunity to see other teachers' work and to discuss teaching with them. However, few of their colleagues had that kind of access to others.

All of the teachers interviewed indicated that they would like more opportunities for professional growth and that they would very much like to have the opportunity to work collaboratively with other teachers. All indicated that they believed they could improve their ability to work with students if they had greater opportunities to engage in professional discussions with their colleagues. These assertions match those of a much larger sample of teachers surveyed in a recent study conducted by the National Education Association (Bacharach, 1986).

Why is it, then, that the leadership positions designed to improve the professional lives of teachers serve so few? Clearly, the assumptions that undergird these positions and the attitudes of those who create them ignore some major systemic conditions that inhibit the actual work lead teachers do.

Assumptions and Attitudes

All three of these lead teacher positions were based on a set of assumptions that reflect the attitudes of those who created them. Ted's case is somewhat problematic in that he held no formal leadership position in his school. Still, he is important because his work reflects the leadership capabilities of entrepreneur teachers. His leadership position was a self-created one, designed to emulate the role of a part-time university professor. Ted's teacher outreach network assumes that the best place to start to change schools is in the classroom and that the best learning takes place when people are voluntarily involved. Thus he goes to local universities in order to gather with like-minded people who are willing to experiment. His approach further assumes that teachers are more likely to change their pedagogy if they have the opportunity to gather with other teachers, and so he provides a structure outside the regular school day for motivated teachers to come together. His approach suggests that teachers should be able to select their own professional growth opportunities and that it is unimportant for a group of teachers from one school to agree on the kinds of opportunities they might provide to improve the collective educational experience of their students.

Mary's original IST position and Gwen's position reflect a different set of assumptions. These positions, created by central office administrators and principals, assume that teachers are not the best source of information when it comes to their own professional development. Two very powerful assumptions follow: (1) Teachers do not know what they need, and (2) teachers are unable to evaluate the effectiveness of a program intended to help them. These assumptions were reinforced by Mary; when she later revised her own position, she consulted with the administrators about the design of the center but did not consult with teachers.

Those creating the positions, when engaged in hierarchical decision making of this nature, assume that teachers are, in Freire's (1968) terms, objects rather than actors in the change process. As a result, things can be done to them and for them without concern for their basic empowerment. This is an extremely limiting view of the way in which learning takes place, of what professional growth is and might be.

The outcome of this kind of decision making is that teachers do not take responsibility for their professional growth over time. Instead, they continue to behave as if those outside the classroom have the expertise needed to examine their practice. Such a stance discourages reflective practice and prohibits a culture of critical inquiry from developing in schools.

These assumptions illustrate the traditional hierarchical nature of decision making in schools. The attitude conveyed to teachers is one that devalues their ability to determine what they need for professional improvement. This in turn discourages any kind of serious reflection on practice as a natural and integral part of their professional life. Such assumptions and attitudes seriously restrict teachers' ability to engage in meaningful professional growth.

No time to grow.   None of these positions builds time into the school day for teachers to practice techniques demonstrated by lead teachers, or time to examine the implications of new techniques on their curricula. Oftentimes, new techniques suggest new materials, fresh performance measures, new assignments for students—all of which take additional planning time on the part of experimenting teachers.

Moreover, the lack of provided time communicates that the act of professional growth is appropriately relegated to individual teachers' prerogatives—that it is not something that should be the professional responsibility of all. If it were really important for all teachers, time would certainly be allocated.

The attitude conveyed here indicates that school time schedules are inviolate and impossible to rearrange, that there is no money in the budget to provide such luxuries as time for professional growth. As a result, many teachers slump in exhaustion as they discover that it is impossible to find the time and resources for their own professional growth while still maintaining their regular classroom responsibilities.

Poor communication. The leadership positions described here were never explicitly articulated to other teachers. The teachers in Ted's building knew little about his work and the opportunities available to them. Gwen's colleagues were never involved in a discussion about the observations she was making, or what criteria she was looking for, or how they might best use her time. Mary was told not to say too much about her position to the teachers in her building, and as a result, they knew very little. The assumption here seems to be that if the roles were made more explicit, they might upset the applecart; because the teaching profession is largely egalitarian, such roles may cause controversy. Given such an assumption, the attitude conveyed is careless of the potential for the position. It suggests that something is being done, but that it is better kept quiet. The lack of communication about the purposes of these positions, and about the ways in which they can provide professional growth for teachers, seriously impedes the possibilities for the positions to have any effect at all.

Acrophobia

These systemic conditions and the resulting attitudes and assumptions indicate that those holding and those creating the positions suffer from a kind of acrophobia—a kind of fear of the professional heights teachers and administrators might achieve if allowed to share a little more responsibility with their colleagues. In the long run, this fear is one that fundamentally contradicts the empowering act of learning. Until teachers are allowed to assess, construct, experiment, evaluate, dismantle, and redesign their own leadership positions and the professional development purposes those positions serve, the potential for professional growth will remain bogged in the lowlands—not a place likely to engender better teachers or better schools.

RECOMMENDATIONS FOR STAFF DEVELOPERS

In order for lead teacher positions to have an impact on the improvement of professional practice for teachers and, as a result, on the school experiences of students, those creating or redesigning such positions should take into account the following insights gained from the problems that plague existing leadership positions.

• Teachers must be engaged in the decision making about their own professional growth. At both building and district levels, this needs to happen in more powerful and convincing ways than simply assigning one teacher to the staff development planning committee. In order for teachers to be truly invested in their own growth, they must have a legitimate voice in the creation, selection, evaluation and reconstruction of the positions intended to serve their needs.

• Those involved in the creation of such positions must engage with teacher leaders and their colleagues to find ways to gain time to work together. In small pockets across the country, school administrators are managing to provide teachers with an afternoon through early release, a morning by orchestrating a late start, a professional development day once a month. Some do it by adding a few minutes to each school day. Others gain time by extending the calendar or the length of the school day. Still others do it by releasing half the building at a time so that one group takes larger classes in order to enable the other half time to work together. The time must be regular and as frequent as possible; there is little hope that one day's early release per year will have the power to effect significant changes. Gwen's case demonstrates that there is little to be gained by providing teachers with one opportunity per year to watch their colleagues teach.

Teachers, like students, learn best when they are allowed to experiment, to think, to discuss, to try again, and to repeat the whole cycle. To assume that instructional improvement will occur without adequate time is ridiculous. We have only begun to explore the possibilities of building legitimate time for professional growth, but that time is critical to the improvement of teaching.

• School people who are responsible for the investigation and the institutionalization of leadership positions for teachers need to ensure that mechanisms are in place to support good communication between teacher leaders, administrators, and other teachers. Good open communication about the roles, their utility, and their possibilities should promote critical inquiry as a norm of practice and should model reflective practice at the same time. At the very least, such dialogue is necessary to model good learning behaviors for students.

The creation of teacher leadership positions that address the kinds of problematic attitudes and assumptions discussed here might well mark the beginning of a radical new stance for teachers, and for students as well. One final caution is necessary. Those creating leadership positions for teachers must ensure that the positions will have some permanence. School districts' well-documented short span of support for innovations might have a significant negative effect on these roles. Teachers have worked in hierarchical systems for the last century. For the last 20 years, all decision making about bread-and-butter issues such as salaries, vacations, and duty times have been the province of association leadership. More recently, many state legislatures have mandated the courses to be taught, the numbers of hours to be spent in each discipline, the texts to be used, and what tests to be administered at what grade level to monitor student progress. As a result, the general teaching force is unused to significant decision-making responsibility as it affects their practice. It is unrealistic to create leadership positions for teachers on a pilot basis and expect them to engage in marked instructional improvement in a couple of years, given their history of noninvolvement. Teachers, like other professionals, must have time to move to better practice through discussion and experimentation without fear that their positions will be eliminated before significant change can take place.

It is not unrealistic to hope that as teachers find themselves legitimately able to reconstruct and improve their own professional practice, they will be able to document the benefits of their self-directed learning. The results might be better outcomes in the classroom, less teacher-centered instruction, improved participation on the part of students, and/or an improved intellectual environment in the school. Such results should lead teachers to examine the legitimate role of students in the classroom, in the same way that they have engaged in the examination of their own role in the educational enterprise. If good learning is, in fact, the act of empowerment, then students should eventually participate in the benefits of the empowerment of teachers.

Not too long ago, I had a glimmer of what this might be like. I was working with a third-grade class as they wrote and raised money for the printing of a book for children at a local hospital. We were struggling with the title; I didn't particularly like their suggestions, and so kept pushing them. Finally, an 8-year-old looked up at me and said, "Pat, figuring out the title of our book is our responsibility, not yours!" I immediately breathed in to bestow upon them my most authoritative, teacher-like voice when I stopped. They were right. They were learning the power of their own voices.

Teachers deserve no less.

REFERENCES

Bacharach, S. B. (1986). *The learning workplace: The conditions and resources of teaching*. Washington, DC: National Education Association.

Boyer, E. L. (1983). *High school*. New York: Harper & Row.

Carnegie Foundation. (1986). *A nation prepared: Teachers for the 21st century* (Report of the Task Force on Teaching as a Profession). New York: Author.

Darling-Hammond, L. (1984). *Beyond the commission reports: The coming crisis in teaching*. Santa Monica: Rand Corporation.

Devaney, K. (1987). *The lead teacher*. Paper prepared for the Task Force on Teaching as a Profession, Carnegie Forum on Education and the Economy.

Dewey, J. (1963). *Experience and education*. New York: Collier. (Original work published 1938)

Freire, P. (1968). *Pedagogy of the oppressed*. New York: Seabury.

Goodlad, J. I. (1984). *A place called school*. New York: McGraw-Hill.

Holmes Group. (1986). *Tomorrow's teachers: A report of the Holmes Group*. East Lansing, MI: Author.

Lambert, L. (1988). Staff development re-designed. *Phi Delta Kappan, 69*(9), 665–668.

Lieberman, A., & Miller, L. (1984). *Teachers, their world and their work: Implications for school improvement*. Alexandria, VA: Association for Supervision and Curriculum Development.

Little, J. W. (1986). Seductive images and organizational realities in professional development. In A. Lieberman (Ed.), *Rethinking school improvement* (pp. 26–44). New York: Teachers College Press.

Lortie, D. C. (1975). *Schoolteacher*. Chicago: University of Chicago Press.

Rosenholtz, S. (1989). *Teachers' workplace: The social organization of schools*. New York: Longman.

Sizer, T. R. (1984). *Horace's compromise: The dilemma of the American high school*. Boston: Houghton Mifflin.

Wasley, P. A. (1989). *Rhetoric and reality: A study of lead teachers*. Unpublished dissertation, University of Washington, Seattle.

10 Developing an Ethos for Professional Growth
Politics and Programs

Judith Schwartz

The rhetoric of school reform has usually included an examination of the conditions that make teaching attractive to talented young people and that sustain talented mature people for the length of a career. Educators have longstanding knowledge about what makes a professional life attractive for people at all stages of their careers: the intrinsic value of the enterprise; the challenge of growth, change, and development; the opportunity for increasing financial rewards, status, and authority as one matures; and the opportunity to mentor young people and thus enjoy a degree of influence on the future of the profession to which one has dedicated one's working life. These conditions represent the general paradigm of professional growth for all adults. Yet, throughout the educational community, this question continues to be posed: What will attract talented people into choosing education as a career, and what conditions will sustain them over a lifetime of professional work?

EXAMINING THE PROBLEMS

Educators also know a great deal about the conditions that must exist to have schools that are effective, caring places in which all children can learn. What, then, creates such a gap between the knowledge of what makes for excellent schools and excellent teachers, and what exists in all too many school districts in the country? Among the host of conditions two major problems stand out—one is the use of money, and the other is the training of teachers. Too much money has been spent in ineffective ways. Oftentimes, contributions from external sources provide add-ons that have little long-term impact on altering the basic organizational structure of schools or altering the worklives of classroom teachers. The solution to many educational problems has been to add another special short-term teacher, hire an aide, develop another pull-out program, or deliver another already packaged program designed by people far away from the school site. Little money has been spent on rethinking the roles of teachers, altering the seven-, eight-, or nine-period high school day, or rethinking the structure and allocation of teacher time, while still providing custodial care for children.

The second major problem in changing schools is the training and acculturation of young teachers. Teachers are trained to think of themselves as individuals operating within the four walls of a classroom. Their training and evaluation has to do with mastering the rudimentary elements of managing the complex organization of the classroom. While they may learn many of the elements for successful classroom management and subject-matter competence, almost nowhere in their training are they taught how to work within an institution as complex as a school. Those training to be teachers should study organizational theory, leadership skills, conflict resolution techniques, group interaction, and group process skills. They need to be given assertiveness training, so that when they interview for positions they can ask of school districts, "What does this school district have to offer me? What are the professional development opportunities available in this district? Where can I be five years from now, if I do a good job?" It is quite possible that if more teacher training institutions practiced interviewing techniques with their best students, greater changes would take place in school districts in shorter periods of time. Prospective teachers should be trained to think of themselves as the future leaders of the profession, imbued with a mission and skilled in negotiating the thorny paths of change. Because they are not trained to think of themselves as powerful, they cannot embrace the uncertainty and challenge of experimentation and oftentimes seek certainty, conformity, sameness, and tried-and-true solutions.

DEVELOPING AN ETHOS
OF CONTINUED PROFESSIONAL GROWTH

Fulfilling the qualifications for the professional life of teachers requires a norm of institutional excellence and an ethic of continued growth as a standard for schools. How does this ethos develop, and how can it be sustained in an organization?

1. We know that it cannot be imposed.
2. It must be a reflection of the collaboration of all parties involved.

3. The stakeholders—students, teachers, parents, and administrators—must feel ownership of the process.
4. This ethos must be true to teachers' vision of their moral and ethical purpose.
5. This purpose must be proclaimed, celebrated, and clearly articulated by the leadership of the school district, particularly the superintendent.

School districts can support and encourage teacher leadership from the preservice experience young people have in their student teaching through the mentoring and other leadership roles teachers need to assume as they mature in their professional life. This teacher leadership enhances the learning environment for students and encourages talented people to remain in the profession. What follows is a description of the program of an upper-middle-class community that supports and encourages teacher leadership even when conditions do not necessitate a change in existing school structure.

A CASE STUDY OF TEACHER LEADERSHIP, COLLABORATION, AND PROFESSIONAL GROWTH

The school district, which I will call Midvale, enjoys a national reputation for educational excellence. It has a highly supportive community, which provides strong financial backing for education, and students who are motivated and, for the most part, hard working. Educational excellence is prized among teachers and students. The staff is well educated; many are leaders in their fields. Yet the school system is essentially conservative and traditional in its curriculum and structure. Change is often difficult in a district that is so successful.

The conditions that sustain the norm of collegial and institutional excellence pervade the system, as attested to by every indicator of educational success. The premise of this chapter is that this ethos of excellence and caring arises and is sustained by the norm of teacher leadership, the maintenance of an expectation of success, and a relationship between the administration and the teachers' association that promote and encourage teacher leadership in the day-to-day workings of the district.

The models of collaboration that exist within the school district create and sustain an institutional norm of excellence that enhances teachers' leadership roles. This collaboration is legitimate and formal. Through the relationship between the teachers' association and the ad-

ministration, based upon collective bargaining, or collective and collaborative problem solving, teachers have a legitimate avenue for seeking
new roles, advocating educational change, and taking risks. The programs now in place in the district are a result of this collective and
collaborative effort. These efforts can be categorized as those that increase teachers' opportunities within the classroom and those that increase opportunities beyond the classroom. The goal of all programs is to
create a norm of institutional growth. These collaborative efforts between teachers and administrators are sustained and made legitimate by
the incorporation of these programs into the teachers' contract, thus
insuring their support and continuation.

The Teacher Center—
Building Teacher Professionalism

A teacher center provides an organizational structure by which
teachers can assume greater control and authority over their professional
lives while enjoying the support of their constituents within the educational community. Collaborative enterprises such as teacher centers enhance teachers' status and authority, thus furthering professional educational goals while providing for sustained risk taking.

The center, an integral part of the professional environment in the
district for more than 20 years, is governed by a board, the majority of
whom are teachers appointed by the teachers' association, and funded by
monies negotiated by the association and the board of education, tuition
payments of teacher participants, and a state competitive grant. The
programs of the center are monitored by this policy board, the board of
education, and an accreditation committee made up of teachers and
administrators. Each semester about 60% of the staff participate in voluntary, afterschool programs. Over a three-year period more than 90% of the
staff participate in teacher center programs. This high level of sustained
involvement reflects the way in which the center has been institutionalized within the school structure. The center program, developed over the
years by the joint efforts of teachers and administrators, has enhanced the
professionalism of teachers, encouraged their growth, and, most importantly, enriched the school system and made it a better place for students.

Participation in the teacher center activities is itself a professional
growth opportunity for teachers. Teachers coordinate all the programs
offered through the center. This means that they are in charge of developing a course or seminar, managing the budget of the program, hiring
the consultants or teaching the courses themselves, evaluating the projects of the course participants, and determining whether participants

will receive inservice credit. A teacher can be a student one day and a course leader the next—thus teachers teaching teachers becomes a reality for a good many of the staff. Teachers recommend programs and often find themselves teaching or managing courses that they have suggested. Since the staff is confident that the center will be responsive to their need, they are quick to assume responsibility. The norm of professionalism is supported in concrete ways by placing teachers in charge of their own professional growth.

Peer Review: A Professional Growth Model

After three years of study, research, and pilot projects, the district and the teachers entered into a new agreement establishing a review system for tenured teachers that operates on a model of success rather than deficit. A joint committee determined that most of the teachers in the district were successful and that the traditional model of supervision—goal setting, two observations, and an end-of-the-year report—did little to meet the requirements for accountability or professional growth. Therefore the committee established a new program designed to provide opportunities for teachers to develop an individual plan for performance review. With the agreement of a supervisor, a tenured teacher may establish a personal plan for professional growth for an evaluation year. Teachers determine the goals they want to meet, design the plan, establish the timeline, and develop the method of documentation. Teachers may choose to work alone, with other teachers, or with an administrator. The basic requirement of the program is that the teacher work on an area of personal growth. The administrator and teacher agree to the elements of the plan, and the teacher is then free to implement the program. At the end of the year a teacher completes a one-page form that asks "What did you do? What did you learn?" Most teachers complete far more documentation than the one page and may offer to serve as resources to teachers who are beginning the evaluation procedure. Teachers often combine courses they are taking at the teacher center with their evaluation procedure so that they can seek additional support as they pursue an area of professional growth.

A teacher, provided with a stipend, offers support to other teachers involved in the program. Each year, about half of the teachers eligible to do so pursue individualized programs that they have designed to enhance their professional knowledge. The program is administered by a joint committee of teachers appointed by the association and administrators appointed by the superintendent. Again, the norm of professional growth is assured by a legitimate collaboration effort between teachers and administrators that can be sustained through a contractual agreement.

Teacher Research

Over the past few years, the teacher center has been training teachers in classroom research. These programs began with the development of a writing-process program. Teachers trained in these procedures for classroom research have spoken at conferences, videotaped and developed archives of effective lessons, and published the results of their work in professional journals.

As more teachers became interested in developing research skills, the center needed to find a way to encourage new participation as well as to continue support for those teachers already engaged in research. In a program called "Research in Curriculum Development," teachers new to the research process were coached by those teachers experienced in classroom research. These research associates are given a stipend by the teacher center for their work with fellow teachers. Thus teachers new to research are individually guided through the process, and experienced teachers are rewarded for their time and knowledge. This program has led to the development of research programs in many areas of school life and to professional publications, so that teachers have developed their own avenues for professional communication with colleagues on matters of educational interest.

Professional Projects

Another longstanding contractual program that provides a sum of money for teachers' professional development is administered by a joint committee of teachers appointed by the association and administrators appointed by the superintendent. This committee awards money for professional projects that teachers choose to do individually or with others. Projects vary and may include summer work, the development of new classroom curricula or schoolwide pilot programs, attendance at conferences or workshops, or provisions for visiting scholars. In all instances, teachers apply for these grants in a competitive program. These funds are separate from district funding for curriculum projects designed to implement district curriculum goals. Adjustments to the program are made by the committee and approved by the teachers' association board and the administration. The legitimacy of these roles for teachers and the knowledge that the teacher members of the committee are selected by the association encourages teachers to work with colleagues to maintain and expand their opportunities for growth.

Teacher Initiative and New Instructional Strategies

Recently, teachers wanted to learn more about strategies for using cooperative learning in the classroom and, as a consequence, develop further skills in using these techniques for department and school groups. Planning began with a committee of teachers who had had some experience with cooperative learning and consultants who had achieved recognition in the district for the work they had already done in other teacher center programs. Based on that meeting, teachers planned a year-long course in cooperative learning that required teachers to register in teams with buildings or departments. In the first year of the program every school in the district was represented by at least one team of people.

In the second year, teachers wanted both a repeat of the introductory course and an advanced program. The teacher coordinators modified the program based on the evaluations of the first-year group and their own experience. Enthusiasm for the program was so great that it was expanded to include a summer program for the high school English department and an all-school, full-year program for two elementary faculties. In each case the elementary principal scheduled the course to meet on faculty meeting days once a month throughout the year. That initial course, based on teacher interest, has now developed into a district commitment supported by funds from the teacher center and the district curriculum office. Thus teachers have had clear evidence in this case, as in many others, that teacher initiative will result in changes and adjustments in district commitments.

A Teacher Mentor Program

Again developed through a joint committee of teachers and administrators, the mentor program provides support for teachers new to the district. Most of the teachers hired in Midvale are experienced teachers who need support in adjusting to a new school and new expectations. The role of the mentor is to help speed up this acculturation process. Mentors are chosen from a list of teachers who have volunteered or been recommended for the assignment. The matches are made by the committee based on school, grade level, or subject area. The mentors meet together for a semester to help them define their role and work out any problems that may occur with their new teachers. This seminar is run through the center and offered for salary credit. First-year mentors receive credit for the program, and second-year mentors receive a stipend for their efforts. A teacher who coordinates the program is also paid a stipend. The mentor program and the mentor role have now been institutionalized in the district through the negotiated contract. The mentor committee is now developing an internship program for new teachers.

Teacher-Administration Collaboration

A few years ago a teacher center seminar conducted by the president of the teachers' association and the superintendent of schools discussed the rash of national reports on restructuring the teaching profession. This seminar was the project of a joint committee charged through a negotiated memorandum of agreement with finding ways of increasing professional opportunities for teachers. The joint committee prepared two reports, which it shared with the faculty at each of the schools in the district. The most recent report accepted by the administration and the association provides for teacher participation in the hiring, supporting, and assessing of all school personnel. Teachers now sit on all committees that interview and recommend hiring of all teachers and administrators in the district. The mentor program provides support for those new to the district, and teachers have requested that they participate in the discussion about retention of new tenured personnel in the district.

The development of most programs within the district is accomplished through joint teacher-administrator committees. In all cases, the teachers are appointed by the teachers' association and the administrators by the superintendent. In this way, teachers have developed a strong sense of their importance in developing school policy and encouraging innovation in the district. These committees have tackled issues such as health insurance, coaching, chaperoning, student teaching, health and wellness, school governance, and budgeting, in addition to all the programs mentioned above. Through this structure teachers have confidence that change within a well-established structure is possible.

These collaborations have been nurtured over a long period of time and sustained because of community support. Essential to the development of these programs has been the articulated goal of the teachers' association to increase professional opportunities for its members. While there exist the usual difficulties of personality conflicts, changing membership of committees and the board of education, economic constraints, and other external pressures, this norm of excellence is prized by all those in the educational community.

These collaborations, established in a positive environment with teachers in charge of their own growth, can overcome some of the problems of "turf and territoriality" that plague much of school reform. Because these roles are temporary, they provide opportunities for people to move in and out of roles depending on interest and other circumstances. Organizations, particularly schools, that depend on hierarchical roles cannot ever create enough rewards to meet the needs of all the talented people within the organization. Through these short-term opportunities, the district is trying to create systems that encourage workgroups of experts in particular fields to solve problems; these are organizations where authority and leadership are lateral, not vertical, and rewards accrue to the group accomplishing the task. These matrix organizations of flexible workgroups may be the model that helps build new collaborative and cooperative roles for teachers and administrators. The institutionalization of programs through the teachers' contract gives teachers the confidence that commitments they make to change and experimentation will not be undermined or limited. While this is only one way in which a district can develop a professional environment that encourages talented people to enter and remain in teaching, it does succeed in supporting professionalism as a norm and making teaching a more attractive career.

11 Foxfire Teacher Networks

Hilton Smith & Eliot Wigginton
with Kathy Hocking & Robert Evan Jones

The conventional way to write about a complex program like Foxfire Teacher Networks is to provide an overview of the program, then get into the specifics—moving from general to specific. Foxfire, though, is not exactly conventional, and neither is its outreach program; so it is not surprising that presentations about it seem to work best when we start with something specific, something that conveys the flavor and major features of the program, then move into generalities. Most readers will associate Foxfire with student-generated anthologies about Appalachian culture, under the general rubric of "cultural journalism." Beginning in about 1967, the success of that instructional venture attracted teachers, primarily of secondary language arts, to Foxfire workshops on cultural journalism. In the process, Foxfire evolved into an approach to classroom instruction applicable to all content areas and all grade levels, and that is what the teacher outreach program intends to disseminate. Now to an event that captures the essence of the program.

During the second and final week of the Foxfire course for teachers we conduct each summer at Berea College, the members of the Eastern Kentucky Teachers Network (EKTN) and their students conduct a showcase—an exhibit of the projects they have completed in their classes during the previous year.

To visit the 1989 showcase is to enter a whirl of student energy. In Berea's student center exhibition area, second-graders hold forth at a table displaying two magazines of "mountain tales" they produced during the year; others in their seven-person team explain the large photo display of their projects, while several work the crowd, selling the magazines. Nearby, two members of a high school social studies class describe their magazine project, *Yesterday's Memories*, answering inquiries by teachers from a graduate course at the University of Louisville. (They are impressed with the students' ability to articulate the what and how they learned from the experience.) Across the room a teacher who travels

193

from school to school on an arts council project plays *Simple Gifts: Songs from Leslie County Schools*, an audiocassette his students conceived and produced. Nearby, three students in a local history project, "Remember When," explain their project "for the umpteenth time" to a knot of other students and teachers. A teacher and her fifth-graders from a parochial school explain the scrapbooks, photo montage, and posters that document their project on family histories, "Time Changes." Across the stage area, seventh- and eighth-graders conduct tours through a huge display about their project, a magazine called *Memories*. Visitors flow through the exhibits, nonstop, for four hours. Adolescent curiosity overcomes shyness, as students from different schools conduct overlapping dialogues about "their project" and "their teacher." And their teachers watch, responding when needed, sharing insights and frustrations with one another.

It is an event that displays the Foxfire approach at its best, often serving as the single most persuasive activity for the teachers participating in the course. It is also a powerful demonstration of the vital role that teacher networks like EKTN play in the professional lives of the teachers seeking to implement that approach to classroom instruction.

About the "Foxfire approach": We settled on *approach* as the most accurate term to describe the shared practices in which we engage when we teach, rather than *method* or *technique* or *style*. We reserve *philosophy* and *pedagogy* for the fundamentals on which the Foxfire approach and similar approaches rest. Each practitioner of the Foxfire approach then designs his or her specific strategies and classroom techniques, built on those shared practices, appropriate to specific teaching assignments, curricula, students, and personal strengths. (See Appendix A for the current version of those shared practices.)

TEACHER OUTREACH PROGRAM

In 1986 three organizations, including Foxfire, received grants from Mr. Bingham's Trust for Charity to see what each could contribute to overall education for literacy. Foxfire's teacher outreach program, funded by that grant, seeks to answer this question: By encouraging and equipping teachers to use the "Foxfire approach" to instruction in their classrooms, K–12, in all content areas, would we contribute to literacy education? Mounting a program like that means that we are one of many groups seeking to influence what goes on in classrooms. Each of those groups is in some way unique, and each contributes to the array of instructional options.

A longer view, moreover, reveals a whole parade of similar endeavors: launched with decennial regularity; fueled with sincerity and fervor; funded by foundations governments, and school districts; endured by pliant, resilient teachers; applauded by the sponsoring groups; and hardly noticed by generations of students. The same view reveals that very few succeeded in fulfilling the goal of changing how teachers teach and what students learn. Someone likened the array of abandoned programs to a roadside junkyard. The analogy is only slightly overstated.

We are mindful, therefore, that if we succeed in some measure, *we also might contribute something useful to the overall pool of strategies for changing how teachers teach.* Groups launching other promising approaches to instruction could consider those strategies in designing their own programs.

One caveat should be clearly understood: Although we have had some success thus far, and although we try to draw lessons from what has succeeded and failed in the past, we do not have a formula or blueprint to follow. Not yet; maybe not ever. Our plan is to start with our best notions, then revise and improvise as needed. If we are thoughtful, and if we document what we do, and if we analyze what we document, maybe we can succeed in some measure. Success, for us, means three things:

1. Teachers involved in this endeavor continue to use and develop this approach to instruction, continue to unfold the underlying principles, and continue to help each other over the rough spots.
2. Their students arrive at subsequent stages of schooling and life with enhanced prospects for making the most of every opportunity, fulfilled as individuals, equipped to learn on their own.
3. The approach is recognized by school administrations as effective.

We also should be able to show *how* all that happened.

That sounds familiar, doesn't it? With slight alterations, that sort of language appears in all sorts of documents and perorations every year. And it probably sounds overambitious. Maybe it is. However, besides being thoroughly chastened by our awareness of the junkyard of previous initiatives, we have two assets that provide just enough confidence to tilt at very large windmills: (1) Nearly all of us involved in this endeavor are classroom teachers, most of us with a number of years in service, and (2) the approach that drives the way we teach seems to resonate with something fundamental in just about everyone—it just seems right.

It is also reassuring to draw on the heritage of past efforts to improve classroom instruction derived from the same pedagogical principles as those that inspire Foxfire. These efforts did not endure as intact programs or organizations, except in small pockets in special circumstances, but the stories of successful classes in that heritage glow like warm coals. It is one time when being new is not the point.

With caveats and basic rationale in place, we can provide a capsule description of our teacher outreach program and how teacher networks fit into the overall scheme. Several of the points in this description are amplified later.

Foxfire Course

The program starts by our acceptance of an offer to provide a Foxfire course for teachers at a university or college, usually for graduate credit. The course is supposed to encourage and equip teachers to use the approach in their respective teaching situations. In our original plan, we considered four or five such courses during the year as manageable, while providing enough variety of populations and schools to really test our assumptions about what might change how teachers approach class-room instruction, especially in terms of improvements in student literacy. Each course is supposed to model the Foxfire approach, so that partici-pants experience first-hand what their own students would experience in a Foxfire classroom as well as observing the techniques of those of us who conduct the courses. (A side comment: It is interesting to notice the teachers who feel acutely uncomfortable with being placed in roles that require participation and ownership of the class process, then observe the stages of insight as they realize that they are uncomfortable because they, like their students, are unaccustomed to a "democratic classroom.")

As texts, we usually use *Sometimes a Shining Moment* (Wigginton, 1986), with emphasis on "sometimes," and John Dewey's *Experience and Education* (1938/1963). Throughout the course, we try to model a prag-matist's perspective of practice enlightened by theory, and theory, in turn, refined by reflection on practice. Most teachers are not accustomed to that perspective on classroom practice, but nearly all, as it turns out, derive considerable satisfaction from that kind of pedagogical engage-ment.

Most of the courses are offered during the summer (10 to 14 intensive days), the rest during the school year (usually once a week, evenings, for a quarter). As a culminating activity to demonstrate mastery of the principles of the Foxfire approach and the underlying pedagogy, and as a running start for the next school year, each participant picks a chunk of curriculum from his or her respective teaching assignment and designs a hypothetical "project" that would engage students in a thorough mastery of that chunk and set them up for the next chunk. The teachers participating in the school-year courses can actually engage their students in designing the project, sometimes completing parts of it before the quarter is over. Those projects, hypothetical and "real," are thoroughly critiqued by their peers in the class and turned in at the conclusion of the course.

For accuracy, we need to note that several of the networks now conduct staff development programs for school districts or consortia of districts—same design, length, and requirements as the graduate course. Whether done as a graduate course for credit or as a staff development program, the participants elect to participate, most out of a genuine sense of need rather than mere curiosity. Basically, we avoid captive or mandated audiences.

Support System

That is the course, but it is only the starting point. After that, there has to be a support system—an organized array of people, materials, resources, guidance, counsel, perspective, encouragement, strategies, and so forth, designed primarily by the participating teachers themselves. We knew that school districts would not be able at this point to provide the kind of support system newly trained Foxfire teachers would need. We also knew that few existing support systems provided opportunities for teacher-to-teacher colleagiality, something many teachers said they needed and wanted. Teacher networks had the most promise of providing the support needed. We learned very quickly that networks simply did not form spontaneously, so we made a point to try to arrange for someone to serve as a network organizer at each site very early in the program. We also learned very quickly that the organizer needed some sort of formal status as a Foxfire teacher network organizer, some operating funds, and continuing involvement with Foxfire. That led to the position of network coordinator, a person who facilitates the beginnings of an entity of some sort that teachers be in touch with and into which they could focus concerns, ideas, and energy. (More about coordinators later.)

Every course and staff development program "graduates" a group of teachers who start implementing the Foxfire approach in their classrooms. Each individual in those groups has unique teaching assignments and constituencies; each has unique talents and perspectives. What they try in their classrooms needs to be documented, captured, and analyzed for the benefit of all of us. Whether another "shining moment" or an utter disaster, and anything between, those efforts need to become part of our shared frame of reference. All of us need to know what worked and why, what did not work and why. To encourage teachers to share their experiences beyond heartfelt encounters at network meetings, we converted our journal for teachers, *Hands On*, into a vehicle primarily for teachers' case studies. Most teachers are not comfortable as documenters, or as writers, so this continues to be an uphill effort. Recent developments in "classroom-based research" or "teacher-as-researcher" have eased the way considerably.

To coordinate all this, we set up a teacher outreach office at the Foxfire Center in Rabun County, Georgia, home base for Foxfire. That office, with a staff of two, maintains files of participating teachers' projects, edits *Hands On*, assumes oversight responsibilities for the integrity of the overall effort, dispenses grant funds to the networks, tracks current trends and research in education as they relate to Foxfire and teacher outreach, coordinates the meetings of network coordinators, and coordinates the evaluation of each component of the program. Until recently, the teacher outreach office practiced "benign neglect" regarding the networks, staying out of the way as much as possible. We will elaborate on this point later.

When we present the teacher outreach program to groups of educators, most start asking questions about the funding of the networks. Foxfire reallocated a substantial portion of its original outreach grant to help the "original" five networks get started. As those networks stabilized, they began to raise some of their own funds, primarily through grants. The host institutions of the newer networks, referred to as type two networks, sign an agreement that obligates the institution to provide most of the initial and continuing funds for the network, including the coordinator's salary. Though the networks, original and type two, are becoming more financially independent, we have realized that at least some portion of the networks' funding will have to come from a coordinated national fundraising effort. We will have more to say about funding in the closing section of the chapter.

THE NETWORKS

Networks of teachers certainly are not new. Foxfire networks may be somewhat different in that they form in the regions around the sites where we offer the courses and staff development programs, then begin to assume responsibility for the course itself and for supporting the efforts of other teachers beginning to implement the Foxfire approach in their classrooms. They have some of the voluntary, spontaneous qualities we associate with networks of the 1960s, with a strong overlay of permanence and professionalism. However, they become interwoven with the educational establishment—conducting staff development programs, writing curricula, making presentations to professional gatherings—rather than assuming the countercultural postures associated with 1960s networks.

Of course, not everyone who takes a Foxfire course joins a network. At some sites we never hear from about half of the members of the class after the last session. Still others take the course, then go to their classrooms to perform exemplary feats of pedagogy with no thought about networking. They are rare, and about 25% selfish; what they do does not become part of the body of experiences to share with other teachers.

Recognizing the Need

As we stated earlier, one thing we knew for sure when we started the outreach program was that simply putting teachers through a course or an inservice program does not change how they approach instruction. They may learn a strategem or two, but their basic approach is not changed. We knew that from personal experiences, too. We ourselves have sat through many hours of staff development programs, rarely rewarded with something we could use. More to the point, we have done a few staff development presentations, with the same results for those in attendance.

The usual pattern of most teachers, including those of us on the Foxfire staff, has been to get through the staff development program on whatever is current, then go back to our classrooms, close the door, and teach very much as we had been. When we did try something novel, it was in approximate isolation and often not the result of a staff development program. If it worked, fine; if it did not, no one knew but us—and maybe the students. There was little sense of participation in something larger, something important beyond our classrooms. If we encountered unexpected adversity, we could easily slip into the default mode of teacher-centered, text-based instruction.

Another perspective came from about 20 years of experience conducting workshops in cultural journalism, resulting in about 200 projects similar to the *Foxfire* magazine. The retrospective lesson was valuable, if chastening, in planning the outreach venture:

> Despite the newsletter Foxfire published [predecessor of *Hands On*], and despite a national conference for [magazine] advisors and their students . . . those of us who were producing magazines were so widely scat-

tered across the land that we were never able to develop a strong sense of mission as a group. Each of us labored alone in his or her classroom, isolated from each other as well as, often, from our own peers. With only the most sporadic of communications possible, *there was no collective momentum, little philosophical growth, and no discernible net change in the way host schools conducted business with their students or their communities.* (Wigginton, 1989, p. 25; emphasis added)

Then we considered the context in which teachers operate currently:

1. Increased state control of schooling, hence loss of local autonomy, hence less teacher autonomy
2. Increased pressure for their students to achieve, especially on standardized tests
3. Teacher evaluation systems, often perceived as unfair and unhelpful
4. Increasingly specific curriculum requirements, hence less latitude in which to be creative
5. Greater teacher visibility and vulnerability because of criticisms of schooling
6. Lack of adequate funding for instruction
7. Little support for trying new approaches
8. Very little opportunity for professional dialogue with peers in the same school

Substantive studies by participant-observers like Seymour Sarason (1972, 1982) confirmed what we intuitively suspected: Encouraging and equipping teachers to adopt a different approach to instruction—as opposed to using a new text or a supplementary classroom activity, such as a simulation—requires that they own the process of adoption, can try the new approach at their own pace, and adapt the approach to their local situations and personal abilities. That requires time and attention well beyond what courses and workshops are designed to provide—quality time and extended attention rarely provided by school district staff development programs, professional organizations, or school administrations. As Joyce (1990) states bluntly in a recent piece, "Teaching was the only complex vocation whose personnel were not provided with time for collegial activity or rigorous and continuing study of their work" (p. 16).

More important than any other factor, however, was *the articulation of confirming sentiments by teachers participating in the outreach courses.* The course critique after the 1989 course at the University of Washington elicited summative comments such as these:

I gained an understanding of a missing link in my teaching style and thinking. Through the presentation and modeling, I learned a great deal about human dynamics, facilitation, and promotion of critical thinking. Being able to ask nitty-gritty questions about classroom functions as well as philosophical concerns was invaluable.

This approach gives me a total structure using strategies for change. It was all useful, memorable, and life-changing. Every activity had a purpose that was evident.

This course started me toward a higher level of learning, teaching, and awareness. It has opened my eyes in a more vivid way into really understanding that every child learns in different ways.

More to the point, the same course critique drew these responses to the question, "What's next?"

It would help me to have a support group I could call to be a sounding board. It would be nice to be able to meet with a group to share our experiences and ideas.

I need to stay in touch. I need support. I need to have a feeling of contribution and completion.

The group needs to form a network; a support group that continues to grow, prosper, and change.

It was that kind of thinking that led to the idea of teacher networks as the major vehicle for the follow-up we knew was necessary for teachers to successfully implement the Foxfire approach on a scale of more than a few inspired, isolated individuals. We did not know how the networks would form, organize, or operate. We did know that the teachers themselves were the ones to decide those issues.

That meant, of course, that there was no model or formula to follow in establishing networks. There would be long conversations and meetings, awkward moments, loose ends, false starts, personality clashes, and several additions to Murphy's Law. We assumed that if the need was genuinely there, and if we helped nurture promising initiatives, that viable networks would form. We knew that the networks would have to be teacher centered in the same way members' classrooms are student centered, and for the same reasons. Members would have to have a direct influence on the networks' directions, programs, and organizations.

Network Coordinators

The network coordinators, of course, are the folks who provide guidance and energy for all that to happen. The selection of the coordinator was different in each of the networks, so their backgrounds and personalities are correspondingly different, often reflecting the characteristics of the region. Most have considerable experience in classroom instruction, several are tenure-track college or university staff members, several have experience with other nonprofit educational organizations, and a few have prior experience as program administrators. All are independent, self-starting, willful, discerning, optimistic, practical, very hard working, durable, and willing to take risks. In most cases, the coordinator set up an office in his or her home, sometimes moving into office space at the sponsoring institution later. Either way, there is an individual with an address, telephone number, word processor, and copier—a base of operations.

Connie Zimmerman, coordinator of the Skyline Teachers Network in Atlanta, shared her perspective on the roles of the coordinator:

> The role of the coordinator? Invite, nudge, nurture, encourage, listen, support, provide Kleenex, ask questions. Be enthusiastic, positive, realistic with an idealistic perspective—practical, in other words. [The coordinator] also has to keep the wheels greased behind the scenes so that the democratic process has the structure in which to develop. I also learned not to provide too much too soon. You overwhelm everybody. For example, no one wanted to deal with the network's budget and finances. You'd think they would want to own the pursestrings from the outset. Only when there were situations about which they cared did they get into finances.
>
> You have to think ahead and you have to be opportunistic. [The university] gave me a chance to teach in the undergraduate teacher education program. It's not part of my coordinator's roles, but it has given me a place in the scheme of things around here that really helps. That goes along with developing friends in key places. That's not in the cynical sense. They are friends because they see things the same way as I do; it's just a matter of developing those relations further, toward mutual benefit.

In the second year of the outreach program the coordinators developed a general list of a coordinator's roles and tasks, so that someone considering becoming a coordinator would have an idea of what he or she was getting into (see Appendix B).

Benefits

Growth of each network has been "organic," varying from region to region, reflecting the personalities of the leaders and members, and responsive to the concerns and visions of the members. Sharon Teets (1989), coordinator of the East Tennessee Teachers Network (ETTN) based at Carson-Newman College, provides a coordinator's view of a Foxfire network. Teets's comments also serve as a summary of recent developments by the networks.

> In the seminars for teachers, the Foxfire approach is modeled by Wigginton, other Foxfire staff, course instructors, and, increasingly, teachers who have completed the seminar in previous years and who have successfully implemented the approach in their own classrooms. After the first summer seminars, some teachers did develop projects with their classes. But after experimenting with the approach many teachers frequently had questions and concerns that they wanted to discuss with Wigginton and other teachers. It soon became apparent that teachers wanted and needed ongoing support from and dialogue with other teachers who were trying to implement the Foxfire approach.
>
> In all of the areas where courses have been offered, teacher networks have now been established, with a paid coordinator, to facilitate the ongoing exploration of the method. Each network assumes responsibility for its own activities, and each has its own character. All of the networks have regular newsletters, small group meetings, retreats for in-depth exploration of topics of interest, and writing workshops to develop articles about their classroom projects for publication in *Hands On*.
>
> In addition, some of the teachers are also participating in a computer-linked network with one another, in which information can be shared with other teachers and students across the states and nation. Individual networks have secured funding to send teachers for additional training experiences, such as participation in the Bread Loaf summer school. As the teachers become more confident in the use of the approach, they have shared their experiences at a wide variety of professional meetings. More importantly, they have also begun to participate actively in teaching the seminars for new teachers each year. Finally, a second Foxfire course is offered for teachers who have completed the first seminar and who wish to explore the approach in greater depth, thus providing for continued professional development. (p. 2)

That description brings the discussion to this question: What do network members derive from participating in Foxfire-affiliated networks? We asked that question on several occasions to groups of active network members. Each network generated slightly different lists, but the results were very similar each time.

The single most common answer: The network provides support and opportunities for members to *continue growth in an approach to instruction.* There were the usual narratives about the value of the emotional support network members provide one another, but the most nods accompanied assertions about the value of sharing classroom techniques and, contrary to those who say teachers are not interested in theory, the value of understanding better the philosophical underpinnings of the approach, of being able to articulate why this works. Knowing that they were participating in the continuing development of the approach, versus implementing something already formulated, heightened the potency of network experience. (It is worth noting that the courses for teachers do attract a fair number of teachers whose whole career has been built on dutiful implementation of instructional designs assigned and expected by their supervisors. Nearly all experience some uncertainty in considering changing their approach to classroom instruction, particularly when they realize that designing such changes involves active collaboration with their students. A few pull back from the edge and make no attempt to change; most at least have begun the process of altering their approach to instruction.)

Networks provide *opportunities for teachers to develop leadership.* The most obvious is the chance to serve in leadership roles in the network itself, especially as part of the executive committee or as members of committees with specific roles, such as planning showcases or reviewing small grant proposals by other teachers. They assist other members with instructional problems, conduct inservice programs for school districts, and participate in presentations about the Foxfire approach to educational organizations. They write case studies that are published in *Hands On* and other journals. Network members often attend professional meetings, giving speeches with their students, representing the network, and bringing back the message of the event to the network. Perhaps the most rewarding form of participation is helping teach the course for teachers.

Another way of viewing participation in a Foxfire-type network is as a form of *teacher empowerment,* at least in terms of classroom instruction, if not necessarily in terms of school-based governance. Teets (1989) points out:

> Virtually all of the reports calling for reform in the schools speak to the need for teacher leadership in the schools (Gross & Gross, 1985). The teaching and research skills acquired in the Foxfire course, combined with opportunities for leadership in the teacher network, would appear to be helpful in fostering the empowerment of teachers to assume leadership roles in the broader educational community.

Just as the most thorough evaluation of the Foxfire approach to date has used qualitative research methodology (Puckett, 1989), the best evidence of the Foxfire potential for teacher empowerment comes from informal conversations with teachers who are active network participants. These lively conversations are often inspirational—teachers talk about the Foxfire approach as changing their personal lives, as well as those of their students. They describe projects that range from in-depth exploration of issues such as homelessness, personal safety, environmental pollution, as well as the use of student-written material as alternatives to the exclusive use of basal readers for reading instruction. One teacher documents a significant increase in the reading level of her second graders as a result of her change in reading instruction.

Teachers' descriptions of qualitative changes in students' behaviors and attitudes, as well as skills, are numerous. Taken together, they are convincing evidence that the teachers using the Foxfire approach feel that they can make a difference in their classrooms. Perhaps it is not the articles documenting student projects in *Hands On*, or the actual content of what the teachers are communicating in conversations that is impressive. Instead, it is the fervor and enthusiasm with which they express themselves.

The Foxfire approach appears to contribute to empowerment through the modeling and the subsequent use of the core practices with students. Reflective thinking, problem-solving, community involvement, and participation in the democratic process are at the heart of the core practices. As teachers help students to become empowered, they, too, seem to develop the skills for their own empowerment.

A significant issue in the empowerment "struggle" is that of being "permitted" to become empowered. The Foxfire seminar grants teachers that permission. Teachers are viewed initially as competent, capable individuals who *can* design, with their students, effective instruction that meets and exceeds state-mandated guidelines. Opportunities for ongoing dialogue with other teachers and professional development activities contribute to enhanced competence and confidence. Recognition of competence, whether in the form of publication in *Hands On* or in other journals (Stumbo, 1989), or in assuming the role of teacher in the Foxfire courses, adds to the teacher's self-confidence as a leader in the profession. (p. 3)

One fact of life for any teacher is the question of *how to deal with a principal and other administrators* who may not understand or appreciate the differences between the Foxfire approach and teacher-text-centered instruction. Helping teachers deal effectively with administrators is one service teacher networks perform, while at the same time serving as a resource for administrators with instructional problems in their schools. The effect is a form of empowerment that does not involve anyone's feeling as though he or she is giving anything up.

Participating in a network gives a teacher the sense of being able to make a difference by *being part of something larger, of being connected with other movements that are complementary to Foxfire, as well as with the other networks*. Many network members claim to have a bigger picture of schooling, reforms, and opportunities in education—and a realization that there is a place in which to share those discoveries—as a consequence of networking. Being funded out of the same grant that funds Foxfire's outreach program, at least in part, tends to incline the networks' members to pursue certain common goals. We attempted to articulate those goals toward the end of the second year of the program, spurred primarily by coordinators' requests to have a clearer sense of mission for the networks. From a coordinator's summary of the meeting:

Hilton [Smith] presented the three expectations FF has for networks:

1. Laboratory settings for the field-testing of this approach (hands-on, community based, student directed) to teaching. It is critical to remember that Bingham provided funds for experimentation within the area of "literacy" enhancement, and that must always be a clear focus. (Literacy is broadly defined to include writing, reading, listening, speaking, research, communication, peer-teaching, "the creation of meaning." This does not exclude projects in math and science.)

2. An arena to conduct ongoing systematic classroom research and then documentation, including such products as case studies, narratives, sharing sessions.

3. Establishment of a two-way dialogue as both a reliable source of information and also a way to uncover conversations already underway. While Foxfire and the coordinators put out information to teachers through courses and other communications, we must be able to get information back from teachers on whether a "practice" is on target or off-base. Teachers are collaborators in this ongoing research.

There are *tangible benefits* from participating in a Foxfire network. Networks sometimes pay for classroom projects, travel to professional conferences, and substitutes so members can attend network events. Networks can arrange for resources for classrooms, such as consultants, experts, and materials.

The result of members' critiques of EKTN's fall 1989 network meeting bring many of those somewhat abstract points to life:

I was able to gather good info for a seventh-grade KY literature study I am developing.

Better working knowledge of what is happening. After having the Berea workshop, then trying to get started at home [school], this weekend has really helped pull it all together. It has been very affirming.

A renewed purpose. It was very frightening to me when I tried some of the things Wig spoke to us about (e.g., memorable experiences) and they flopped royally. I tried every terminology [on the students] and could never connect. I now feel that was okay and now I can go on and try from another [angle].

Many times I have felt that our organization was somewhat unorganized. I'm learning that "unorganized" is a poor evaluation. We are becoming, still.

That I'm not the only one having fear as I begin; that I am not alone out there. Even the veterans are still learning (there are no experts); that we will progress, helping each other. A renewed zeal to return to school and push forward.

Throughout this program we conducted evaluations, from simple "course critiques" after each of the courses for teachers, to a systematic assessment of the overall effectiveness of the course conducted largely by an outside evaluator (phase-one evaluation), to an ambitious effort to assess the extent to which the teachers participating in the courses for teachers and networks actually implement the Foxfire approach in their classes (phase-two evaluation) (Eddy, 1989; Eddy & Wood, 1989). We used the results, usually confirming but also often chastening, to revise the course and to alter the ways both teacher outreach and the networks did business. (Our only regret is that we did not allocate nearly enough funds for evaluation in the original grant proposal.)

These excerpts from the "Final Thoughts" section of Eddy and Wood's (1989) pilot study for the phase-two evaluation suggest the kind of searching analysis we have received from that evaluation:

What I am saying here is not directed at the network, nor at any of the hard, diligent, and difficult work any of the coordinators are doing. Rather, it is to raise a question about the overall direction of this thing. Is our intent to really help change the way children are treated in schools? If so, let's not forget this is a difficult process—and it occurs classroom by classroom, school by school. It only happens when the real workers in the struggle, . . . [the] teachers, are supported, nurtured, and promoted everyday. If that is our intent, then we need to rethink some of what we are doing. We need to go at this from the bottom up, with the teachers working on building the networks to be what they want them to be.

In only one school [in this network] did we find the philosophy moving out to other teachers. This school also seemed to have the greatest connection with the coordinator, Wigginton, and [Foxfire]; it also had an involved and supportive administrator. However, even in this setting most of the philosophy was limited to "Foxfire projects."

The bottom line for me is that the [Outreach] Program makes sure it doesn't wake up one day and find itself operating in a kind of splendid isolation, its teachers "doing their own thing" and talking only to one another—unaware that there were "fellow travelers" elsewhere moving in the same general direction.

It did seem to me that a good many teachers were finding they actually *could* teach effectively by giving up more and more control and letting their students take on greater responsibility for the *way* things were taught, if not yet for *what* was taught. It wasn't a major change certainly, but it was beginning to happen.

Benefits to and gains by teachers are of little value unless those benefits and gains show up as gains by the students in their classrooms. We are beginning to accrue evidence, both anecdotal and empirical, that students in Foxfire classrooms gain at least as much in academic knowledge and skills as students taught in more conventional, teacher-text-centered modes, and considerably more in the affective domain, especially manifested as enhanced attitudes toward learning. One of the tasks for the networks is to develop ways to accrue that kind of data, a task that has frustrated many educational researchers. Whether those gains will endure as those students move through later grades, college, and vocations we will not know until and unless we conduct some sturdy longitudinal studies of those students. We are developing plans for that now.

TO BALANCE THE VIEW

As the phase-two evaluation comments suggest, none of what we described above has happened easily, or painlessly. In each network there were times when all of us began to doubt that the network would become anything more than a coordinator and a small group of skeptical teachers with very tentative commitments. At times, the process had a two-steps-backward-one-step-forward feel. In other words, it was not a matter of providing the course for teachers, then watching while groups of eager teachers banded together into a potent pedagogical force. Network members occasionally withdraw or simply fade away; some lose patience with the pace of growth and development; for some the network is not political enough (Foxfire networks are consciously and firmly nonpolitical with regard to the educational systems in which they operate); sometimes the direction of the network becomes incompatible with some members' values and priorities; and sometimes a teacher just does not have the energy to add another commitment on top of career and family.

Now that we can see what the networks are becoming—professional organizations with the wide range of programs and services outlined above—it is clear why each was slow to attain "critical mass" and become a viable organization: Teachers are interested in participating in a venture that promotes professional and personal growth; they are not interested in simply getting together to share classroom stories, nor in replicating their school district's staff development programs. In other words, what teachers wanted and expected was much more than we had calculated—more than a support group, but more like a support group than the other professional organizations to which they belong.

In a proposal narrative, Reva Luvaas-Hess, coordinator of the Bitterroot Network, makes this point clear:

> Given the fact that the network teachers actually own the network and insist on both quality control and quality service to them as practitioners, the networks may have the power to change the way schools of education intersect with the field of education. No longer content to be "trained" and then dropped, alone, into the fray, these teachers will insist on a continuing dialogue [and] quality attention to their continued growth and expertise.

Developing such an organization is a daunting task in itself, especially when participation is voluntary on the part of people who are already overworked and overcommitted. Participation in a Foxfire network means helping organize and run the network, unlike organizations in which you pay your dues, get a newsletter, and decide whether to attend the national convention in Miami. There's no headquarters office in D.C., with a staff of 200. Instead there is an awareness, sometimes uncomfortable, that the only way for a network like this to succeed is to make commitments to provide mutual support for present and future members. We are not accustomed to joining an organization like that, especially one in which we would be charter members—without a clear charter to follow.

Zimmerman, as a network coordinator, provides an analysis of why critical mass was so difficult to attain and what she thinks provided the impetus for enough momentum for the Skyline Network to coalesce into a working unit:

> First of all, distractions abound: (a) A lot of these folks see gradu-ate courses as a means, not an end. Getting through the courses and getting the degree is *the* point. So they're not really taking the course with the idea of getting involved. [Note: Of the 16 teachers who took the Georgia State University course in spring 1987, Con-nie is the only one who participates in the network.] (b) School districts have their own programs, of course, and many of them are not voluntary. (c) Then there's university bureaucracy. In our case, the course can be taken only as an elective, so it doesn't fit into many teachers' programs of study. That gives us really low enrollments in our courses, so we're not getting the numbers we need for the network. And they haven't done much to promote the course, either. (d) Then sometimes the problem is ours: Some members of the network become "protectionist" about the net-work and maybe turn off people who might otherwise join.
>
> I'm not really sure what happens for a network to get critical mass, but I know there were several things that helped us. First was just getting enough people through the course so that 50% par-ticipation was enough to be a network, not just buddies. After that was the retreat where we met the EKTN members; that gave everyone the realization that we were in something national. And our first real live working session, where we were *doing* some-thing, and the presentations with their kids to other teachers, with press coverage. The best experience for several of them was help-ing teach the workshops last summer.

A coordinators' discussion generated a list of additional hazards:

1. Geographic distances and the reluctance of school districts to provide substitutes for teachers to travel make it difficult to get members together. Telephone discussions, letters, and computer linkups cannot substitute for face-to-face interactions.
2. The membership question: Who are the members? Everyone on the mailing list? Only those who participate? Those who say they are members? Sometimes these questions intersect with the personalities

of the members, resulting in divisiveness or a sense of exclusion felt by some potential members. Then, who decides who are members?

3. That, in turn, contributes to the identity problem: Just what is this organization? The obvious answer, it is what the members make it, turns out not to be obvious at all. Each member has his or her own concerns, teaching assignments, memorable experiences, and world-view. Some are more vocal and demonstrative; some are looking for a cause in which to enlist; some are arming themselves for battles with the system; some are walking, talking bundles of uncertainty, seeking alignment; some are veterans, just about burned-out, seeking renewal. The network, then, tends to become many things to many people—too many things, so that no one is quite sure whether it is worth the commitment.

4. Without a core of shared perceptions, the network is slow, sometimes agonizingly slow, to develop a sense of mission. Until the members somehow broaden their perceptions to embrace issues and concerns beyond those of their own classrooms, the identity, personality, and membership problems are difficult to overcome.

A Skyline Network member's letter to the coordinator, following a network meeting that dealt with some of those issues, provides a personal perspective that undoubtedly conveys what most network members feel:

> On the way home, I was thinking about what you had asked regarding little or no involvement in Skyline by some who have taken the course. In retrospect, I can see the "stages" I've gone through with this new way of teaching. There came a time, as you know, when I really "caught on" and got so excited I couldn't wait to implement some of these things I was learning. At the same time, all of us are sort of treading water just to keep up with everyday duties.
>
> So when you start asking things like, "Can you attend a retreat? A Spring meeting? Do a newsletter? Contribute articles? Etc . . . ," it is a little frightening *at that point*. I remember thinking, "This may be too much of a commitment for me right now."
>
> However, now that I have gotten my feet wet and tried a few Foxfire-type activities (big and small), I feel more "qualified" to do and contribute to some of the above-mentioned things. At first, it was just too overwhelming.
>
> You continued to call, write, and boost my confidence, and that is probably what kept me involved (little as it was) in Skyline. Your visit to my school really helped, too. I liked the way you got

right in there with the kids and got to know them so easily. I think
it made them feel a part of it also. I realize, however, that you
can't do it all. So, I was thinking perhaps we could sort of pair up
with another county and have a coordinator in each one who
could occasionally get everyone together, say on that side of town.
Or, maybe it wouldn't have to be geographically close . . . I don't
know . . . I was just thinking . . .

The letter conveys the apprehensions and the emergence of a cautious commitment. It serves as a poignant summary of much of what we
have said above—and a reminder that schooling involves people, not
automatons who can be reprogrammed to do different tasks. It also
confirms our initial assessments: that the need and potential are out there,
that this would be a difficult task, and that teachers would see it through.

THE PROSPECTS FOR THE FUTURE

The primary teacher outreach grant runs out in June 1991. We plan to
continue, albeit in an altered fashion. The staff of the Foxfire Fund will
pursue a different agenda after June 1991 (completing its twenty-fifth year,
coincidentally), with a continuing commitment to the outreach program.

Nearing the end of the fourth year of this endeavor, we have seen nine
networks form, with several more prospective networks taking their first
steps. (A list of networks and coordinators is available from Foxfire Teacher
Outreach, Rabun Gap, Georgia 30568.) Inquiries and overtures continue to
arrive at a rate of about one a month, to which we respond carefully,
avoiding the tendencies of both the one-quick-hit event and the teach-one/
tell-ten paradigm. The consensus of all of us associated with this endeavor
is that we will be cautious about adding new networks, staying well within
our resources to make sure we do not lose the integrity of the approach or
the process, thus maintaining the grass roots orientation of the program. (As
of this writing, we have just begun our first venture in training the staff of
an entire school, with prospects for several others.)

Recent developments in the governance of some of the networks
suggest some patterns for the maturing of the networks and the solution
to some of the problems of growth. The Bitterroot Network initiated a
system of "area contacts," network members who agree to be responsible
for maintaining contact with the other network members nearby. Each
"area" also agrees to take on particular chunks of the network's business,
for example, coordinating the showcase. Bitterroot is also considering a
more formal arrangement of regional coordinators, network members
who agree to oversee the area contacts in their region of Idaho. (Bitter-

root is spread over the entire state of Idaho, which means up to a twelve-hour drive, one way, to get to some of the network members.) Skyline, somewhat more compact geographically but seriously fragmented by the presence of over 20 school districts in the metropolitan area, set up a core group, similar to an executive committee, to conduct its business. EKTN, the oldest and largest network, set up an executive committee about two years ago, then found funds to release one of its members, Jenny Wilder, to serve as a teaching associate. Jenny takes on the responsibility for working with teachers in the network, while the coordinator, Debbie Bays, focuses on fundraising and administration.

One observation from the pilot for the phase-two evaluation turned out to be prescient about our future directions (Eddy & Wood, 1989):

> Although "management" may not be precisely the word for the continuing relationships the [Teacher] Outreach Office will be working out with each of the networks in the next few years, the pressures on it will surely mount on other scores as new units are added. [Long list of tasks follows.] All this and probably much more will compound the pressures and demands on Teacher Outreach as each new network . . . is established.

That happened. In addition, as the networks became larger and more stable, they insisted on more coordination of the whole outreach effort, including the networks themselves. That was the end of the policy of benign neglect described earlier.

The networks will affiliate into some sort of federation of networks and teachers, with a headquarters staff to coordinate the whole operation. Most of the networks will become more closely affiliated with the sponsoring institutions, hence becoming more financially independent.

With the cooperation of various members of the networks who have used and critiqued some of our Foxfire course guides, we will convert them into a series of handbooks to be published by Heineman-Boynton/Cook. A video or two about the Foxfire approach will complement the handbooks.

In the summer of 1990, we offered the basic course for teachers 14 times, at sites in ten states. Most of those courses and workshops were conducted by the network coordinators and network members, assisted by "mix-and-match" teams of teachers from other networks. Formats for the courses have become increasingly imaginative, responding to what we have learned from the evaluations and to the exigencies of local circumstances. For example, several of the networks now require attendance at several follow-up sessions during the year following participation in the course. Others build network involvement into the commitment prospective participants make in order to be considered for participation in the course. In some cases, the demand for the course is such that the network can screen participants, seeking teachers whose performance seems to indicate real interest in using the Foxfire approach, trying to create classes with equal representation of elementary, middle, and secondary teachers, and creating cadres of Foxfire teachers in the same school.

One surprising development was the request from members of several networks for a follow-up course, one that digs deeper into the pedagogy and provides connections with other, complementary approaches. In the summer of 1990, we offered that course, referred to as the level-two course, at three different sites around the United States. Combined with courses and staff development programs offered during the school year, we offered the level-one course about 20 times and the level-two course about 6 times from June 1990 through May of 1991.

Whatever the direction, locations, and programs, the teacher networks will continue to be the primary vehicles for outreach—at least for the forseeable future.

The preceding phrase holds two caveats. First, we could come upon other, more promising support systems for outreach. It is doubtful that this will happen, but the pragmatic premise on which this whole edifice is built says that we attend to what works, not necessarily what we have been doing. (Imagine *that* premise becoming the operational paradigm of education!) Second, we have not set this endeavor up as a necessarily enduring parallel to the systems states and school districts already operate. If teacher performances and student achievements support the contention that this approach should be one of the approved and supported approaches to classroom instruction, then its practitioners will weave it into the organizational structures of the educational establishment. Then some of the resources and energies that currently support more traditional modes of instruction will flow into the classrooms and support systems for those teachers who elect to use it. Will that happen? It may be hard to imagine, but it is not unthinkable. In the meantime, there are new networks to develop, current ones to secure, and lessons to learn.

Appendix A
THE FOXFIRE APPROACH
PERSPECTIVES AND CORE PRACTICES

Perspectives

This revision of what was entitled "Nine Core Practices" reflects the latest in our collective thinking about the principles and practices characteristic of the approach to instruction we pursue. The principles and practices are not scriptural; they are not oracular. They come from reflections and discussions on the results of classroom instruction. In time, we will refine them again to reflect the best of our thinking.

This approach to instruction is one of several promising approaches, some of which share many of the same principles. We've found that as each of us explores this approach in our classrooms, we broaden the base of experience from which we all work, often engaging other, resonant approaches and strategies. The approach never becomes a "recipe" for any teaching situation, nor a one-best-way teaching methodology that can be grasped through one-shot, inservice programs or teacher "handbooks."

In the contexts in which most of us work, few of us will be able to say that our instruction manifests all of these "core practices." Being able to assert that is not the point. The point is to constantly review our instructional practices to find ways to engage each core practice. For when that happens, we and our students experience the most elegant and powerful results this approach can deliver.

The goal of schooling—and of this approach to instruction—is a more effective and humane democratic society. Individual development through schooling is a means to that goal. Often given rhetorical approval while being ignored in practice, that goal should infuse every teaching strategy and classroom activity.

As students become more thoughtful participants in their own education, our goal must be to help them become increasingly able and willing to guide their own learning, fearlessly, for the rest of their lives. Through constant evaluation of experience, and examination and application of the curriculum, they approach a state of independence, of responsible behavior, and even, in the best of all worlds, of something called wisdom.

Core Practices

1. *All the work teachers and students do together must flow from student desire, student concerns.* It must be infused from the beginning with student choice, design, revision, execution, reflection and evaluation. Teachers, of course, are still responsible for assessing and ministering to their students' developmental needs. Most problems that arise during classroom activities must be solved in collaboration with students. When one asks, "Here's a situation that just came up. I don't know what to do about it. What should I do?" the teacher turns that question back to the class to wrestle with and solve, rather than simply answering it. Students are trusted continually, and all are led to the point where they embrace responsibility.

2. Therefore, *the role of the teacher must be that of collaborator and team leader and guide* rather than boss. The teacher monitors the academic and social growth of every student, leading each into new areas of understanding and competence. And the teacher's attitude toward students, toward the work of the class, and toward the content area being taught must model the attitudes expected of students—attitudes and values required to function thoughtfully and responsibly in a democratic society.

3. *The academic integrity of the work must be absolutely clear.* Each teacher should embrace state- or local-mandated skill content lists as "givens" to be engaged by the class, accomplish them to the level of mastery in the course of executing the class's plan, but go far beyond their normally narrow confines to discover the value and potential inherent in the content area being taught and its connections to other disciplines.

4. *The work is characterized by student action*, rather than passive receipt of processed information. Rather than students doing what they already know how to do, all must be led continually into new work and unfamiliar territory. Once skills are "won," they must be reapplied to new problems in new ways. Because in such classrooms students are always operating at the very edge of their competence, it must also be made clear to them that the consequence of mistakes is not failure, but positive constructive scrutiny of those mistakes by the rest of the class in an atmosphere where students will never be embarrassed.

5. A constant feature of the process is its *emphasis on peer teaching, small group work and teamwork.* Every student in the room is not only included, but needed, and in the end, each student can identify his or her specific stamp upon the effort. In a classroom thus structured, discipline tends to take care of itself and ceases to be an issue.

6. *Connections between the classroom work and surrounding communities and the real world outside the classroom are clear.* The content of all courses is connected to the world in which the students live. For many students, the process will engage them for the first time in identifying and characterizing the communities in which they reside. Whenever students research larger issues like changing climate patterns, or acid rain, or prejudice, or AIDS, they must "bring them home," identifying attitudes about and illustrations and implications of those issues in their own environments.

7. *There must be an audience beyond the teacher for student work.* It may be another individual, or a small group, or the community, but it must be an audience the students want to serve, or engage, or im-

press. The audience, in turn, must affirm that the work is important and is needed and is worth doing—and it should, indeed, *be* all of those.

8. As the year progresses, *new activities should spiral gracefully out of the old*, incorporating lessons learned from past experiences, building on skills and understandings that can now be amplified. Rather than a finished product being regarded as the conclusion of a series of activities, it should be regarded as the starting point for a new series. The questions that should characterize each moment of closure or completion should be, "Now what? What do we know now, and know how to do now, that we didn't know when we started out together? How can we use those skills and that information in some new, more complex and interesting ways? What's next?"

9. As teachers, *we must acknowledge the worth of aesthetic experience*, model that attitude in our interactions with students, and resist the momentum of policies and practices that deprive students of the chance to use their imaginations. We should help students produce work that is aesthetically satisfying, and help them derive the principles we employ to create beautiful work. Because they provide the greatest sense of completeness, of the whole, of richness—the most powerful experiences are aesthetic. From those experiences we develop our capacities to appreciate, to refine, to express, to enjoy, to break out of restrictive, unproductive modes of thought.

    "Scientific and artistic systems embody the same principles of the relationship of life to its surroundings, and both satisfy the same fundamental needs." (John Dewey).

10. *Reflection*—some conscious, thoughtful time to stand apart from the work itself—is an essential activity that must take place at key points throughout the work. It is the activity that evokes insights and nurtures revisions in our plans. It is also the activity we are least accustomed to doing, therefore the activity we will have to be the most rigorous in including, and for which we will have to help students develop skills.

11. *The work must include unstintingly honest, ongoing evaluation for skills and content, and changes in student attitude.* A variety of strategies should be employed, in combination with pre- and post-testing, ranging from simple tests of recall of simple facts through much more complex instruments involving student participation in the creation of demonstrations that answer the teacher challenge, "In what ways will you prove to me at the end of this program that you have mastered the objectives it has been designed to serve?" Students should be trained to monitor their own progress and devise their own

remediation plans, and they should be brought to the point where they can understand that the progress of each student is the concern of every student in the room.

Appendix B
NETWORK COORDINATOR RESPONSIBILITIES

The following list of tasks came from network coordinators. The tasks listed are those that seem to be common to all networks, and do not include tasks that are unique to each network and coordinator's situation.

1. Help teach the Foxfire course for teachers, working with network teachers to accept increasing responsibility for the course each year; make logistical arrangements for the course, including scheduling, lodging, meeting rooms, etc.
2. Coordinate recruitment and selection of teachers for the Foxfire courses.
3. Serve as the contact person and negotiator with the sponsoring institution.
4. Serve as a member of mix-and-match teams to teach the Foxfire course at other sites.
5. Critique course participants' units of study or projects submitted for the course.
6. Review minigrant proposals and monitor progress of minigrant projects.
7. Keep track of equipment purchased with minigrant funds.
8. Help teachers write and edit case studies to fulfill minigrant obligations and for publication in *Hands On*.
9. Seek resources and connections for network members.
10. Prepare an annual budget with the network, maintain accurate financial records, submit financial reports as required by the Teacher Outreach Office.
11. Prepare quarterly reports of network activities; distribute to the Teacher Outreach office, foundations, and other networks.
12. Obtain copies of any publicity that network members receive and send copies to Teacher Outreach.
13. Maintain an accurate network mailing list and send a copy to Teacher Outreach.
14. Develop a network newsletter and other communications as needed. Share with Teacher Outreach and other networks.

15. Coordinate professional presentations by network members and their students; watch for opportunities for network members to make presentations and conduct staff development workshops.
16. Serve as an advisor in network members' classrooms, helping them and their students to develop projects, deal with classroom problems, and locate resources for classroom instruction.
17. Promote the growth of the network through meetings, newsletters, workshops, etc.
18. Participate in decisions regarding overall development of the Outreach programs, including new networks, new courses, etc. Participate in coordinators quarterly meetings.
19. Secure funds for the network budget.
20. Participate in evaluations of the network and of Outreach in general.
21. Participate in developing the "teacher-as-researcher" component of the Outreach program.
22. Work in collaboration with the other Foxfire-affiliated networks and network coordinators.
23. Lend expertise to newly forming networks.
24. Continue own philosophical and professional growth.
25. Avoid burnout. . . .

REFERENCES

Dewey, J. (1963). *Experience and education.* New York: Collier. (Original work published 1938)

Eddy, J. (1989, Fall/Winter). Evaluating Foxfire's teacher outreach program. *Hands On,* pp. 7–15.

Eddy, J., & Wood, G. (1989). *Piloting the phase two assessment.* Unpublished manuscript for Foxfire phase two evaluation.

Gross, B., & Gross, R. (Eds.) (1985). *The great school debate: Which way for American education?* New York: Simon & Schuster.

Joyce, B. (1990). Prologue. *Changing school culture through staff development* (1990 ASCD Yearbook). Arlington, VA: ASCD.

Puckett, J. (1989). *Foxfire reconsidered.* Chicago: University of Illinois Press.

Sarason, S. (1972). *Creation of settings and the future societies.* San Francisco: Jossey-Bass.

Sarason, S. (1982). *The culture of the school and the problem of change.* Boston: Allyn & Bacon.

Stumbo, C. (1989). Beyond the classroom. *Harvard Educational Review, 59,* 87–97.

Teets, S. T. (1989, June). *Partnerships with small colleges.* Paper presented at the annual meeting of the Association of Independent Liberal Arts Colleges for Teacher Education, Indianapolis.

Wigginton, E. (1986). *Sometimes a shining moment.* Garden City, NY: Doubleday.

Wigginton, E. (1989). Foxfire grows up. *Harvard Educational Review, 59,* 24–49.

12 Individual Growth and Institutional Renewal

Robert M. McClure

This is the best staff development I've ever experienced. (Teacher in the Mastery In Learning Project, 1985)

The NEA Mastery In Learning Project (MIL) is a site-based, faculty-led, school improvement project. It attempts to learn what happens to educational quality when a school faculty, organized knowledge, and the authority to act are brought together in the school. Thus a claim that an individual's professional growth had been so positively affected by the Project, as expressed in the above comment, was surprising. The teacher's observation, though, came to dominate much of the work of the Project: Professional growth *is* at the heart of the school renewal and, ultimately, the restructuring of American education.

This chapter is organized around three major topics: the conceptual nature of the Project; the procedures that were developed to understand the local setting and initiate the change process, along with illustrations of their subsequent impact; and the development of collegiality and the use of the knowledge base as essential elements in school restructuring.

There was very little involvement of teachers or other practitioners in the several commissions that shaped the effort to renew schools in the early 1980s. In an attempt to bring the voices of teachers to the national discussion, Mary Hatwood Futrell, president of the National Education Association (NEA), in 1983 appointed a commission to make recommendations about the future of schooling. Comprised of 20 classroom teachers from across the country, the task force produced *An Open Letter to America on Schools, Students, and Tomorrow* (National Education Association, 1984). Nine principles were proposed, four of which guided the Mastery In Learning Project when it began in the spring of 1985:

- *Students must be active participants in learning.* There must be high expectations for student performance, learning environments free from disruptive behavior, and learning activities designed to improve student initiative. Students must be involved in questioning and exploration rather than be passive recipients of information.

- *Full learning opportunity must be available for all students.* All students must be provided varied and appropriate learning opportunities enabling them to realize their individual potential, irrespective of economic, social, physical, or psychological conditions.
- *Authority must be vested in the local school faculty.* More appropriate decisions about teaching and learning are made by those closest to students and the community.
- *Students must master what is taught.* The objective of education should not be mere passing grades, but a demonstrated grasp of fundamentals, the competent use of skills, and command of subjects. Mastery of what is taught is the standard of excellence, with schools offering a comprehensive and significant curriculum, organizing time, and providing resources for this purpose.

The wording in this last proposition from the task force provided the Project's name, a title that caused confusion among educators about the Project's intent. Since "mastery learning" (Bloom, 1976) was a concept familiar to many in the field, it was understandable that such confusion should exist. A difficulty was describing an orientation to school change and improvement different from that which is implied by the Project's title. To suggest such a difference, the word *In* was added to the title.

MASTERY IN LEARNING

The focus of the Project is on the essentials of schooling—learning, curriculum, teaching—and how these interrelate to define the culture or climate of the school. The resources of the Project are used to enable the faculty to create the conditions necessary for students to master important knowledge and skills. MIL asks the faculty and its community to re-create their school to reflect:

- The best that is known about teaching, learning, curriculum, and climate
- The faculty's and community's best aspirations for its students

In other words, the Project did not predetermine what schools should be like as a result of reformation and then set out to achieve that vision.

Rather, it set out to test the idea that school faculties that had access to current knowledge, research, and exemplars of good practice could, given the authority, "grow a school" that would better serve its students than one reformed by outside mandates.

To provide initial guidance to the effort, a beginning definition of mastery was developed. It is more comprehensive than that typically used in education:

> Mastery in learning implies the facility and confidence, judgment and strength, and command of knowledge and skills achieved through education. It means that each student has deep understandings in several subjects, the psychological "ownership" of at least one area of study, and the ability to organize knowledge to solve problems. (McClure, 1986, p. 1)

To publicly emphasize this view of learning, a log was created to represent the Project. It is a rectangle in which the name of the Project is surrounded by several synonyms of the definition, such as *judgment, reason, confidence, facility, command, competent, relevant, holistic, empower, understand,* and *apply.*

The nature of the curriculum that would be created in the school and the way in which teaching would occur were also suggested:

> A curriculum that encourages mastery helps students acquire and use the basic skills of communication, computation, and thinking to understand, interpret, and contribute to their culture and to appreciate other cultures. Mastery in teaching means going beyond mechanistic, rote schooling. It means cultivating higher order thinking, particularly the abilities to analyze, critique, synthesize, problem-solve. (McClure, 1986, p. 1)

Description of Network Schools

Following publication of the National Commission on Excellence in Education's *A Nation at Risk* (1983), many school renewal efforts, particularly those initiated by state legislatures and governors' offices, relied on a mandated, top-down approach to improvement. To demonstrate to policy makers and others the efficacy of another approach, MIL created a demographically representative network of schools. At the outset, six schools were chosen to participate in an 18-month pilot effort. In them, the concept of faculty-led school renewal was explored in considerable depth with teachers, principals, other faculty members, and community representatives.

At the completion of the pilot phase, a full-fledged network of 26 schools was formed. Selected from a pool of 1,400 applicants, the schools were chosen according to criteria designed to produce demographic representativeness. Upon selection, each school received an invitation to participate in the Project, stipulating that the faculty must vote in excess of 75% in a closed ballot to accept the invitation. All of the invited schools exceeded this requirement.

As a group, schools in the network are representative of all schools in the country regarding socioeconomic levels, ethnicity, race, type of community, and nature of the school's organization. The total student population is 20,280; there are 1,198 teachers, 454 support staff, and 64 site-based administrators. The student populations in 8 of the schools are racially balanced; in 6 of the schools, blacks, Hispanics, Native Americans, and/ or Pacific Islanders are in the majority; and in 12 of the schools, Caucasians are in the majority.

There are 12 different grade-level patterns in the network, including a K–2 and a K–12 school, as well as the more usual arrangements. Thirteen of the schools are elementary; 8 are middle or junior highs; 5 are high schools. They are in 20 states and in 25 school systems.

As the teachers and administrators talked about curriculum, teaching, learning, and school climate at the outset of the Project, several characteristics emerged (McClure, 1988a):

- "Principals and teachers relied heavily on textbook manuals, mandates from outside the school, directives from supervisors, and advice from others in similar roles. They accepted the status quo and doubted that challenges to it would have much impact" (p. 60).
- Most of the practitioners in the network knew about or had experienced previous efforts to improve schools and believed that much of that work had been misguided and done more harm than good. They believed that it was their responsibility to resist efforts that would, once again, do damage to educational quality.
- "Most staff members did not describe themselves as risk takers. They saw their school systems as closed organizations uninterested in input from 'low-level' staff, organizations that punished those who took risks" (p. 61).
- "School staffs accepted, almost unquestioningly, the technologies that control schooling: behavioral objectives, textbooks, and standardized tests" (p. 61).

When asked to select words that described their school, the following were often used: *memory, textbooks, uniform classrooms, separate subjects, broad curriculum, student testing that stresses recall, central decision making, teacher burn-out.* In "Dinner at Abigail's: Nurturing Collaboration," Madeline Grumet (1989) describes the experience of one school in the MIL network and comments on how these teachers felt about their situation:

> It is less about being overworked than about feeling responsible for the experience of children and forbidden to shape that experience. It is the frustration of being harassed and hampered by the organization of space and time and materials that are essential to your work without having any say about how these resources that shape schooling are distributed. (p. 21)

For the most part, faculties in the network schools are different now from the way their inventories described them at the outset of the Project. They are increasingly aware of the knowledge base that undergirds their work and are more likely to consider it useful in solving their problems. They see themselves as powerful shapers of the future of their school; they are more collegial and less isolated, more savvy about the politics of school systems, and better able to view their school in a comprehensive manner. They think that they can be influential in affecting student learning. They are more passionate about the values they hold.

Processes Developed by MIL

Although the local faculty (defined as teachers, administrators, and others at the school responsible for the educational program) design the reform agenda, the Project provides the processes by which restructuring occurs:

1. *Profiling the School* (several weeks). Through structured interviews with teachers, students, parents, and administrators, a description of the school is created to serve as a benchmark for the Project's efforts.
2. *Inventorying the Faculty* (several days). Through a process that reveals similarities and differences in priorities and aspirations among faculty members, the school faculty establishes initial priorities for improvement.
3. *Faculty Enablement* (two to three years). The faculty works to create the skills, attitudes, and inclinations necessary for sustained inquiry into the assumptions and practices that define their school.
4. *Comprehensive Change* (ongoing). Having developed skills and habits of collaboration and collegiality and a clearer vision of

what is desirable for their school with regard to learning, teaching, curriculum, and school climate, the faculty engages in ongoing systemic school improvement.

In the following sections, the process of Inventorying the Faculty is described. There are three parts to this process. The procedures developed here have also been used by schools not enrolled in MIL as they initiate their own improvement and staff-development efforts.

FACULTY INVENTORY: PART ONE

What is so wonderful about your school that you would not want it changed?
What is wrong with the school that everyone knows and should be changed immediately?
What is wrong, but we don't know how to fix it?

These three simple questions shape the opening exercise of Mastery in Learning's Faculty Inventory, the Project's initiating activity. All faculty members were required to participate in this and the five other procedures that constitute the Inventory.

Diad/Triad

The first activity is called the "diad/triad" because of the method used to explore the three questions. In the first round, the faculty, congregated in one room, was divided into teams of two to respond to the questions, trying to achieve consensus between themselves. After a few minutes, these diads were asked to complete their answers and to form triads—a group of six persons (combining three of the diads). Each group shared their answers from the first round, and then attempted to achieve consensus around their answers to the questions.

Finally, after about 15 minutes, a third round of the activity was conducted, this time joining as many as half of the faculty on one side of the room and the other half on the other. Although depending on number of persons involved, this third round usually took about 30 minutes.

Why take an hour of a faculty's scarce time to ask three rather obvious questions—and not just once, but three times? From what was learned in the field-test and in later observations of the effects of the activity on faculty work, five reasons emerged:

1. *Context.* Movement into the beginnings of faculty-led renewal needs to be comfortable, contextual, and interactive. In almost all of the 26 schools in the network, this was the first time the faculty had dealt with issues of the kind represented by the questions. Most teachers saw the diad/triad as the beginning of the something quite different in their school; most, after five years, remember this single activity above all others that constitute the inventory.

2. *Norms.* The process begins, at least in most schools, to change the norms, to place a value on interchange among faculty about their school, to suggest that faculties have a role in determining the nature of this place.

3. *Collegiality.* The diad/triad helps to create the conditions from which collegiality can emerge. It allows individuals to see their peers in a different perspective, to expand beyond the social and into the professional.

4. *Perspective.* It helps faculties understand that their school is perceived differently because of roles or orientations held by individuals and that if change is to be comprehensive, these perspectives constitute an important part of the system to be affected by the restructuring effort.

5. *Complexity.* Going through the process three times also helps to demonstrate the complexity and depth of many of the school's problems. For example, in the first round teachers will often identify student discipline in the halls and on the playground as a target for immediate improvement. In subsequent rounds, the understandings of the causes of student disruptive behavior will surface, and the target will become, instead, better communication among staff about expectations or learning how to teach for more positive and independent behavior. One teacher described the effect of going through three rounds of answers to the questions as "peeling the onion until you find the tears."

The activities described in the following three sections complete the first two hours of the faculty inventory.

Conditions That Encourage Mastery in Learning

From six conditions presented, individual participants were asked to consider the desirability, practicability, and extent to which such conditions presently existed in their school (Mastery In Learning Project, 1985):

1. Great range of student instructional materials (books, tapes, films, programmed instruction, simulations, games, and so forth), thus allowing a variety of ways for students to achieve objectives
2. Many opportunities for teachers to work with small groups of students
3. Students working more independently—more often using teachers as resources than as direct instructors
4. Teachers' teaching of basic skills supplemented by computers, teacher aides, and peer coaching, thus enabling teachers to devote more time to helping students acquire higher-order skills
5. Student assessment becoming more a province of the school community, employing a variety of techniques and measuring outcomes that are germane to the school's community and its students
6. Schedules for students allowing opportunities for more depth in curriculum (e.g., six-week blocks with students concentrating on two or three subjects, or trimesters, or four weeks on and two weeks in tutorials)

The purpose of using this activity was to help create an understanding that there are a variety of options available to faculties as they consider the restructuring of their school.

In the beginning of the Project, network faculties saw conditions 1 and 2 as highly desirable but not very practical, since both would seem to require additional revenues. Generally they did not view the other four conditions as desirable. Four years later, when MIL teachers and administrators designed their national meeting, they asked for help in implementing projects directly related to the other four conditions—a marked change in perspective.

Teaching and Learning Practices

In this exercise participants were asked to place a check next to each item on a list that described a practice that was in place in their school most of the time. The list, culled from the literature on effective schools (e.g., Kyle, 1985), included 42 items and was grouped in five categories:

- *Environment*—orderly school climate, few classroom interruptions
- *Program*—goal-oriented instructional program, basic skills are learned, taught, used
- *Teachers and support staff*—knowledge of content taught, spend time actively teaching

- *School principal*—assertive instructional role, conveys high expectations for students and staff
- *Assessment and revision*—ongoing assessment of student progress, communication of progress to students and community

In their tallying of the existence of the 42 listed conditions, faculties from schools in the network ranged from a low of 8 checks to a high of 32.

There were two reasons for including this instrument in the Faculty Inventory. The first was to help faculties understand that there was an important body of literature drawn from a research base that spoke to their situation. Further, many influential policy makers and school administrators, in addition to researchers, were using the language of this approach. It was important for practitioners to know that language and what it represented if they were to be players in their community and in the broader efforts to reform schools.

Second, it was important that these teachers and administrators understood that research on effective schools started from a value that high standardized test scores were a very important measure of school effectiveness. Different values might produce a different direction as they thought about how to improve their program. This was the beginning of an important theme in the Project: When using research to help plan a program, it is important to know the values underlying that research and whether it fits the shared vision of the faculty about the school.

No school in the Mastery In Learning Project has chosen to adopt an effective schools plan; however, many have adapted those findings that match their agendas, particularly those related to orderliness, parent involvement, and curriculum continuity. They have also questioned some of the findings from this body of literature, suggesting, for example, that collegial instructional leadership is more desirable than the hierarchical one suggested by much of the research on effective schools.

Imagining Success

In this activity, adapted from the work of Susan Loucks-Horsley and Leslie F. Hergert (1985), participants were asked:

> Imagine you are hovering over your school in a helicopter. What you see is a close-to-ideal school—one that has participated in the Mastery In Learning Project for four years and made a number of significant changes. What might one of those changes be? (The helicopter is figurative—you are to describe any kind of important change whether visible or not.) (Mastery In Learning Project, 1985, p. 27)

Following the identification of the one desired change, each participant
responded to six questions about that particular change:

1. What is going on in the classroom?
2. How is the room organized?
3. What materials or equipment are available, in use?
4. Who is working with whom?
5. What are teachers doing?
6. What are students doing?

Teachers and other faculty members were asked to engage in this process
of describing a desirable future because it was important for them to
establish an initial personal goal for the school. Most of these visions
focused on relationships among teachers and students and not on the
content of the program. Most often the responses called for

- Greater opportunities to work in small groups and with individuals
- More opportunities to help students acquire depth in content
- New relationships among the adults—less isolation, less hierarchy
- Instructional materials that were in greater abundance, more var-
  ied, and more timely; easy access to equipment such as photo-
  copiers, telephones, computers, and design labs

Their vision became the beginnings of a personal map, and, although
most changed their ideas and their visions over time, the targeting in itself
became an important act of empowerment for them.

These four activities constituted the first two hours of MIL's Faculty
Inventory—although it was not uncommon for several individuals to
remain in the room and spend another hour or more working on Imagining Success. Dreaming about what their school could become was an
unusual and arresting activity for many of the teachers, counselors, librar-
ians, principals, specialists, and others who participated in the beginnings
of the Project in their school.

FACULTY INVENTORY: PART TWO

At the conclusion of the session described above, all individuals were
asked to complete a questionnaire designed to assess teachers' and other
staff members' perceptions of practices and conditions in their school.
Faculty members were given a week to complete the questionnaire since

it was extensive, requiring at least two hours to complete. Individual anonymity was assured.

Participants assessed the extent to which a practice or condition was present in the school and rated the importance of the item. The questionnaire consisted of 121 statements arrayed across four categories—students/learning, school/faculty, teachers and teaching, and curriculum. Figure 12.1 provides a representative statement from each category.

After tabulating these data, the results were returned to the faculty with the complete list ordered from those items with the greatest discrepancy to those with the least. A second listing provided information on those items that were seen as most important, that is, those receiving the highest ranking on "what should be."

Although data were analyzed within the individual schools (not across school sites), there were a few findings that pertained to many of the schools:

- The highest discrepancies usually occurred in the school/faculty and students/learning sections.
- Specific high-discrepancy items often called for more opportunities for teachers to plan together, orderly/safe environments, instructional materials, students more actively engaged in learning, administrators working more directly with the educational pro-

FIGURE 12.1   Representative Statements from the Faculty Inventory, Part Two, Questionnaire

STUDENTS/LEARNING

| Students can work in a variety of ways to achieve learning objectives. | What is: | 1 2 3 4 5 6 7 8 |
| | What should be: | 1 2 3 4 5 6 7 8 |

SCHOOL/FACULTY

| Teachers work together across grade levels, disciplines, and departmental groupings. | What is: | 1 2 3 4 5 6 7 8 |
| | What should be: | 1 2 3 4 5 6 7 8 |

TEACHERS AND TEACHING

| Teachers have opportunities to expand their repertoire of teaching strategies. | What is: | 1 2 3 4 5 6 7 8 |
| | What should be: | 1 2 3 4 5 6 7 8 |

CURRICULUM

| The content and skills to be taught are intellectually valid. | What is: | 1 2 3 4 5 6 7 8 |
| | What should be: | 1 2 3 4 5 6 7 8 |

gram, opportunities for shared decision making, and access to relevant professional development programs.

- Low-discrepancy items usually had to do with curriculum goals, content validity, and curriculum content.
- Those items that received highest ranking for importance had to do with orderly student discipline, opportunities for teachers to individualize instruction, and bringing instructional materials and technologies into the school to help students learn.

Eight items in the questionnaire related directly to opportunities for staff development and, in almost all of the schools, were rated as important and with relatively high discrepancies between what existed and what was desired (Mastery In Learning Project, 1985):

> Staff development opportunities are related to faculty goals.
> Staff development is practical and focuses on specific skills and abilities.
> Staff development assists teachers to understand and use new curriculum and materials.
> Teachers participate in planning staff development opportunities.
> Teachers incorporate ideas and information from staff development activities to improve their planning and teaching.
> Administrators support and encourage teacher participation in staff development.
> Teachers have opportunities to expand their repertoire of teaching styles.
> Staff members recognize the need for continuous professional development.
> (p. 35)

FACULTY INVENTORY: PART THREE

A few weeks after the initial two-hour meeting and completion of the questionnaire, the faculty again met together. In this session, they listened to a presentation about the findings, debated their accuracy and relevance, determined the ways in which they would launch their school improvement work, and decided on a structure to support their decisions. What follows is a brief summary of what happened in one of the network schools during this session—a somewhat representative picture of others in the network.

An analysis of the Faculty Inventory revealed a number of problems, unresolved issues, and aspirations for this junior high school staff. These included the following:

- *Problems*—several kinds of communication problems, chiefly among staff; physical space; lack of materials; lack of cooperation between board and teachers; lack of community involvement; student placement; lack of follow-up of inservice workshops; and teacher burn-out
- *Unresolved issues*—ability versus heterogeneous grouping; the nature of the student discipline program; teacher professionalism versus labor/management arrangements; internal versus external control of curriculum; and the nature and source of professional development
- *Aspirations*—learning environment more closely matched to their students; better balance between student- and teacher-directed instruction; teachers using various teaching methods and styles; teachers, parents, and administrators working as a team

After a lively discussion about the information presented, the faculty agreed to three initial targets for improvement. The first was to improve the ways in which students were placed in classes; the second, to improve communication across the faculty and between them and the central office staff and school board; and the third, to create a staff development program that was school based and faculty led.

Following the procedures that had been established by the Project, a steering committee was formed to give direction to these three tasks, to coordinate the resources necessary for their accomplishment, and to move the work toward increasing comprehensiveness. They subsequently mounted action research projects, came to agreement about a long-term renewal plan, became active consumers of educational research, and began to address problems of communication in forthright ways.

In succeeding years, this faculty became a coherent group, focusing their energies on collegiality, sharing responsibility for the quality of the school's climate, becoming expert on the change process. They reversed their initial stand on grouping, moving from homogeneous to heterogeneous and in the process learning how research can affect school improvement. Individual faculty members organized and chaired faculty meetings on a rotating basis. For one semester, they managed the school in the absence of any administrators and learned that they wanted and needed a principal in the school. They developed a new job description for a principal, the criteria for selection, and an interview protocol—and they hired the person.

For the most part, the accomplishments of this school's work have been directed at improving the conditions of teaching. There are indications, however, that students have also benefited (McClure, 1989):

- There is an increased acceptance on the part of students for "non-frontal teaching methods" and an understanding on their part that "that's the way the outside world works."
- Parents and faculty report opportunities for these adolescents to explore alternative forms of learning, careers, and friendship patterns—all resulting in improved attitudes.
- High school faculty report large differences in the ninth-grade class (i.e., those in the MIL project for three years); much more accepting of new instructional strategies, these students "aren't fighting it."
- In regard to the school's climate, there has been a "real turn around"—reduction in graffiti, increased student-led recognition programs, and very good discipline (even with the changes in administration).
- Students indicate greater empowerment, being more in control and having more influence over what happens to them.
- The school has moved from the bottom quartile in the system on the statewide achievement test to being the top-scoring school in the area.

SCHOOL RESTRUCTURING:
SELF-RENEWING CENTERS OF INQUIRY

The definition of restructuring in the Mastery In Learning Project was shaped by Ted Sizer when he admonished MIL faculty leaders to "challenge the regularities. Nothing is beyond questioning. Even those things with which we are most comfortable have got to be, not hyperbolically attacked, just questioned—undefensively" (McClure & Obermeyer, 1987, p. 6).

At a faculty retreat of one of the schools in the network, what was to be questioned in the name of restructuring was explored:

Curriculum, behavioral objectives, tests, lectures, chalk boards, ten-month school year, fifty-minute hour, six-period day, faculty meetings, bulletin boards, classrooms, pep rallies, grade levels, inservice, drill, student tracking, bookrooms, playground duty, science labs, workbooks, advisories, homerooms, recess, parent-teacher conferences, detention, study halls, classroom management, assemblies, bells, lesson plans, departments, dittos, hall passes, intercom announcements. . . . These and countless other such topics define the forms of schooling, and they are not sacrosanct! (McClure, 1988b, p. 1)

In MIL schools, restructuring is not seen as having a beginning and an end. Most faculty members see it as an ongoing process of comparing current practice with what is known and what is valued and moving to make the necessary changes. This definition of restructuring is changing the norms in MIL schools: They are becoming, as Robert Schaeffer suggested 25 years ago (1967), self-renewing centers of inquiry.

The building of collegiality and the use of the knowledge base are critical attributes to significant school improvement. The extent to which school faculties have acquired these attributes predicts the depth, breadth, and success of their efforts to achieve significant improvements in educational quality. The following sections discuss these attributes.

Collegiality

The Project builds on the principle that every decision about learning and instruction that can be made by a local school faculty should be made by that faculty (Bentzen, 1974; Goodlad, 1984; Sarason, 1971). To make sound educational decisions, however, requires a faculty that sees itself as responsible for the school and not just as a group of individuals who close the doors of their classrooms and do the best possible job without reference to the total institution. As Madeline Grumet (1989) states: "Implicit in the MIL agenda is the assumption that what goes on in the classroom is linked to what goes on in the corridors, the lunchroom, principal's office, the teacher's room, even the buses" (p. 20).

Faculty in MIL schools began their participation in the Project with high degrees of sociability. When responding to the diad/triad question, "What is so wonderful about this school that you wouldn't want it changed?" answers from every faculty said something about their close personal relationships with one another. Their closeness as a group, their camaraderie, probably had something to do with the decision to apply to become an MIL school in the first place.

Later, however, it became clear that these relationships were primarily social and, though school based, not firmly rooted in the business of schools—learning and teaching and curriculum development. In the early days of the Project, new definitions of conduct had to be worked out in the schools. Some faculties were not able to develop new ways of working together, to build collegiality, and even suffered a diminution of their former sociability.

Individual teachers and administrators have sometimes chosen not to accept the responsibilities that came with the new ways of relating to one another and withdrew, or banded with persons of similar thinking to become opponents of the renewal work, or escaped by transferring out of the school. Interestingly, school faculties that describe themselves as successfully engaged in school restructuring handle dissidents differently than do other faculties. They are seen as an important balance to others prone to moving the reform agenda more quickly, and that role is acknowledged and respected. Individual faculty members in MIL schools were, for the most part, able to build on their social cohesion and become professionally engaged with one another.

The progression to collegiality developed through several stages, with some consistency across the 26 sites (McClure, 1988a). At the outset, when informed that their faculty had been invited to participate in the Project, most teachers engaged in testing of intent, trying to figure out motives and hidden agendas. The trust level was low. Later, with such questions satisfactorily answered, exhilaration set in and commitments were made when the faculty felt they were to be treated as professionals and given the authority needed to improve conditions of learning and teaching. Often individuals emerged as leaders at this time who had not served in such capacities before. This phase generally lasted a few months, during the conduct and implementation of the Faculty Inventory and the initial planning.

A couple of months into the first school year, toward the end of October, most faculties experienced the "Halloween syndrome." A phase of dispiritedness came about as the staff began to discover that no one from the outside was going to direct them in this effort, that responsibility for the vision, the work, and the results was theirs. At this point, many dropped from active participation in the Project, returning to what they knew best, teaching solo in their classroom. Now, as few as 20% of the faculty remained actively committed to the idea of faculty-led school reform.

What occurred next—regeneration—appears to have been a critical phase in the life of these 26 reform efforts. In effect, they began the work over again, revisiting the data from the Inventory, getting interested in the change process, learning that there was a body of literature about how to overcome such obstacles (e.g., Miller, 1988) and using it. Most faculties then sought to achieve small successes, acting on a few simple, straightforward ideas (e.g., rules for student behavior in public areas, barring classroom interruptions for most of each class period, beautifying an area of the campus). These small, visible, campuswide successes recaptured the interests of a larger number of faculty and were often used as springboards for more comprehensive outcomes.

As the faculty gained experience and confidence in themselves and became more collegial, three other phases emerged that supported their restructuring efforts. One was their use of research, which will be discussed in the next section. Another, with profound impact on drawing the faculty together around professional issues was experimentation, that is, interested persons banding together to test an idea and serve as an "R&D party" for the faculty. Some have improved integration of content by combining subjects not usually taught together (e.g., music and math, art and history), developing a new syllabus, teaching it, and reporting the results to the faculty. Others have worked on scheduling, grouping, "less-is-more" approaches to curriculum, integration of students with special needs into the mainstream, new forms of student evaluation, differentiated staffing and teaming, expanded teaching repertoires, new forms of governance, greater student authority, and improved parent involvement programs.

Finally, many school staffs in the Project have moved from separate improvement efforts to a more comprehensive approach. They see that the school is a system, that to attend to one aspect of it affects another. Through these phases, strong professional relationships across the faculty have supported these schools' renewal efforts. Leaders in these faculties say that this developing collegiality provides the glue that will maintain their school as a self-renewing center of inquiry.

Using the Knowledge Base

Three rules governed a faculty's initial participation in the Project: 75% staff approval; full faculty participation in the Faculty Inventory; and commitment that no decision about a reform initiative would be made without consideration of the options available. This last requirement diminishes the all-too-frequent "bandwagonism" that has characterized so many school improvement efforts in the past. Improvements chosen for implementation can, therefore, be undergirded by evidence of worth. As teachers seek these options through assaying what is available, there is also a strengthening of collegiality and professionalism.

In "Teachers Using Research: What Does it Mean?", Carol Livingston and Shari Castle (1989) defined the MIL view of the knowledge base as "the full range of knowledge resources available to the profession. These include theoretical, philosophical, empirical, and practical resources" (p. 14). They go on to conclude, however, that if the school is to be the center of change, it is inappropriate to conceive of a research utilization paradigm in which the practitioner is solely a user and the researcher is the producer. As Ken Sirotnik and Richard Clark (1988) contend:

> We must reexamine the idea of schools as centers of decision making and renewal, or we will find that all our discussions of school-based management will simply propel us further along the path toward unsuccessful efforts at change and renewal. If we don't understand the significance of the school as center of change, we will continue to see it only as the target of change. And we will fail to recognize and tap the reservoir of knowledge and talent that already exists there. (p. 664)

To combine the latent desire and need by school people for knowledge to aid school restructuring with the resources generated by the research and development community, the Project created a resource base for its schools. This system, designated TRaK (for teaching resources and knowledge), has as its purpose to collect and make available to MIL schools in one accessible, user-friendly form the best that can be taken from research reports, other educational literature, and the field of practice.

"TRaK packets" were created as participating faculties identified improvement agendas and sought to learn what is known about the direction they wish to take. Each packet contains an overview of the literature, a few complete documents regarding the topic (usually articles from journals), suggestions about staff development resources (names, materials, self-help guides, and a list of institutions such as ASCD that offer staff development programs), and detailed references of ways to learn more about the subject.

As faculties developed their priorities, MIL staff and consultants responded with packets on a wide variety of topics, including critical thinking, integrated curriculum, discipline, learning styles and teaching models, faculty communication, parental involvement, writing across the curriculum, effective schools, empowerment, community involvement, class size, computers in education, cooperative learning, homework, language development, scheduling, self-directed learning, self-esteem, standardized achievement testing and its alternatives, student grouping, and teacher planning. The packets range in size from 30 pages to as many as 200.

Schools used the packets in a number of ways. In some, the contents were to be parceled out to faculty members at work on the particular topic; reports were then given to the total group—a kind of "jig-saw approach" described in literature on cooperative learning. Another school used "updates" in which small parts of a packet were shared with the faculty in short weekly bulletins.

For the most part, however, these one-way delivery systems were an incomplete solution to the problem of narrowing the gap between practitioners and the knowledge base. Too often, there was not the process expertise in the schools to help people use the material, and, of course, the process did not foster the objective of creating healthy interaction between researchers and practitioners.

There were also greatly varying definitions of what constitutes research and its uses. Many teachers thought that access to research would provide them with specific answers to persistent problems and were disappointed when they found ambiguity. Others sought to justify current practice ("research says . . . ") and were displeased when contradictions or ambiguities occurred.

To use the knowledge base interactively, MIL schools are now connected with one another through computer technology, the IBM/NEA-Mastery In Learning Project School Renewal Network. In addition to the 26 MIL schools, other participants in the network include the federally funded research and development laboratories, several universities, and schools participating in other site-based renewal projects. The system, designed for interaction around topics germane to school restructuring, was conceptualized primarily by assessing the research and development needs of the MIL faculties. Participants dialogue around such topics as critical thinking, instructional strategies, at-risk students, authentic student assessment, and parent involvement.

Each of the ten focus topics is facilitated by a researcher and practitioners from two or three network schools. It is anticipated that this technologically supported interaction will have a synergistic effect on the knowledge base underlying teaching, learning, curriculum, and school culture.

As faculties have become more sophisticated in their interactions with research, other "uses" of research come to be important—for contemplation and deliberation (the practitioner as critical adapter), for transformation (research as a stimulus for paradigm shifts), and for production (active collaboration among faculty and between practitioners and researchers) (Livingston & Castle, 1989).

Charles Thompson (1989), who examined reports of several MIL faculties' efforts to interact with organized knowledge to improve their educational program, commented on the enabling, empowering aspect of this work:

> The revolutions reported in this book are not, however, simple redistributions of power. These revolutions do not so much redistribute power as

multiply it. New knowledge ... emboldens teachers to think, to examine their practice, to believe that they are competent to change existing practice. And there is an almost electric sense of energy release that accompanies this realization, a sense of excitement that raises the energy level throughout each building. (pp. 91–92)

Faculty-led school improvement efforts that are context specific, student-outcome oriented, intellectually valid, and professionally enabling embody the essence of effective staff development programs.

REFERENCES

Bentzen, M. M. (1974). *Changing schools: The magic feather principle.* New York: McGraw-Hill.

Bloom, B. (1976). *Human characteristics and school learning.* New York: McGraw-Hill.

Goodlad, J. I. (1984). *A place called school: Prospects for the future.* New York: McGraw-Hill.

Grumet, M. R. (1989). Dinner at Abigail's: Nurturing collaboration. *NEA Today,* 7(6), 20–25.

Kyle, R. M. J. (Ed.). (1985). *Reaching for excellence: An effective schools sourcebook.* Washington, DC: U.S. Government Printing Office.

Livingston, C., & Castle, S. (1989). Teachers using research: What does it mean? In C. Livingston & S. Castle (Eds.), *Teachers and research in action* (pp. 13–28). Washington, DC: National Education Association.

Loucks-Horsley, S., & Hergert, L. F. (1985). *An action guide to school improvement.* Washington, DC: Association for Supervision and Curriculum Development and NETWORK.

Mastery In Learning Project. (1985). *Procedures manual.* Unpublished manuscript. Washington, DC: Author.

McClure, R. (1986, April). *Defining mastery of the academic disciplines.* Paper presented at the annual meeting of the American Educational Research Association, Chicago.

McClure, R. (1988a). The evolution of shared leadership. *Educational Leadership,* 46(3), 60–62.

McClure, R. (1988b). Restructuring schools: Taking inventory and charting direction. *Doubts & Certainties: Newsletter of the Mastery In Learning Project,* 2(4), 1.

McClure, R. (1989). [Interviews with selected staff of one of the schools in the Mastery In Learning Project network]. Unpublished raw data.

McClure, R., & Obermeyer, G. L. (1987). *Visions of school renewal.* Washington, DC: National Education Association.

Miller, L. (1988). *Restructuring: How formidable are the barriers?* (MIL Occasional Paper No. 2). Washington, DC: National Education Association.

National Commission on Excellence in Education. (1983). *A nation at risk.* Washington, DC: U.S. Government Printing Office.

National Education Association. (1984). *An open letter to America on schools, students, and tomorrow.* Washington, DC: Author.

Sarason, S. B. (1971). *The culture of the school and the problem of change.* Boston: Allyn & Bacon.

Schaeffer, R. J. (1967). *The school as a center of inquiry.* New York: Harper & Row.

Sirotnik, K. A., & Clark, R. W. (1988). School-centered decision-making and renewal. *Phi Delta Kappan, 69,* 660–664.

Thompson, C. L. (1989). Knowledge, power, professionalism, and human agency. In C. Livingston & S. Castle (Eds.), *Teachers and research in action.* Washington, DC: National Education Association.

AFTERWORD

Interactive
Staff Development
Using What We Know

Gary A. Griffin

The history of schools in the United States has been accompanied by concerns about quality, often expressed in such terms as the relation of instruction to student outcomes, the personal character and professional preparation of teachers, the nature of the human interactions among teachers and students, the relevance of school curriculum to student interests and needs, the role of school in society, and the intellectual capabilities of teachers. Much of the time, the concerns for quality were seen as easily dealt with through systems of oversight, remediation and professional development programs, and ongoing teacher evaluation. In other words, "supervision of teachers," a construct with multiple meanings and rooted in diverse paradigms, had as its primary focus ensuring that safe practice was the standard in the teacher cadre. And assuring safe practice by teachers was seen as the goal of the work of a set of administrative-supervisory roles in a school or school system (Griffin, 1982).

To some, supervision is what is practiced when the term *staff development* is invoked. Supervision, whether so named or engaged in as staff development, despite some dramatic examples to the contrary, has carried over the years some pretty heavy intellectual and practical baggage. It has suffered from competing goals (helping teachers grow in directions they believe desirable and ensuring that system-determined minimum standards are maintained), multiple functions (assistance versus assessment), role confusion (helper and evaluator), organizational role schizophrenia (supervisor, coordinator, administrator), institutional placement (district office, school, department), and, most recently, serving as the vehicle for carrying forward the so-called first wave of educational reform (Hoffman et al., 1986).

243

Although not labeled "supervision," many of the action proposals that characterized the response to recent criticisms of schools and teachers were rooted in a similar safe practice paradigm and depended for implementation success on strengthened and, indeed, more comprehensive enactment of traditional supervisory work. That is, teachers in general, but particularly new teachers, were called on to demonstrate certain "desired" teaching behaviors, provide evidence of modest levels of literacy, and be able to answer written questions about pedagogy. Securing the data to verify these minimal levels of teaching expertise fell most often to school supervisors and administrators. And, importantly, when teachers already in practice were found wanting, conventional supervisory practices were called into play. The teachers were given specific help to attain certain levels of targeted teaching behavior. This help took such conventional forms as workshops, conference/observation/follow-up meetings with system officers (supervisors), microteaching practice sessions, and the shaping of teaching to correspond to selected manuals of teaching effectiveness. Clearly the mechanisms for treating teachers from a deficit perspective were in place, as, indeed, they have been for over a century in large numbers of the nation's schools.

FORCING THE FIELD:
CONCEPTION AND INQUIRY

Starting before the 1980s version of school reform began to pervade the discourse of schooling in this country, two other paradigms for bringing about school improvement and teacher effectiveness were gaining ground in some school settings and universities, approaches that bore little resemblance to the somewhat stereotyped picture of supervision presented here. I will call these two approaches *staff development* and *teacher empowerment*.

Staff development is a much discussed but variously interpreted activity (Griffin, 1983). For some, *staff development* is the rubric under which any effort to engage individual or groups of teachers with improvement exercises is included. For others, staff development is a serious and systematic effort to engage a group of professional educators who work together, a staff, in activities designed specifically to increase the power and authority of their shared work. I accept the latter perspective for reasons that will be apparent later in this chapter.

Staff development offered a focus for improvement efforts (Wideen & Andrews, 1987). Rather than working from the belief that central office supervisors and administrators could or should direct improvement activities, staff development centers its work in a particular school. The problems to be dealt with, the issues to be faced, the resources to be marshaled, the information to be gathered—all are found in a school. This attention to the influence of context problems and possibilities has its roots in both common sense (*our* problems are believed to be more important and urgent than what *they* perceive to be our problems) and in a number of descriptive studies of school change, one of the most influential being the effort led by John Goodlad (Bentzen, 1974). Also, knowledge about school variation became much more dramatic and, hence, more widely known as influential upon school outcomes as student populations within individual schools became characterized more by diversity than uniformity in terms of language, race, and culture. Staff development, then, made sense to school professionals as a construct to focus teacher and school improvement work.

At about the same time that *staff development* came to be an accepted phrase in educational parlance, researchers, usually university based but with some exciting school-based exceptions, were asking questions about the underpinnings of school and teacher effectiveness (Doyle, 1987). The answers to those questions, it was believed, lay in the classrooms and schools themselves, not in the propositional-theoretical pronouncements of members of the academy. For the first time, large-scale studies of actual schools and classrooms were designed to isolate, when possible, or aggregate, when necessary, the actual work of the effective teacher, the verified events and activities of the effective school. As the results of this research became known, a set of themes emerged, themes suggesting strongly that effectiveness, most often defined as stronger-than-predicted student outcomes on standardized measures of achievement, was influenced by interactive context variables (Schlechty, 1987). And, interestingly, conventional "supervision" was *not* associated with effectiveness. In fact, the practices of top-down and heavily hierarchical practices typical of schools were seldom, if ever, found to be related to school or teacher effectiveness (Schlechty, 1990). (It is unfortunate that the "strong leadership" factor in effective schools research came to be interpreted by some as an authoritarian principal.)

Instead, effective schools were found to be educational settings where teachers were professionally collegial (rather than simply socially and personally compatible), where administrators arranged the context (schedules, times, rewards, incentives) to support that collegiality, where teachers were deeply involved in goal setting, where teachers worked together on self-initiated improvement activities such as peer coaching or school- and classroom-oriented inquiry, and where the initiative for experimentation and innovation rested most often with the faculty group rather than in an administrative or supervisory cadre (Rosenholtz, 1989).

The consequences of these research findings were powerful in several ways. First, largely because of the imagination and effort of the American Federation of Teachers, the National Education Association, and a small group of researchers, the findings were made available and accessible to large numbers of teachers and other school leaders (see Chapter 12, this volume). This infusion of research findings into practice settings was unprecedented. With very few exceptions, research about schools and teachers has usually remained firmly lodged in universities and other research and development organizations. The research-practice "gap" was widely decried but seldom ameliorated.

Second, and less salutory, the research findings also became part of the repertoire of policy makers who, unfortunately, too frequently used the findings to formulate another set of hurdles for teachers to stumble into or over on their way to certification, tenure, and, in some extreme instances, so called mastery status (Hoffman et al., 1986).

Third, the research findings became a significant part of the platform from which teachers, in groups and as individuals, developed a sense of empowerment. That is, the research offered substance to an argument that went something like this: If teachers assume major responsibility for their own development and the nature of their work, and carrying out this responsibility is associated with effectiveness, we need to develop both political and intellectual agendas to ensure that these associated conditions are made a part of every teacher's worklife. Indeed, the research findings helped many of us to think more seriously about "professionalism" for teachers in that a profession, by definition, works according to a codified knowledge base, typically research-derived, and such a knowledge base, although incomplete and fragmented, was emerging and available for thinking about and doing teaching.

I believe it is timely to think about the *functions, nature, and expected outcomes* of staff development as a school improvement strategy that can rest in large measure on research findings suggesting how that improvement comes about and is supported. This is in contrast to staff development that derives its *content*, usually in the form of templates for effective teaching practice, from research findings.

FROM SUPERVISION
TO INTERACTIVE STAFF DEVELOPMENT

I have selected the term *interactive staff development* to describe this perspective because it characterizes what I believe are essential features of working with teachers in schools, features suggested by research findings and pointing to the centrality of treating effectiveness as a situation-specific, cumulative, and coherent issue. *Interactive* focuses attention on the reality that people, ideas, events, outcomes, expectations, beliefs, purposes, and perceptions are in constant mutually affecting motion and sets forth the requirement that this motion be accounted for and, when possible, mobilized to attain desired ends. *Staff* defines the core group of professionals who are participants in the process and situates them in a meaningful context, a school. *Development* indicates forward motion, links activities and events in coherent ways, considers people as individuals at varying stages of expertise, and focuses attention on working toward an end in view, a vision of the possible.

Understanding of improvement practices and a cautious reading of research findings about effectiveness suggest a set of assumptions that should direct decision making in interactive staff development. The assumptions that follow begin with the teacher, place the teacher in a school context, and then deal with the interaction of context and teacher in terms of professional growth and development. These assumptions are informed directly by much of the other material in this book.

Assumption 1: Teachers, more often than not, are perceptive about their shortcomings and strong points. It has been an implicit tradition in so-called improvement or reform strategies to second-guess teachers, to stand apart from the teaching cadre and offer pronouncements about strengths and weaknesses, pluses and minuses. This, in fact, is what school supervision was all about in that a layer of school bureaucracy was developed and supported toward the end of inspection and rating of teachers.

In the current thinking about teacher professionalism, some argue that *education* has already been professionalized through the superintendency. This view of what it is to be professional assumes that the central feature of professionalism is access to knowledge that can be used to control other workers. Therefore, when the superintendency was conceptualized as requiring advanced degrees (gaining access to advanced knowledge) and those degrees ensured that the successful candidates would know how to develop evaluative (control) systems to use with teachers, a condition for thinking of education as a profession was met.

These two phenomena, passing judgments on teachers and offering administrators the opportunity to develop schemes for such ratings, are both rooted in a theory about teachers as relatively nonreflective workers, people who need someone with more authority to pass judgment on the quality of their practice.

This theory is seriously flawed in one sense but, unfortunately, predictive in another. It is flawed because teachers as individuals are more often than not sensitive to their shortcomings and justly prideful of their accomplishments. It is predictive, however, because the organizational structures that have been created for teachers and students depend on this theory to justify much of their in-built bureaucracies and, consequently, create the conditions necessary to silence teachers' views about their teaching (Sarason, 1971). In most schools, for example, admitting shortcomings and seeking advice are seen as admissions of inadequacy. In most schools, too, forums or organizational arrangements for teacher reflection, individually or collectively, are absent. Even though teachers are more self-conscious about their teaching than certain control theories might admit, the situations that surround their work define them as unthinking.

Research on teacher thinking, on teachers' implicit theories, and on expert teachers supports a view of teachers as persons who are thoughtful about their work, their impact on students, their strong points and their vulnerabilities (Carter, 1990). This research, in part, also points out how teachers, particularly veterans, are often less than precise about these thoughts and considerations, in large part because of the absence of any need to become articulate, to be communicative, to use the thoughts as objects of systematic attention with their colleagues.

Interactive staff development would depend on and account for ongoing reflection, using teacher judgments about their own practices as bases for working toward improving educational opportunity for children and youth. The stories teachers tell, the successes they recount, the frustrations and dilemmas they face would become a significant source of ideas for improvement or change or "reform" activity. Teachers' thoughts and personal accounts of their work would influence the process of formulating (rather than mandating) ways to act toward school change.

Assumption 2: Teachers value highly their interactions with students. A longstanding strand of educational research and practice points to the importance of teacher-student interactions (Doyle, 1984). This importance has been associated with teachers' sense of efficacy, with teachers' views about their place in the larger society, with their willingness to participate in individual or school development activities and strategies (Griffin, 1987).

Suggesting school change for its own sake, considering restructuring the ways that teachers and administrators work together independent from enhancing student learning, and proposing curriculum improvement without also considering the curriculum's relation with students are all potentially futile avenues of pursuing school improvement. The futility lies in the divorce of the primary objects of attention from the implicit and explicit *raisons d'être* of most schoolteachers (Buchmann, 1984). Although these or other innovative ways of thinking about the work of teachers may have some face value, they quickly lose their attractiveness unless they are yoked in some obvious fashion to teacher-student interactions and the relation of those interactions to student achievement.

Using this understanding is not patronizing; that would only be the case if this knowledge about what teachers value is seen in a patronizing, condescending manner. Unfortunately, a tradition of educational research has been a kind of distanced commentary on teachers and their worklives. That is, researchers sometimes report teachers' talk or behavior and then demean that talk by categorizing it or ignoring its contextual relationships or otherwise applying intellectual frames around it that diminish its importance, its value to teachers (Cooper, 1988).

In the instance of teachers' value of their interactions with students, that large part of being a teacher has been categorized as sentiment, as storytelling, as unimportant reminiscence. And yet, why should anyone be surprised that teachers dwell on their relationships with students, successful and problematic, when it is exactly those relationships that make up the core of the teaching enterprise? Why is it unimportant for teachers to think and talk about "what works" when their societal role depends on knowing how to bring about successful learning? Why should teachers sometimes be chastised for lack of eloquence about their implicit theories of instruction, largely unarticulated, when discourse systems that might make those theories explicit are systematically absent from their work settings?

A new conception of staff development that considers seriously the interaction of teacher work, workplace conditions, theories-in-use, and engagement with personally held and new ideas as basic elements of good schools would not ignore the importance of teachers' beliefs about their work with students. Instead, it would capitalize on that knowledge, make it public and explicit, and use it to develop criteria for judging the worth of teaching, of curricula, of student organization. It would be a primary data source for deciding what is of worth and for determining "what works" in making what is worthy accessible to students.

Assumption 3: Teachers' worklives are enhanced by professional interactions with other adults. It is no longer necessary to comment on the isolation factor in relation to teaching, although there are some naive observers of teaching who still wonder how a teacher can be "lonely" in the persistent presence of student groups. For too long, teachers, unlike most other professionals, have been compartmentalized, much like workers in a cottage industry, with few opportunities for meaningful and sustained interactions with one another.

Yet recent research points strongly to the power of teacher-teacher professional collegiality as a key to school success and to effective school change (Lieberman, 1988). When teachers work together to develop common bonds around shared goals, interactive decision making, and mutual inquiry, there develops a school culture that is rewarding for teachers as well as beneficial for students. When teachers are engaged together in thinking aloud about their work and its consequences, the results are not simply a greater sense of professionalism on the part of teachers, although that certainly is the case, but a stronger and more coherent instructional program for children and youth (see Chapter 12, this volume).

Interactive staff development would capitalize on and provide on-going opportunities for teachers to learn from one another and learn together. Learning from one another makes sense in that what is most deeply known *about teaching* is known *by teachers*; a way for that knowledge to infuse groups of teachers must be devised. But learning together is a different concept. Of course, in most inservice education programs, teachers are expected to learn together, but the knowledge is determined not by teachers but by school system officers. Interactive staff development, using the assumption about the power of teacher-teacher interaction, would focus opportunities for learning together on becoming expert about those issues that the teacher group itself deems of most future or current worth.

Assumption 4: School leadership, as currently conceptualized, is an increasingly impossible task and must be reconstructed to include teacher leadership. A great deal has been written and said about the importance of leadership in schools. Until recently, the concept of leadership was limited to the principal (and, perhaps, assistant principals and department chairpersons). The common pattern in schools is for teachers to earn advanced degrees, with specializations in supervision or administration, apply for and be appointed to a principal role, move out of teaching, and then use system-derived authority to direct the work of an elementary or secondary school.

This pattern, admittedly oversimplified, has several flaws. First, the idea that one should be away from groups of students in order to be influential upon school work denies the importance for school success of first-hand and cumulative knowledge about students, the nature of instruction, and the curriculum. (Effective principals, almost to a person, are usually praised because of their deep knowledge of the nature of the student population and the dilemmas of providing instruction.) Second, the advanced degrees are more commonly rooted in conceptions of leadership that derive from out-of-date industrial models of management and labor, a conception that business and industry have abandoned but that school systems cling to (Griffin, in press). Third, decisions about which principal would be most effective for which school are seldom influenced by the teachers with whom the principal must work but controlled by system-level officials. Fourth, principals depend most for their authority on the system rather than the school; they do the work of the larger organizational unit, often to the dismay (and detriment) of those with whom they work daily. Running through all of these problematic conditions is the disregard that the steps in the typical pattern display for teachers, teachers who today are concerned about increasing their professional status and their active participation in influencing their own and their students' daily lives (Cooper, 1988).

The heart of the leadership dilemma for most schools today is the overwhelming demands it places on individual school principals. Although probably only in rare instances, school principals at one time may have had a manageable job. The school was a less complex organization. It was not required to be so directly responsive to societal and cultural demands. It dealt with a narrow range of school subjects. It had an easily identified neighborhood clientele of parents and students. And so forth.

Contrast the long-ago picture of schools with today's multicultural settings. Schools are expected to respond to a wide range of societal concerns, from teaching students to drive to ensuring they are knowledgeable about how to remain AIDS-free. Schools receive students from a wide geographic area, often covering entire cities or counties. Schools are caught up in trying to stay abreast of the knowledge explosion. Schools have available for use a bewildering array of technological support for instruction and management. Schools are *not* the simple, straightforward organizations of yesteryear.

For success in today's world, schools need a wider and deeper leadership cadre than is found in the single principal. Interactive staff development would recognize this and promote leadership among teachers, leadership that is specialized and that is regularly and systematically accessible to colleague teachers (Holmes Group, 1986). (Recall that interactive staff development is less something that is done to teachers than it is a way to engage teachers interactively with the issues they must address in their worklives. Teachers must interact with one another in a variety of ways, including provision of school-level leadership.)

In such a situation, it is reasonable to assume that a school might have teacher leaders with specializations in such persistent school issues as curriculum improvement and test construction and use, as well as special-izations that can be helpful with recent schooling phenomena such as multicultural education, developmental differences, and instructional technology. At issue is devising a means by which teachers can be directly involved with the life of a school, wherein an impossible organi-zational conception of leadership can be improved, and whereby the dilemmas of a complex organization can be dealt with efficiently and effectively.

Assumption 5: The success of interactive staff development must be a consequence of ongoing reconceptualization of responsibilities for school and student success.   As is implied above, the interactive staff develop-ment process proposed here calls for a major change in the ways that schools are organized, led, and prepared to do their important work. Some of what I have proposed is present in current reform agendas. What is often missing from these agendas, however, is a focus on the issue of accountability. Who or what body is responsible, in the end, for the degree to which a school meets public and professional expectations?

One of the elements of an interactive staff development strategy must be accountability. There is a logical and desirable conceptual and intellectual interaction between responsibility and outcomes. If, as I have proposed, teachers assume greater collective and individual responsibil-ity for school-level decisions and activities, it is logical to extend that concept to include shared responsibility for the effects of those decisions and activities.

The issue of accountability has been confounded for decades by the externally imposed criteria for determining school success. Further, the criteria are most often nonvarying and unchanging. Typically, a stan-dardized test of student achievement is adopted by a district, used across sharply different school settings, and kept in place for years. This prac-tice of accountability denies school-specific differences in student popu-lations, curriculum emphases, faculty strengths and weaknesses, organi-zational histories, and school-community expectations. It also ignores the irrefutable fact that schools, like the communities they serve, change over time, altering their characters as a consequence of proactive decisions or as responses to changing social conditions.

Interactive staff development depends in large measure on school professionals working together to determine what they want to accom-plish and how they will realize their expectations. This mission-action relationship is informed by focused and specialized teacher leadership as well as the institutionalization of ongoing forums for learning from one another and learning together. To complete the equation, it is necessary that the interaction include systematic and disciplined attention to the degree to which the school-determined outcomes are achieved.

The most dramatic departure from business as usual in this scheme is that interactive staff development would focus accountability objectives, criteria, and measures on school-level expectations rather than solely on district or system ones. (Obviously schools would be obliged, for efficiency as well as district-level accountability purposes, to attend seriously to district purposes and accountability mechanisms. But, unlike current practice, that attention would be only part of the accountability process, not the only way of judging school effectiveness.) In such a scheme, a school with large numbers of recent immigrants, almost all of whom come to school as non-English-speakers, would develop/adopt/adapt curricula that took this feature into account and would develop accountability measures to match. In another school, one whose professional staff has decided that higher-order thinking and problem solving should infuse the school subjects, an accountability strategy would be devised that would include such opportunities for students to demonstrate their conceptual abilities well beyond the recall items that appear on most standardized tests. A school with large numbers of disengaged students might decide that faculty mentors be used as a strategy to connect students to the life of the school and, consequently, examine the nature and consequences of such a program in terms of school attendance, students' participation levels in school activities, and student persistence in long-term academic projects.

While it is impossible to ignore the desirability of devising ways for teachers to become central participants in school decisions, it is also impossible to ignore the relationship that such participation must have with the outcomes of schooling. The proof of any "reform" in public education will lie in the degree to which what was changed has some positive bearing on the purpose of schools, helping students become knowledgeable, skillful, and thoughtful citizens.

Assumption 6: Participating in interactive staff development will require new knowledge and skill on the part of all involved and will be accompanied by considerable anxiety, stress, tension, and conflict. Interactive staff development, as proposed here and in cases where one or more of the pieces of the proposal have been implemented, appears at a distance to be a significant change for the better for all concerned. What enlightened teacher would not want to be a part of such a revitalized educational environment? How could experiments with these elements fail?

But the truth of the matter is that school professionals who engage in departures from the norm such as discussed here encounter a set of knowledge and skill requirements that are unprecedented in their experience and, indeed, in most of the long history of schools throughout the nation. In fact, teachers are not prepared by universities or by their own districts to be leaders (Griffin, in press). They are not seriously connected to the knowledge they need to work with adults rather than children. They are systematically and persistently separated from new knowledge about instructional strategies, curriculum theories, and organizational development. They are, in effect, the $2 \times 4 \times 6$ teachers Ole Sand talked about 25 years ago: Teachers whose worklives are determined by the 2 covers of a book, the 4 walls of a classroom, and the 6 periods of a school day. Most know how to work in this limited space; few know how to navigate the larger school context and the even larger intellectual educational environment.

For interactive staff development, or any other similar model of participatory professional and school improvement, to work, it is necessary that the actors learn about and how to enact a new and unfamiliar repertoire of ways of engaging with their workworlds (Tikunoff, Ward, & Griffin, 1981). They must connect to knowledge sources, among themselves and outside their institutional boundaries. They must learn how to cope with competing claims. They must learn how to work together, conflicts and all. They must become producers of meaning, inquirers into their own practice. They must, in effect, learn what is needed to capitalize on their own strengths and shore up their own shortcomings in intellectually sound and practically reasonable ways.

Teachers who have come to accept their roles as receivers of others' wisdom may chafe at this role but, when confronted with the need to learn the new knowledge and skill necessary to meaningfully break out of it, are often frustrated, confused, uncomfortable, and otherwise disoriented. When this occurs, as it almost inevitably does, it becomes necessary for some mechanism to be in place (or instituted) that can be a sounding board and resting place for teachers and others who begin to believe that they just may have bitten off more than they can chew. In some cases, an external agent, such as might be represented by a union-sponsored teacher center leader or a teacher colleague who has "been through it all," is helpful (see Chapter 10, this volume). In others, linking with a neutral organization, such as a nearby university or regional laboratory, can be helpful in thinking through the issues to be confronted. Chapter 12 notes the value of teachers' establishing computer-linked relationships with researchers.

Interactive staff development does not assume that problems will not be encountered, that frustration will not occur, or that some participants will not report that they feel "burned out" as a consequence of working under the interactive conditions. Rather, it anticipates these natural phenomena as teachers learn new ways to work more productively together and singly and accounts for it as a matter of course, rather than using the dilemmas and tensions as reasons or excuses to abandon the enterprise.

Assumption 7: Despite the problems associated with learning new knowledge and skill, participants in interactive staff development will be more fully and productively engaged in teaching and schooling than is typical. A number of attempts at reconstructing the ways that teachers work together toward professional growth and school improvement, although involving considerable personal anxiety and intellectual frustration, are reported by teachers as being ultimately rewarding, well beyond expectations or imagination.

Teachers in an intensive knowledge production experiment encountered a bewildering array of new ways of thinking about and doing schooling and an equally unfamiliar set of ways of inquiring into teaching, but they testified that they had never had more satisfying school-related experiences (Tikunoff et al., 1981). Teachers engaged in taking more control over curriculum and instruction in their schools reported the enormous challenge of dealing with intellectual ambiguity as well as their own interpersonal relationships, but they also reported that they would never go back to "the old ways" again. Teachers adapting research-derived teaching strategies to their own classes and student groups told researchers how important it was to be connected to the world of ideas and to be considered as "grown-ups" in the process. Teachers using unfamiliar computer technology to track down teacher colleague and researcher colleague advice on school improvement provided testimony to initial fear and frustration but eventual pleasure in having command over another tool for improving their chances at doing well in their work (Griffin & Barnes, 1986).

How can we account for these oxymoronic combinations of frustration and satisfaction, tension and gratification, exhaustion and exhilaration? I believe the explanation lies at the heart of what it is to be human. That is, we all seek out opportunities to be of value, to be considered worthy, to accept and overcome challenges, to solve problems, to feel ourselves a valued part of an important enterprise. For too long, teachers have seemed to be considered cogs in a wheel, passive participants in a social enterprise that has lost its way. As teachers, we sometimes forget (or are forbidden to remember) that "the realities of teaching are multiple" (see Chapter 1, this volume). We come to believe that "they" are right, that there *is* one best way, that our voices are unimportant in the grand scheme of things. In short, we become infantalized; we are not "grown-ups" in the places where we are expected by our clients and our patrons, if not our superiors, to be expert. We fall into the $2 \times 4 \times 6$ syndrome.

Obviously, though, our humanness—our search for better ideas, more exciting possibilities of practice, a greater sense of worth among peers—can take over. In the right conditions, we can forge new perspectives, create new visions, encourage ourselves and others to greater aspirations, and along the way we can reawaken our pride in what we do, how we do it, what we accomplish. The conditions for that reawakening lie partly, I believe, in the assumptions underlying the idea of interactive staff development.

CONCLUSION

This chapter has considered some of the problems of typical staff development, particularly when staff development is acted out as yet another version of conventional supervision. As a contrasting case, it has promoted the concept of interactive staff development, a proposal that incorporates selected recent research about effective schools, proposals for changing teachers' worklives, experiments in altering schools as work and learning places, and developments in the larger society that influence schools. The interactiveness proposed goes well beyond the conventions of people working with other people; it includes the multidirectional influence of the mix of ideas, places, people, events, structures, and inquiry.

We have learned a good deal since the publication of the first edition of this book. We will learn more in the coming years. It is my hope that we will learn whether the proposals put forth here, and others like them elsewhere, have value in helping to make teaching and schooling more satisfying and productive for participants in the processes and for the society as a whole.

REFERENCES

Bentzen, M. M. (1974). *Changing schools: The magic feather principle*. New York: McGraw-Hill.
Buchmann, M. (1984). The priority of knowledge and understanding in teaching.

In L. G. Katz & J. D. Raths (Eds.), *Advances in teacher education* (Vol. 1) (pp. 29–50). Norwood, NJ: Ablex.

Carter, K. (1990). Teachers' knowledge and learning to teach. In R. Houston (Ed.), *Handbook of research on teacher education* (pp. 291–310). New York: Macmillan.

Cooper, M. (1988). Whose culture is it, anyway? In A. Lieberman (Ed.), *Building a professional culture in schools* (pp. 45–54). New York: Teachers College Press.

Doyle, W. (1984). How order is achieved in classrooms: An interim report. *Journal of Curriculum Studies, 16,* 259–277.

Doyle, W. (1987). The classroom as a workplace: Implications for staff development. In M. Wideen & I. Andrews (Eds.), *Staff development for school improvement: A focus on the teacher* (pp. 38–54). New York: Falmer.

Griffin, G. A. (1982). *Supervision in preservice, induction, and inservice settings.* Paper presented at the annual meeting of the American Educational Research Association, New Orleans.

Griffin, G. A. (Ed.). (1983). *Staff development* (82nd Yearbook of the National Society for the Study of Education). Chicago: University of Chicago Press.

Griffin, G. A. (1987). The school in society and social organization of the school: Implications for staff development. In M. Wideen & I. Andrews (Eds.), *Staff development for school improvement: A focus on the teacher* (pp. 19–37). New York: Falmer.

Griffin, G. A. (in press). Teacher education and curriculum decision making: The issue of teacher professionalism. In M. F. Klein (Ed.), *Curriculum issues in legislating and centralizing curriculum.* Albany: State University of New York Press.

Griffin, G. A., & Barnes, S. (1986). Using research findings to change school and classroom practice: Results of an experimental study. *American Educational Research Journal, 23*(4), 572–586.

Hoffman, J., Griffin, G., Barnes, S., O'Neal, S., Edwards, S., Paulissen, M., Salinas, A., & Defino, M. (1986). *Teacher induction: Final report of a descriptive study.* Austin: University of Texas at Austin, Research and Development for Teacher Education.

Holmes Group. (1986). *Tomorrow's teachers.* East Lansing, MI: Author.

Lieberman, A. (Ed.). (1988). *Building a professional culture in schools.* New York: Teachers College Press.

Rosenholtz, S. (1989). *Teachers' workplace: The social organization of schools.* New York: Longman.

Sarason, S. (1971). *The culture of the school and the problem of change.* New York: Allyn & Bacon.

Schlechty, P. (1987). *Schools for the twenty-first century: Conditions for invention.* Washington, DC: Council of Chief State School Officers and American Association of Colleges for Teacher Education.

Schlechty, P. (1990). *Schools for the twenty-first century: Leadership imperatives for educational reform.* San Francisco: Jossey-Bass.

Tikunoff, W. J., Ward, B. A., & Griffin, G. A. (1981). Interactive research and development as a form of professional growth. In K. Bents & D. Corrigan (Eds.), *School-focused inservice: Descriptions and discussions* (pp. 112–133). Reston, VA: Association of Teacher Educators.

Wideen, M. F., & Andrews, I. (Eds.). (1987). *Staff development for school improvement: A focus on the teacher.* New York: Falmer.

About the Editors
and the Contributors

Index

About the Editors
and the Contributors

Ann Lieberman is a professor in the Department of Curriculum and Teaching at Teachers College and co-director of the newly formed National Center for Restructuring Education, Schools and Teaching (NCREST). She was elected president of the American Educational Research Association (AERA) for 1991. Her major interest is in understanding how to restructure schools in New York City and throughout the nation. She has been involved as researcher, policy maker, and practitioner in attempting to build collaboration between schools and universities. Her many publications include *Teachers: Their World and Their Work* (with Lynne Miller), *Building a Professional Culture in Schools*, and *Schools as Collaborative Cultures: Creating the Future Now*.

Lynne Miller is a professor of education and executive director of the Southern Maine Partnership (a school/university collaboration) at the University of Southern Maine, where she also directs teacher education. She worked as a secondary English teacher and as a building and central office administrator prior to her faculty appointment. Miller has written widely in the areas of staff development, school improvement and restructuring, and the social realities of teaching. She is co-author, with Ann Lieberman, of *Teachers: Their World and Their Work*.

Myrna Cooper is the founder and director of the New York City Teacher Centers Consortium, a collaboration of the United Federation of Teachers, the New York City Board of Education, the New York State Education Department, and local colleges of teacher education. Cooper has served as consultant and advisor to numerous organizations, school districts, and agencies, which have sought her counsel on issues of teacher leadership, school improvement, and knowledge utilization. She has represented the American Federation of Teachers on NIE and OERI advisory panels, providing a practitioner's point of view in the formulation of their agendas regarding teaching and learning in inner-city schools. Cooper is the author of numerous publications and position papers. Her most recent article, "Whose Culture Is It Anyway?", appears in *Building a Professional Culture in Schools*, a publication of Teachers College Press.

Maxine Greene is Professor Emeritus of Teachers College, where she has been professor of philosophy and education since 1973. She is past president of the American Educational Research Association, American Education Studies Association, and the Philosophy of Education Society. Her major interests include aesthetic education, teacher education, and social theory and philosophy. She is best known for her numerous books and articles that represent a unique blend of social philosophy, aesthetics, teacher education, and teaching. Her best-known books include *Teacher as Stranger: Educational Philosophy in the Modern Age* and *The Dialectics of Freedom*.

Gary A. Griffin is a professor of teaching and teacher education at the University of Arizona. He has conducted numerous large-scale research studies of student teaching, teacher induction, and staff development. In addition he has been program director at the Research and Development Center for Teacher Education and dean of the College of Education at the University of Illinois at Chicago. He has written numerous articles, reports, and monographs. Recent writing and research focus on teacher education, school improvement, and the professionalization of teaching.

Kathy Hocking is an elementary school teacher trained in the Foxfire approach in 1987. She specializes in fourth-grade integrated curricula and developmentally appropriate uses of the Foxfire approach. She is in a graduate program at the University of Idaho, completing work on a handbook on the application of the Foxfire approach for primary grades.

Peter Holly was tutor in curriculum studies at Cambridge Institute of Education in England. He is currently a freelance consultant working in the United States in the areas of evaluation and action research. He is working with school districts within the Puget Sound Educational Consortium in the state of Washington and the National Education Association.

Robert Evan Jones is a fifth-grade teacher in Woodinville, Washington. He is currently job-sharing a fifth-grade classroom. He is project director of Soundfire—the Foxfire teacher network within the Puget Sound Educational Consortium. He is in the graduate program in education at the University of Washington.

Susan Loucks-Horsley is program director for teacher development at the Regional Laboratory for Educational Improvement of the Northeast and the Islands and associate director of the National Center for Improving Science Education. She received her doctorate in curriculum and instruction from the University of Texas at Austin. Her research and development interests include innovation and change, staff development, and program improvement. Co-developer of the Concerns-Based Adoption Model while at the Texas Research and Development Center for Teacher Education, she has addressed narrowing the gap between research and practice in two recent publications: *An Action Guide to School Improvement* and *Continuing to Learn: A Guidebook for Teacher Development*.

Robert M. McClure is director of the NEA Mastery In Learning Consortium, a school-based national program for school transformation. He has taught at all levels in the public schools as well as in higher education.

Milbrey Wallin McLaughlin is a professor of education at Stanford University. She received her Ed.D. at Harvard University and has worked at the Rand Corporation as a senior social scientist. Her research interests include planned change, school context, policy implementation, and at-risk youth. Among her many publications, she is best known for: *Federal Programs Supporting Educational Change, Steady Work: Policy, Practice, and the Reform of American Education* (with Richard Wilmore), and *Teacher Evaluation: The Contexts of Teaching in Secondary School.*

Sharon Nodie Oja, an associate professor in the University of New Hampshire's five-year Teacher Education Program, received her Ph.D. from the University of Minnesota in 1978. Oja has been a principal investigator in two nationally funded school-university projects: A Collaborative Approach to Leadership in Supervision and Teacher Stages of Development in Relation to Collaborative Action Researching Schools. Her research interest has focused on adult development as a deliberate goal of teacher/staff development projects. She has written on topics of teacher development, adult cognitive-developmental stages, school-university research, and collaborative supervision. Her co-authored book *Collaborative Action Research: A Development Process* was published in 1989.

Anna E. Richert is an assistant professor of education at Mills College in Oakland, California. Before coming to Mills she was associate director of the Teacher Education Program at Stanford University, where she received her Ph.D. in curriculum and teacher education. She received the 1989 Outstanding Research in Teacher Education Award from the Association of Colleges and Schools of Education in State Universities and Land Grant Colleges for her research on case methodology. "Case Methods and Teacher Education: Teaching the Novice to Reflect" will appear in *Issues and Practices in Inquiry-Oriented Teacher Education.* Her case methods research is part of her ongoing study on teacher learning and teacher education.

Judith Schwartz is the director of the Scarsdale Teachers Institute and president of the Scarsdale Teachers Association. She served on the New York State Commissioner of Education's Taskforce on the Teaching Profession and the New York State Taskforce on the Implementation of Education Reform. She received her B.A. from Syracuse University, did graduate work in political science at the University of California, Berkley, and holds a master's degree from Teachers College, Columbia University, and from Pace University. She is a frequent speaker on teacher professionalism and education reform.

Hilton Smith is a high school social studies teacher with 30 years of experience. He is currently serving as coordinator of the Foxfire's Teacher Outreach Program.

Suzanne Stiegelbauer combines experience in a number of different fields, including anthropology, education, fine arts, and art history. She holds two master's degrees and a doctorate in anthropology from the University of Texas at Austin. She worked on the research team of the Research on the Improvement Process Program at the Texas Research and Development Center for Teacher Education from 1979 to 1985. In her role as a consultant for school districts and organizations throughout the United States and Canada, she has served as evaluator, researcher, and staff developer. Also an instructor at the Ontario Institute for Studies in Education, she has published articles on leadership and change in schools, minority and multicultural concerns, and Native American education in several professional journals. She is assistant author of *The New Meaning of Educational Change* (Michael Fullan).

Patricia A. Wasley is senior researcher for Change at the Coalition of Essential Schools, Brown University. She is the author of a number of articles on teacher leadership as well as *Teacher Leadership: Problems, Paradoxes and Possibilities*. She is currently engaged in work documenting the changes that occur for teachers, administrators, students, and policy makers as they work collaboratively to redesign schooling. She has held a variety of positions in public education both in the United States and overseas.

Eliot Wigginton teaches high school in Rabun Gap, Georgia. He is best known for the creation of the Foxfire magazine produced since 1966 by his students. Wigginton has received national acclaim for his writing, which includes, among scores of articles and books, *Sometimes a Shining Moment*. He has received numerous awards, among them the prestigious MacArthur Award.

Index

recommendations for staff developers
about, 180–82
and research/theory, 165–71, 189
rewards of, 165
and school reform, 158, 159
and support, 165–71, 181, 182
and teachers as learners, 181
Learning
action, 136, 143
and action research, 134, 142–44, 145–46
and adult development, 37
assessing, 108
and CBAM, 32–33
climate for, 37
as context dependent, 119
and cooperation/collaboration, 86, 121,
127–29, 133, 134, 190, 238, 252
and experience, 113, 114
as a focus of the 1990s, 16
and human development, 107–8
and interactive staff development, 250,
252
nature of, 106
organizational barriers to, 113
by principals, 134
and reflection, 113–15
by students, 107–8
support for, 113, 114–15
and teachers as learners, 107–8, 113–30,
134, 181
and teaching, 68–70, 93–94, 106–8, 228–
29
See also Mastery in Learning (MIL)
Learning schools, 134, 143–44
Levine, Sarah, 44
Levinson, Daniel, 38
Lewin, Kurt, 136, 137, 140, 150
Lewis, J., 144–45, 146, 149
Lieberman, Ann, 139, 140, 142, 158–59
Life structure, 38–41
Little, J. W., 61, 69, 70, 71, 72, 104–5
Livingston, Carol, 237–38
Loevinger, Jane, 41–44
Lortie, D. C., 93, 158–59
Loucks-Horsley, Susan, 16, 229
Luvaas-Hess, Reva, 209

McKernan, J., 135, 140–41
McLaughlin, M., 105–6

McTaggart, R., 150
Marsh, D. D., 30
Maslow, Abraham, 19, 44
Mastery in Learning (MIL)
assumptions in the, 235
and centers of inquiry, 225, 234–40
characteristics of the, 223
and climate, 222, 228, 231, 233, 234
and collaboration, 225–26, 227, 233,
235–37, 239
and conditions that encourage Mastery
in Learning, 227–28
and the curriculum, 223, 228, 232, 235,
237
and decision making, 222, 231–32, 235,
237, 238
and empowerment, 234, 239–40
and evaluation, 228, 229, 230–32
and futuring, 229
and instruction, 232
and inventorying the faculty, 225,
226–34, 235, 236, 237
and knowledge, 225, 235, 237–40
and the network schools, 223–25
and norms, 227, 235
outcomes of the, 236–37
principles of the, 221–22
processes developed by the, 225–26
purpose of the, 221, 222
and research, 229, 233, 237–40
and restructuring of schools, 225, 234–40
and staff development, 232, 233
and teacher–student interactions, 227–28
and teaching/learning practices, 228–29
and technologies, 224, 228, 239
and TRaK, 238–39
Mentoring, 57, 186, 190–91
Merleau-Ponty, M., 7
Miles, M. B., 147, 148
Moral development, 44–46, 51
Motivation, 62, 63–64, 78, 80n4
Myers, M., 143

National Education Association, 178, 246.
See also Mastery in Learning (MIL)
Nebraska State Department of Education,
31
Networking, 78, 197, 198–208
Neugarten, Bernice, 38, 40